EDUCATION IN URBAN AREAS

EDUCATION IN URBAN AREAS

CROSS-NATIONAL DIMENSIONS

EDITED BY
Nelly P. Stromquist

PRAEGER

Westport, Connecticut
London

Library of Congress Cataloging-in-Publication Data

Education in urban areas : cross-national dimensions / edited by Nelly
  P. Stromquist.
        p.   cm.
     The subject of this book derives from a western regional
  conference of the Comparative and International Education Society
  (CIES), held on 15–16, November 1991.
     Includes bibliographical references and index.
     ISBN 0–275–94658–4
     1. Education, Urban—Cross-cultural studies—Congresses.
  I. Stromquist, Nelly P.
  LC5101.E39   1994
  370.19′348—dc20   93–17626

British Library Cataloguing in Publication Data is available.

Library of Congress Catalog Card Number: 93–17626
ISBN: 0–275–94658–4

First published in 1994

Praeger Publishers, 88 Post Road West, Westport, CT 06881
An imprint of Greenwood Publishing Group, Inc.

Printed in the United States of America

The paper used in this book complies with the
Permanent Paper Standard issued by the National
Information Standards Organization (Z39.48–1984).

10 9 8 7 6 5 4 3 2 1

Contents

Part II. Bureaucratic Dynamics in Urban Educational Systems

Part III. The City and Educational Politics

Part IV. The Educational Experience of Women and Marginal Students

Figures and Tables

Preface

The subject of this book derives from a western regional conference of the Comparative and International Education Society (CIES) held on 15–16 November 1991. At that time, given its sponsor (the School of Education at the University of Southern California) and its location (Los Angeles, California), it seemed appropriate to organize a conference that would highlight the particular physical, demographic, and social features of the city that have substantial implications for the educational system. Living in Los Angeles does convey a sense of "urban-ness" that is inescapable. The vast spread of its population, the large distances between points of interest, the rich cultural and ethnic diversity, and the strong differentiation among neighborhoods are features that permeate everyday living, give a particular feeling to urban life and fill the people on its contrasting streets and crowded freeways simultaneously with hope and despair. In many ways, Los Angeles is at the threshold of the future.

Professor Michael Dear, from the Department of Geography at USC, gave the keynote speech at this CIES conference and entitled his presentation "Taking Los Angeles Seriously: Time and Space in the Post-Modern City." He described Los Angeles as postmodern in the sense that it is characterized by complication and fragmentation: "In post-modern thought all rationalities disappear. No new single rationality emerges and a tremendous diversity rushes to fill this vacuum." Social life, he said, is engraved in a space/time fabric, and in Los Angeles this fabric has been stretched to such a point that we cannot now recognize its coordinates. His view of Los Angeles was that of "a First-

World city sitting on top of a Third-World city." The heterogeneity, chaos, and vitality of Los Angeles, building "an accretion of local communities," were "not an exception, but probably a prototypic example of the new world." If so, it is a reality that poses many challenges not only to the individuals living in it but also to the social sciences trying to understand what goes on in the city.

Education, of course, seeks to identify the educational repercussions of urban-ness, yet the whole set of effects is multifaceted and thus complex. The major civil unrest of April 1992 in Los Angeles, which occurred as the manuscripts for this book were being reviewed and edited, brought out in a dramatic way the tensions and possibilities linked to urban life. The surprising extent of damage—destroyed property and lost livelihoods, not to mention the human casualties—that resulted from the Los Angeles "riots" were also indications of the pent-up frustration and ease of mobilization that cities can generate. And in the aftermath, for the residents of Los Angeles it is most illuminating to witness how diverse interests mesh and crush to render socioeconomic change at the same time an immediate challenge and a distant reality.

The collection of articles presented in this book represents but an initial attempt to unpack what city features really represent for education. In assuming this claim we note two facts: One is that most urban education studies so far have occurred in developed countries and thus have acquired a particular emphasis, that of centering on marginalized groups, particularly those of minority ethnic groups; the second is that the configuration of issues derived from urban features in developing countries is much larger than in the West, and these have been taken for granted rather than subjected to close scrutiny.

The twelve chapters that comprise this book cover realities in both industrialized and developing countries, thus enabling the reader to notice similarities, contrasts, and nuances. The contributors, like myself, embarked on a relatively new subject by exploring the facets that "urban" per se would bring to the educational enterprise. Over several months, long after the CIES conference took place, we struggled to isolate urban features that impinge on education and that should not be taken as givens but be examined empirically and questioned normatively. As a point of departure, the authors worked with the framework provided by Stromquist (presented in Chapter 2 of this volume), sometimes expanding on a specific concept identified in this chapter, sometimes bringing out a manifestation of urban-ness not covered by it. In these endeavors, the contributors were patient and eager to respond to questions and criticisms.

The studies are not intended to be comprehensive or exhaustive in their treatment of urban features, but we hope that, by bringing into the light specific dimensions of urban life, our understanding of and sensitivity to educational experiences in the city will have increased.

ACKNOWLEDGMENTS

Without the eager participation of the fifteen other contributors to this book, this "urban" exploration would have not begun. I am most grateful to them for their steady pursuit of new knowledge. Beyond their authorship, there are contributions in other forms I wish to acknowledge. First of all is the support of my close colleague William Rideout, who encouraged me to think of the urban context as a major force shaping the nature of the educational system and to expand this concept to the analysis of developing countries as well. My thanks go also to Gerald Grace, a renowned authority in urban education, who accepted willingly the invitation to reconsider the concept in light of recent global political and economic events. I am grateful also to my husband, Eric, whose "first reading," in this work and always, has been fundamental to my productivity.

EDUCATION IN URBAN AREAS

Introduction

Nelly P. Stromquist

Our contemporary world is becoming increasingly urbanized. United Nations projections affirm that the urban populations of developing countries will represent 50 percent of their total population in the next decade and that the levels of urbanization of these developing countries will approach those of the industrialized countries by the year 2020. Unquestionably, urbanization is here to stay and grow.

A key characteristic of the urbanization process in developing countries is that it is taking place in the absence of concomitant transformations in the job market and the urban infrastructure. Castells (1979) reminds us that urbanization in Latin America, a phenomenon repeated in many African and Asian countries "is not an expression of a process of 'modernization,' but the manifestation, at the level of socio-spatial conditions, of the accentuation of the social contradictions inherent in its mode of development—a development determined by a specific dependence within the monopolistic capitalist system" (p. 63).

With large numbers of urban residents outside the formal economy and living in conditions of poverty and hopelessness, the dream linked to urban residence is far from being realized by millions of persons. They keep moving to the cities despite the harsh realities that will greet them because no matter how meager the rewards, they will still be larger than those in the countryside. A dream realized partially is better than no dream at all.

The city does consume larger amounts of resources than rural areas but it also has a greater array of problems and needs. The features of urban-ness have been explored primarily in industrialized countries, where attention has been paid to the conditions of marginalized populations, usually comprising minorities of color or primarily individuals of low income. Education in the cities of the more industrialized countries has been examined mostly in terms of the problems facing the populations served, such as low achievement, violence in the schools, and language needs. It has also been examined in terms of the inequality of the educational inputs: crowded facilities, high teacher turnover, and so forth. Finally, it has been studied for the political tensions that it reflects: school-community conflict, battles for desegregation, financial scheme, issues of parental choice. These problems suggest that the focus of attention of urban education has been placed on the users of and actors in the educational system who happen to reside in an urban area, rather than on how the features of the city itself bear a particular imprint on the way educational systems work or education is provided. In other words, the location, space, and texture of the city have not always been the focus of analysis in urban education.

Even approaches expressing great concern for equality such as Marxism have been lacking an urban-spatial dimension. Yet, it is accepted that social relations become fixed in space as the city space becomes highly segregated by social status. In the words of Katznelson, "What has been missing [in Marxism] is the linkage between the economic system and the social and spatial specificity of the structuring of working-class lives" (1992, p. 230). But a major exception to Katznelson's assertion can be found in the works of Castells (1979 and 1983), who offers an examination of the urban, not as a focus on space or the urban as a site, but on space as a social product. Castells says in this regard: "Space, as a social product, is always specified by a definite relation between the different instances of a social structure, the economic, the political, the ideological, and the conjuncture of social relations that result from them" (1979, p. 430).

This kind of analysis calls for paying attention to such factors as dimension, density, social heterogeneity, and information diffusion as mechanisms that mediate between urban residents and social outcomes. Seeing urban from this perspective makes us alert to a critical question regarding everyday life: "What is the process of social production of the spatial forms of a society?" Or, posed in another way, the question becomes: "What are the relations between the space constituted and the structural transformation of a society?" (Castells, 1979, p. 19). The analysis of educational systems in the light of this framework, in my view, is in its initial stages. This analysis is also difficult because often the content of the problem tends to draw importance away from the context that caused it in the first place.

This collection brings together articles on urban education from both developed and developing countries. It presents five studies focused on the United States and other industrialized countries, two studies on Asia, two on Africa, and one on Latin America. The juxtaposition of these different realities is illuminating because it allows a more territorial focus than that provided by urban education from industrialized countries. Nonetheless, the collection presents only a taste of the main issues regarding the urban context. It does not pretend to offer an exhaustive treatment of the array of urban issues.

In trying to analyze urban-ness, a distinction should be made between educational events that happen in a city but could also happen elsewhere (the urban as a site) and those events that could happen only in a city as a result of a variety of inherently urban features (the urban as a space produced by social forces). Urban education is an area that needs further treatment in terms of the impact produced by population and housing density, convergence of rich and poor social groups, coexistence of dominant and marginal cultures, the distance between the urban centers and rural areas, distances between points of interest within the city, the response of bureaucracies in dealing with dominant/subordinate groups, and the role of neighborhood movements in the promotion of sociocultural change.

The contributions comprising the book are arranged in four parts. Part I, "Concepts and Trends," begins with a discussion by R. Murray Thomas on the meaning of *urban* and its multiple definitions and varying assumptions. The ambiguity, the taken-for-granted, and the conflict in meanings at times show how elusive social reality can be in the final analysis. Our precision is challenged by a world that is much more complex than our bounded logic. The second chapter, by Nelly P. Stromquist, identifies a number of features characterizing the urban context and contrasts the manifestations of these features in developed and developing countries. She examines the urban features of developing countries as a by-product of their colonization experience and the current prevailing model of development, which continues to give priority to industrial growth while regarding rural areas primarily as sources of food, cheap labor, and export earnings. The third and final chapter of Part I is presented by Gerald Grace, who, taking mostly a First World perspective, scans the political ideologies that account for the limited attention that disadvantaged people in the cities receive. Using Galbraith's concept of "culture of contentment," he offers a sober prognosis of urban educational problems and their likely lack of solution.

Part II, "Bureaucratic Dynamics in Urban Educational Systems," also comprises three chapters. Deirdre M. Kelly offers a finely woven account of the strategies implemented by a large school district in dealing with potential dropout students, and shows that programs ostensibly designed to help these students in fact enable the schools to retain a preferred type while making it possible to eliminate those seen as problematic from a performance or discipline point of view. W. O. Lee and Li Zibiao's chapter documents the economic and educational inequalities that emerge in a large city despite its embeddedness in a socialist regime with strong and genuinely egalitarian goals. As long as cities remain high in the hierarchy of social services and employment opportunities, no socialist planning can deter people from flowing into them. Malongo R. S. Mlozi's study focuses on the provision of a particular type of nonformal educa-

tion, that of agricultural extension. He shows that even a form of education
that originally was meant to address the needs of low-income groups ends up
serving the interests and needs of more advantaged social classes who can command the attention and services of the state bureaucracy. Mlozi's chapter also
shows how the rapid expansion of urban areas is bringing rural features to the
city, thereby creating vague boundaries in city/urban cultural practices in the
African context.

Part III, "The City and Educational Politics," covers important manifestations of state power and response. The chapter by Roger Boshier illustrates the
hermetic deployment of education and schooling that can happen in city-states
whose survival depends exclusively on its human resources. The city, through
its manageable size, makes possible a high degree of control and surveillance.
The chapter by Nelly Moulin and Isabel Pereira gives insight into the evolution
of neighborhood movements in the city and how their development shapes the
type of educational demands they make when they perceive a state that will be
responsive to their claims. Moulin and Pereira's study also shows how urban
areas can become a terrain for the most heated disputes of equality. The changing demographics of the city also brings out some clear strategies and counter-
strategies in the political arena. This is reflected in the study by Roslyn Mickelson, Stephen Smith, and Carol Ray, who offer an in-depth account of how
economic interests in a rapidly growing city can generate demands for change
in educational services, though these may reverse earlier efforts to attain equity
through an integrated school system. Mickelson and her associates show that
growth is an urban dimension that can become a strong element in the local
political agenda; using the concept of the "growth machine," these authors
analyze the set of coalitions that emerge to shape educational services.

Part IV, "The Educational Experience of Women and Marginal Students,"
brings up issues totally peculiar to developing countries. The chapter by N'Dri
Assie-Lumumba explains how limiting the existence of secondary schools only
to the cities (a situation that characterizes much of Africa) functions especially
to the detriment of rural girls, whose mobility is constrained by sociocultural
norms and whose lives as students in the city can be very difficult and can
make them vulnerable to sexual exploitation. The chapter by Magaly Lavadenz
shows how diverse populations of the city create many needs. Those needs
identified as pertaining to minorities (meaning here a group of small size),
especially when mixed with other factors such as language, recent geographical
dislocation, and introduction to a new culture, get lost in the response. Lavadenz offers a qualitative study focusing on three Central American students to
demonstrate how their traumatic experiences with war in their countries have
affected them and how these children pass through the urban school system
completely undetected and thus untreated. Finally, the chapter by Adrian Blunt
brings into the academic debate a relatively new subject, that of street children.
Blunt explains the various urban factors that have resulted in the growing
homelessness of children; he also shows that their educational needs at present
are met only by nongovernmental organizations, usually with the support of

external donors, and covering only a small number of these children. He raises the critical question of whether the fact that the street children's education is operating outside the state with a substantial advocacy role on the part of street educators may foster class consciousness and thus produce counter-hegemonic knowledge.

In tying together the themes and actors in the studies presented in this book, several useful insights emerge, as discussed in the following sections.

THE BRUTALITY OF URBAN POVERTY

Many cities contain vast areas of transposed rural poverty, even though cities as a whole may have better resources than villages. The growing visibility of street children throughout the world is a clear manifestation of the horrors of city life. These children have fallen from a class that is already considered to represent the lowest level of the social scale in countries with limited economic resources or with governments that assume minimal social responsibility. Too young to defend themselves, unable to find meaning and support in their own families, or faced with no family ties, children take to the streets in search of survival. Under these conditions, education is distant and, to make things worse, not offered to the children by the state. Unserved by the formal educational system, they receive attention only from nongovernmental groups, which by their very nature cannot cope with the massive scale of the young homeless problem. Nonetheless, important educational experiments are taking place and the potential for emancipatory education is there.

In the case of girls, the promise and reality of the city are full of tension. Urban poverty is felt by rural girls who find themselves in the city, although they are less likely to be on the street and more likely to be victimized within homes. The lack of sufficient boarding schools for the young Ivorian women who must leave family and home in the countryside in search of secondary schooling in the city makes them vulnerable to preventive measures by parents who, fearful of negative consequences, decide against further schooling of their daughters. Protection by parents leads to the exclusion of large numbers of girls from secondary schools. And when the girls are allowed to go to the cities, they become sexually vulnerable to economic needs which force them to accept the questionable patronage of older men.

In general, the response of the urban poor to education supports a fact political decision makers tend to gloss over, that unless reasonable support mechanisms are there to facilitate the physical existence of individuals, the acquisition of formal knowledge will be seen and treated as a distant luxury.

THE NONNEUTRAL ROLE OF THE STATE

In the interaction between urban structure and urban politics it is clear that the state does not always opt for the common good. In the struggle for educational services, some social classes are more successful than others in receiving attention from the state. The urban orchards and farms of Tanzania in hands of elite groups command greater services from government agricultural extension agents because the elites can provide greater incentives, rewards, and prestige to attract the agents, whereas the urban farmer who is poor—the one for whom the services were originally intended—finds it difficult to get help. The elite's productivity grows and a vicious cycle of the state-elite connection and mutual support is maintained. The Tanzanian examples show that it is not distance but power and accessibility which shape the dynamics of nonformal education in the city.

The experience of Charlotte, North Carolina, makes transparent the tendency by the state (local government in this case) to respond primarily to economic interests. Gearing many of its actions to respond to initiatives by the "growth machine," the state shifts gradually from a commitment to desegregation to one of magnet schools as a way to provide for ethnic heterogeneity in the schools.

The vulnerability of the state to organized social pressure also exists and is well exploited by the neighborhood movements in Rio de Janeiro. The ability of people who live in close proximity to each other to exchange experiences, opinions, and ideas facilitates the development of community organization to demand better services by the state, in this case, basic education. The Rio experience also suggests a possible hierarchy of educational needs, by which demands on the system have to be met first at the quantity level (access) before moving into qualitative demands. This interesting phenomenon reveals a paradoxical situation in which mobilization for more schooling by popular movements may result in attaining merely more reproductivist education, which provides knowledge that scarcely contributes to social transformation.

The nonneutral role of the state assumes various forms, depending on the particular context in which it operates. In the study on Tanzania it appears as favoring the privileged social class. In the case of Singapore the state is an entity that carefully plans its every move. For street children, it is a state with little interest and sympathy. In the case of Charlotte the local government appears willing to play along with the economic interests, since they are the main source of revenue and thus material support.

The cases reviewed in this book, by focusing on urban phenomena—relatively visible and easier to document than those which occur in rural areas—make transparent the interests of the state in responding to economic leverage.

THE SCHOOL'S RESPONSE TOWARD THE MEAN

Urban educational systems, characterized by large enrollments and large schools, tend to develop standard operating procedures that differentiate among their student population, but this differentiation is limited to groups that attain a certain magnitude and importance. The study of Central American children reveals a school system that is impervious to the needs of students with a traumatic war experience. Because these children have had an experience that is totally different from those of other students in the school system and because, after all, they represent a small number in the large mass of students, there is no consciousness or effort made to detect these students' psychological problems that clearly affect their school performance. These children never become a particular target for support and go through the system untreated.

Another instance of the response of urban school systems toward the mean is provided by the study of U.S. continuation schools. Confronted with students who are likely to fail in high school, the schools (administrators and teachers) establish unwritten categories of students and eliminate all those whom they do not wish to serve while appearing to provide these students with especially tailored programs. While this could be an instance of responsiveness by the school—though we saw this was not the case with the Central American or the street children—closer analysis of the second-chance schools provided by the school district in Kelly's dropout program study reflects strategies of least effort. Students are classified into two or three types and made to fit into them.

It is unclear how flexible an educational system can be. The examination of urban educational systems presented in this book shows that rather low levels of flexibility prevail.

THE POLITICAL POWER OF ECONOMIC FACTORS

The case of Singapore, a city-state with no other resources than its people, illustrates the economic rationality that informs much of educational policy. For Singapore to compete with other countries, the adoption of a technocratic and functional education is paramount. This in turn sets in motion a highly competitive and examination-focused schooling experience. The strong social Darwinism that shapes much of this urban education calls for strict control by the state not only in the regular schooling but also in the nonformal education offerings. The city-state adopts a high-level defensive stance, leading to an educational system characterized by coherence, control, and uniformity. The diversity promised by city life does not materialize when the city is simultaneously a nation and when it faces vital survival needs.

Economic considerations are also at work within socialist regimes. The case of Guangzhou gives evidence that despite highly egalitarian objectives of service for the city and the rural areas alike, the city manages to receive more support. This situation is a product of current policies giving priority to key point schools in China and to the city's function as a major locus of employment, which attracts a growing influx of adults and their children into Guangzhou despite a rather strong control of the population's movements.

The focus on urban phenomena, by moving to a very concrete level of analysis, shows that economic factors affect both free market and planned economies. Ultimately, then, it is the common features of intense growth and access to better services that make cities function in similar ways whether they operate within capitalist or socialist political systems.

INTERNATIONAL INFLUENCES ON THE CITY

Although cities themselves create important social and economic dynamics, these dynamics are also influenced by international forces or by responses to international conditions. The educational policies and programs of Singapore clearly respond to the city's international situation and prepare the country for economic competition. The migration toward Guangzhou despite the legal difficulties associated with it is a response to the role of the city in job creation; and the busy nature of the city's economy is linked to its many factories, whose products no doubt reach the global market.

There are also international links between a raw materials–based economy with low export revenues on the one hand and the adoption of structural adjustment programs on the other. Prescriptions under structural adjustment calling for the elimination of boarding schools in many African cities, for instance, which affect girls considerably, ultimately derive from the country's performance in the global market. In a more extreme fashion, the country's participation in the world economy also results in a growing number of poor people, including street children. This situation is reflected in the cases of Côte d'Ivoire (Chapter 10), Kenya (Chapter 12), and the Philippines (Chapter 12) reviewed in this book.

CONCLUSION

The analysis of educational conditions and issues in the framework of the urban space in which they appear opens opportunities for taking a second look at both educational policies and programs. The coding of the *urban* in terms of structural and spatial dimensions that bear on how knowledge and training are offered by the state and others is a task that this book only begins. Yet, we believe that the composite picture that emerges in this book is good evidence that we are facing a fertile terrain for further interrogation and empirical study.

REFERENCES

Castells, Manuel. (1979) *The Urban Question: A Marxist Approach*. Cambridge: MIT Press.

Castells, Manuel. (1983) *The City and the Grassroots*. Berkeley: University of California Press.

Katznelson, Ira. (1992) *Marxism and the City*. New York: Oxford University Press.

PART I

CONCEPTS AND TRENDS

1

Defining *Urban* in Educational Studies

R. Murray Thomas

My concern is the question of how to define the term *urban* so as to enhance the efficiency of research on urban education issues. The event that first drew this matter to my attention occurred when I worked with a team of Indonesian scholars studying the vocabulary and syntax knowledge of pupils at various levels of the Indonesian school system. The research was intended to help textbook writers adjust the contents of schoolbooks to the language abilities of pupils in the nation's multilingual society of 150 million people at that time (today the population reaches 180 million). Most Indonesian children in their own homes speak a local tongue, but at school they use the national language, Bahasa Indonesia, which is a sophisticated version of traditional Malay. With few exceptions, textbooks are written in the national language.

The textbook authors' problem of writing in language understood by pupils throughout the country resulted chiefly from the fact that certain of the nation's 350 or so local languages are very close to Bahasa Indonesia in vocabulary and structure, while others are only vaguely similar, and still others are quite different. Hence, the central research question became: Which Bahasa Indonesia words and sentence forms will children in different sections of the nation already know when they open their textbooks, and which words and structures will need to be explained within the text itself or in the teacher's guidebook?

As the research team considered how they would select samples of pupils to represent different levels of language knowledge, one member proposed an urban-rural dimension. His assumption was that urban children command more advanced national-language skills than rural children. This opinion was based on evidence that in many societies rural peoples lag behind city dwellers in modernization, including education and technological development. By drawing samples of children from both urban and rural settings, the investigation would cover the range of language ability from the most skilled (urban) to the least skilled (rural) pupils.

However, when the team began to identify specific geographical settings, it became clear that using a bare urban-rural dimension based solely on population size and density would be too crude to yield suitable data. The key variable affecting pupils' command of Bahasa Indonesia was not simply the size of a community but, rather, children's opportunities to hear and use the language. Thus, samples should be drawn to reflect different degrees of experience with the national tongue.

As team members adopted this new tack, they agreed that their original urban-rural dimension had not been entirely wrong. People from all over Indonesia immigrated to such large cities as Jakarta, Surabaya, Medan, and Bandung, where the national language became the medium of communication that people of all language backgrounds used in common. In such settings, children daily heard and used Bahasa Indonesia, even though a local dialect might also be common in their homes. However, in some rather large inland towns whose residents were almost entirely from one language background, the local language predominated in daily communication throughout the community. Children in such settings might encounter Bahasa Indonesia only in school. Furthermore, the amount of children's Bahasa Indonesia experience in the largest cities was certainly no greater than that in remote rural sections of the nation in which the local language was nearly identical to Bahasa Indonesia. In such villages, the only language children heard in either their homes or the broader community was the national tongue. In effect, choosing samples of respondents simply on the basis of population size and density would not suffice.

To solve their dilemma, the research team adopted two criteria intended to reflect three levels of opportunity to hear and use Bahasa Indonesia—a high level, a medium level, and a low level. By investigating children's command of vocabulary and syntax in geographical settings representing three such levels, the researchers believed they could discover the words and sentence types that textbook writers needed for preparing language-appropriate reading materials. The criteria focused on:

1. the degree of similarity between (1) Bahasa Indonesia and (2) the chief mode of daily communication among people of the community, and

2. the amount of mass-communication media in Bahasa Indonesia available in the community (newspapers, magazines, books, and radio and television programs). This second standard was added to the first on the assumption that a more sophisticated knowledge of the language would be gained in communities blessed with greater quantities of mass media.

Thus, settings were chosen to reflect three levels of these two elements. As a consequence, there was something of a rural-urban flavor to the final selection of sampling sites. The largest urban centers scored high on both criteria. The lowest scoring sites were in remote rural areas where a local language unrelated to Bahasa Indonesia predominated and mass communication media rarely if ever reached the residents. But the choice of sites was not identical to that which would have resulted if sampling had been based on only the size and density of a community's population.

The Indonesian case, then, illustrates a general research concern reflected in the three questions that serve as the center of discussion in the following pages: How have researchers studying urban matters defined the word *urban* as well as other terms related to it? In what ways can the decision about how to define *urban* be important? What guidelines for defining *urban* might be adopted to promote the value of research on education in urban settings?

COMMON WAYS OF DEFINING *URBAN*

A review of books and journals featuring research on population concentrations reveals that authors vary considerably in the way they define such terms as *urban, metropolitan, city, large city, capital city, inner city, ghetto, suburban, rural, country, town,* and *village.* Consider, for example, the following six definition options.

A first method, frequently found in both professional and popular literature, is to use a term that is unaccompanied by any explanation of precisely what it means in the study under discussion. The author apparently presumes that the meanings of such words as *urban* and *rural* are so universal that they require no clarification. This results in such phrases as "Fifty-four million individuals live outside America's designated urban areas" (Nachtigal, 1982, p. 5). What readers lack here is an exact meaning for *designated.*

A second common approach is that of publishing a study in a journal or book whose title includes the word *urban,* such as *Urban Education* or *Urban Studies,* without identifying what makes the content and conclusions specifically urban. However, the fact that the article or chapter appears in such a publication suggests that the contents are assumed to apply in urban settings. For example, in the 1990–91 issues of *Urban Education,* authors of twelve articles followed such a practice.

Another popular method involves selecting a site which by apparent common sense is a city and thus qualifies as urban—Berlin, Tokyo, Buenos Aires, Seoul, Hong Kong, and the like. A review of two years' issues of *Urban Education* revealed New York as that journal's most frequently mentioned city in studies of urban issues. However, this method suffers from want of precision, since places referred to as cities or towns can vary greatly in even such basic characteristics as numbers of residents and their geographical concentration. For example, one report of a study in *Urban Education* identified the research sites as Nebo and Park City, Utah, with no indication of why these sites qualified as urban (Petersen, Deyhle, & Watkins, 1988).

A fourth common technique consists of defining *urban* or *rural* numerically in terms of population size and density. Frequently a size is designated, such as "population over 25,000," without the density specified more precisely than that suggested by such a phrase as "100,000 living in close proximity" or "a closely settled area containing 50,000 or more inhabitants." In other cases, density will be indicated by the number of people per square mile or square kilometer.

A fifth option is that of adopting a definition used in conducting a population census. Consider, for example, how *urban* and *rural* were delineated for the 1980 and 1990 U.S. population surveys:

The urban population comprises all persons living in urbanized areas and in places of 2,500 or more inhabitants outside urbanized areas (see definition of urbanized areas). More specifically, the urban population consists of all persons living in (1) places of 2,500 or more inhabitants incorporated as cities, villages, boroughs (except in Alaska and New York), and towns (except in the New England States, New York, and Wisconsin), but excluding those persons living in the rural portions of extended cities; (2) census designated places of 2,500 or more inhabitants; and (3) other territory, incorporated or unincorporated, included in urbanized areas. The population not classified as urban constitutes the rural population. (*1980 Census of Population*, 1983, pp. A1-A2)

This, however, is not the entire census definition. A page of additional, somewhat complex distinctions among forms of *urbanized areas* has been designated in order to "provide a better separation of urban and rural population in the vicinity of large cities. An urbanized area consists of a central city or cities and surrounding closely settled territory (urban fringe)" (*1980 Census of Population*, 1983, p. A2).

More precisely, an urbanized area is identified as:

one or more places ("central place") and the adjacent densely settled surrounding territory ("urban fringe") that together have a minimum of 50,000 persons. The urban fringe generally consists of continuous territory having a density of at least 1,000 persons per square mile. The urban fringe also includes outlying territory of such density if it was connected to the core of the contiguous area by road and is within 1½ road miles of that core, or within 5 road miles of the core but separated by water or other undevelopable territory. Other territory with a population density of fewer than 1,000 people per square mile is included in the urban fringe if it eliminates an enclave or closes an indentation in the boundary of the urbanized area. The population density is determined by (1) outside of a place, one or more contiguous census blocks with a population density of at least 1,000 persons per square mile or (2) inclusion of a place containing census blocks that have at least 50 percent of the population of the place and a density of at least 1,000 persons per square mile. (*1990 Census of Population and Housing: Summary Population and Housing Characteristics, California*, 1991, p. A12)

A further variant of the Census Bureau's definition is the concept labeled "Standard Metropolitan Statistical Area," a designation that may appear simply as "SMSA" in research reports, so that readers must already know the specific meaning of this term if they are to understand what sort of region is represented in the report (example: Galster and Keeney, 1988). Although the detailed definition of SMSAs is rather complex, their general nature is suggested by one or both of two criteria they need to meet. They must (1) include a city with a population of at least 50,000 within its corporate limits or (2) include a "Census-Bureau-defined urbanized area (which must have a population of at least 50,000) and a total SMSA population of at least 100,000 (or, in New England 75,000)" (*User's Guide*, 1982, p. 45). More broadly, "an SMSA includes a city and, generally, its entire UA [urbanized area] and the remainder of the county or counties in which the UA is located. An SMSA also includes those additional outlying counties which meet specified criteria relating to metropolitan character and level of commuting of workers into the central city or counties" (*User's Guide*, 1982, p. 45).

When authors of a study merely note that they have adopted a census definition, and they fail to offer more precise information about the area investigated, readers can still be puzzled about exactly what *urban* is intended to mean. Puzzlement can result if (1) the readers are not well acquainted with the details of the complicated census definitions, (2) the authors have not identified which of the definitions (urban, UA, SMSA) they intend, or (3) the authors have not adopted all of the nuances of a complete census description. Furthermore, a reader may be misled if the authors have not explained which year's census definition they used, a problem resulting from the fact that the Census Bureau on different occasions has altered the way *urban* differs from *rural*. For example:

Since 1960 there has been an increasing trend toward the extension of city boundaries to include territory essentially rural in character. The classification of all the inhabitants of such cities as urban would include in the urban population persons whose environment is primarily rural in character. For the 1970 and 1980 censuses, in order to separate these people from those residing in the closely settled portions of such cities, the Bureau of the Census classified as rural a portion or portions of each such city that was located in any urbanized area. To be treated as an extended city, a city must contain one or more areas that are each at least 5 square miles in extent and have a population density of less than 100 persons per square mile. The area or areas must constitute at least 25 percent of the land area of the legal city or include at least 25 square miles. These areas are excluded from the urbanized area.

Those cities designated as extended cities thus consist of an urban part and a rural part. Only the urban part is considered to be the central city of an urbanized area.

However, the term *central city* . . . refers to the entire population within the legal boundaries of the city. (*1980 Census of Population,* 1983, p. A2)

A sixth approach to defining *urban* involves combining population size with descriptive characteristics chosen as indicators of the kind of urbanization or ruralization the investigators had in mind. Authors may either limit their choice to one descriptive characteristic beyond population size or extend it to more than one. As an instance of a single characteristic: ''Guadalajara and Puebla were selected as case studies because both have a high level of tenancy and non-ownership by Mexican standards and both are in metropolitan areas of over one million people'' (Gilbert and Varley, 1990).

An extreme proposal of multiple indicators for distinguishing urban from rural is Nachtigal's list of ostensible correlates of urban and rural that he derived from summaries of past investigations:

Rural Americans lag behind their metropolitan counterparts in terms of wage levels, family income, adequate housing, and access to education and health care. Rural systems have relatively fewer support staff and services, less revenue, and lower per-pupil expenditures. Children in rural America begin school later, progress more slowly, and attain fewer years of education than their urban/suburban counterparts. In addition, rural residents are less likely to enter college, receive vocational training, or enroll in adult education programs. (Nachtigal, 1982, p. 5)

An author drawing on Nachtigal's approach could be expected to define urban in terms of population size as well as several of Nachtigal's correlates, then choose to study research sites that are comparable in size and correlates.

In conclusion, then, there is no standard practice among researchers for defining *urban, rural,* or other terms associated with population size and density. This lack of uniformity causes problems for both the producers and the consumers of research.

EFFECTS OF DECISIONS ABOUT HOW TO DEFINE *URBAN*

With few exceptions, the purpose of every social-psychological research project is not merely to describe a given group of people in a particular setting. Instead, the purpose is to derive generalizations that can usefully be applied to people other than those who were directly studied. Thus, the intent of virtually all urban research is to produce information helpful for understanding people in urban settings other than the one originally investigated. If this goal of generating useful generalizations is to be achieved, then the other people and environments to which the research results can properly be applied should display the same—or very similar—*significant characteristics* as those exhibited by the group and the setting on which the research was originally conducted.

Figure 1.2
Educational Aspects as Causal Variables

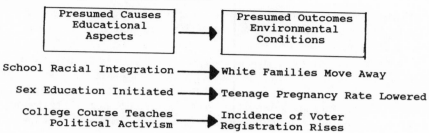

cational establishment or of the urban setting that may not cause an outcome but are still correlated with the outcome variable. Oftentimes the aim of a research project is to determine which variables that are correlated with an outcome are probably causes and which are related to the outcome but are not contributing causes. In other words, the research task is to differentiate between *causal* and *casual* variables. For example, if a higher degree of child neglect was found in families in which both parents were employed than in families in which one parent stayed home, is the causal factor "both parents work versus one parent works," or does this factor just happen to be somewhat correlated with degrees of child neglect, while the real cause is something else, such as a combination of such variables as (1) the type of after-school supervision of the child, (2) the quality of parents' interaction with the child, and (3) the child's level of social intelligence.

A fourth conception of cause-effect relationships proposes a symbiotic relationship in which educational aspects and environmental conditions reciprocally influence each other. For example, Galster and Keeney (1988) studied factors affecting economic opportunity in representative Standard Metropolitan Statistical Areas. Included among the variables they investigated were access to schooling, educational attainment, racial discrimination, housing and housing-price discrimination, occupations, and interracial differences in incomes. They concluded that these factors mutually influenced each other in a complex web difficult to disentangle and assess. Race and economic status affected housing location, which itself affected educational opportunity and attainment. Educational attainment influenced occupation, which affected housing quality and location, and so on. Hence, in such a case the investigator's challenge becomes that of trying to evaluate the directions and amounts of influence of these multiple variables.

In summary, the educational aspects on which a researcher focuses can play the roles of outcome variables, presumed causal factors, noncausal correlated variables, or both cause-and-effect variables. It is important that investigators indicate which of these roles they intend a given variable to fulfill. It is also important that authors tell why they have chosen each of the variables and have assigned them their roles.

Correlations among Variables

Of the possible relationships between (1) specified aspects of education and (2) specified aspects of the environment, which ones interest me and why?

In educational studies, the essence of explanation consists of demonstrating why certain variables are related to each other while others are not. Or more precisely, explanation involves offering a line of reasoning that shows why there is a higher degree of correlation between certain factors than between others. Consequently an investigator's problem becomes that of (1) deciding which of the possible correlations among aspects of education and features of the environment warrant attention and then (2) positing a line of reasoning that might explain the degree of relationship found among the variables. As an example, consider a study involving two education aspects—students' level of academic success and students' use of drugs. The investigator's choice of these two variables has been founded on the hypothesis that youths who do poorly in their studies are more prone to use drugs than those who do well.

However, the research is more specifically *urban* when there is a comparison of an education aspect with one or more characteristics of an environment defined as *urban*. For instance, an investigator might assess the relationship between the extent of gang violence in the community (as a feature of the environment) and the ability of pupils to concentrate on their studies (an educational outcome), with this choice of factors being based on the theory that an uncontrolled, destructive social atmosphere in a community distracts learners from academic pursuits.

In effect, I am suggesting that in research on urban education there is typically embedded in the study's meaning of *urban* a selection of educational aspects that are thought to be related to characteristics of an urban setting. If the hypothesized correlations are actually found in the study, then it becomes the researcher's task to suggest whether the relationship is causal or simply casual and then to adduce an argument in support of this suggestion.

Methods of Identifying and Assessing Education Aspects

Definitions used in research studies are most specific when they are carried to the operational level. In other words, the most precise way of conveying the meaning of a particular variable is to describe the operations involved in recognizing or measuring it in real-life situations. For instance, we best understand what is intended by the term *academic success* when we learn that a student's grade point average throughout high school has been used as the indicator of academic performance. We know what the phrase "ability of pupils to concentrate on their studies" means when we are told that the researcher measured concentration by observing how consistently selected pupils in a classroom carried out individual assignments at their desks on ten successive school days. We understand what is intended by "incidence of drug use" when the researcher reports that incidence was judged by means of questionnaires filled out anonymously by high school students during one social studies class period.

WHAT ARE THE SIGNIFICANT CHARACTERISTICS OF THE URBAN ENVIRONMENT?

As in the case of education aspects, the task of identifying and assessing the significant characteristics of an urban setting can be directed by three questions, focusing on (1) selected features of the environment, (2) correlations among variables, and (3) methods of identifying and assessing those features. For convenience of discussion, the first two questions will be considered together. The third will be presented separately.

Selected Environmental Features and Correlations among Variables

The two guide questions are: Which features of the environment do I think exert significant influence on the characteristics of education that I have identified (or vice versa) and why? What relationships do I consider important between (1) specified aspects of the educational establishment and (2) specific features of the environment, and why?

Like education aspects, environmental variables can be conceptualized as outcomes (effects), causal factors (causes), noncausal correlates (casual relationships), or both causes and effects. An example of an environmental factor serving as an outcome variable would be found in a study focusing on how students' attitudes about conserving natural resources will influence a city's waste-product recycling practices. Although, as in this example, educational research can center on the environmental outcomes of people's behavior, the majority of studies view the variables the other way around. Most investigations treat questions of how urban conditions affect students or affect the conduct of the education system. In most studies, the researchers are seeking to discover the magnitude of correlations between (1) hypothesized causal factors in the urban setting and (2) some aspect of the people involved in education (learners, teachers, administrators) or of the educational establishment's policies and practices.

The problem for researchers, then, is one of identifying which urban features they believe might have an important effect on the aspect of education in which they are interested. Cast as a question, the problem becomes: What is the nature of the relationship (and particularly the magnitude of correlation) between (1) one or more estimated causal factors in the urban setting and (2) one or more selected education outcomes? The way this question is answered is intimately linked to the way *urban* will be defined in the study at hand. Why this is true can be demonstrated with the following example.

To begin, let us assume that our problem is a typical one in urban-education research—that of discovering a causal relationship between (1) one or more features of an urban environment and (2) an education outcome. Our education outcome is the incidence of respiratory disorders in school children. The variable *respiratory disorders* is the significant education aspect which serves as our initial guide to choosing the urban-environment characteristics we will hypothesize as significant. Our research project will then consist of collecting data to test our hypotheses about the degree of influence those environmental factors likely have on respiratory infections among pupils. Our choice of environmental features is guided by information from the past about such breathing disorders as the common cold, influenza, asthma, lung cancer, and the like. The two environmental variables we choose to study are air quality and weather conditions. More precisely, we wish to learn more about the effect of those two variables on pupils' respiratory infections in urban versus rural settings.

As we set out to define *urban* and *rural* for this investigation, I suggest that our study will yield the most precise results if our definition focuses on environmental characteristics that are probably *causal*. This means that we will not be satisfied with defining *urban* and *rural* in terms of population size and density, since neither of those is a cause. It is true that, in general, there is a higher proportion of respiratory difficulties in crowded cities than in sparsely settled country villages. However, population size and density are not causal factors in themselves. They are merely noncausal correlates of something else that contributes to respiratory disorders. In our study we are hypothesizing that the *something else* could be air quality and weather conditions as truly causal factors. In other words, any correlation between population size/density and breathing problems is the result of differences in the contents of the air and the weather conditions in large and small concentrations of people. But not all cities of similar size are alike in either air quality or climate. A smoky factory city to which many workers commute by car can have far more air pollution than does a city of similar size which has outlawed polluting industries and whose residents travel mostly by public transportation. Likewise, weather conditions in a Minnesota farming district can differ markedly from those in a Texas ranching area, though both may be called *rural*. As a result of such differences, any correlation between population size/density and pulmonary infections will be considerably lower than the correlation between any truly causal environmental features and pulmonary disorders.

If we wish to base constructive social action on the results of our study, we should recognize that simply computing the relationship between population size/density and the incidence of respiratory problems furnishes us no useful information. Seeking to reduce the population of a community is not only an unrealistic endeavor, but such a reduction in itself does not get at the cause. In contrast, if we define the environmental factors in terms of air quality and weather, we can take constructive social action. If poor air quality is found to be at least a partial cause of respiratory disorders, we can take steps to improve the air (reduce auto and industrial emissions). If we find that weather conditions also contribute significantly to respiratory infections, we can conceivably improve people's protection from inclement weather (suggest suitable clothing, housing, work habits, and forms of recreation).

Methods of Identifying and Assessing Urban Characteristics

What methods should I use for recognizing and assessing each of the significant aspects of people, and why these methods?

As noted above, the initial guide to choosing urban characteristics is the aspect of education on which the research is to focus. If this aspect is viewed as the outcome variable, then the question becomes: What features of the urban environment do I believe are at least partial determinants of that particular aspect of education? The identification of such features can be guided by (1) commonsense observations of urban conditions as related to the education aspect, (2) generalizations from past research studies which the present investigators believe should be verified, refined, or refuted, or (c) a social-psychological theory which the investigators wish to apply or test.

Once the environmental features have been identified, each needs to be defined operationally. For example, in our hypothetical research on pupils' respiratory disorders, the variable *air quality* needs to be specified in terms of the percentages of different chemicals in the atmosphere and the way these amounts will be measured. Likewise, the variable *weather conditions* or *climate* needs to be specified in terms of temperature, wind, humidity, precipitation, and the like. Furthermore, the techniques for measuring amounts of each of these factors need to be described.

WHAT EXPLANATION OF *URBAN* SHOULD READERS RECEIVE?

I have suggested in the foregoing discussion that a definition of *urban* in educational research is most useful if it specifies characteristics of any setting labeled *urban* that are likely significant determinants of the particular educational outcome that interests the researcher. At the operational definition level, this means not only that the significant environmental aspects (the urban factors) and educational outcomes be identified, but also that the techniques used to recognize and assess each aspect be explained in detail. Such a working definition serves as the researcher's clearest guide to sampling, instrument construction, and the interpretation of results. That type of definition is also of great aid to readers who might wish to replicate the study in another setting or to estimate how well the results of the reported investigation might fit their own situation. However, a detailed definition of this variety may be rather lengthy and complex. The question then may be asked: How much of such an extensive definition should be included in reports of the research study? I would propose that such a decision be guided by three criteria—most significant features, available space, and nature of the readership.

Most Significant Features

If the procedures suggested in this chapter are followed, then *urban* will not be defined simply by such a term as *city* or *metropolitan area,* by the name of a community (Bombay, Lima, Beijing), or by population size and density. Instead, the definition will include a description of environmental features that are presumed to be significantly related to specified educational variables in a causal manner. If these features differ markedly between large and small population concentrations, then their description might be prefaced with such a phrase as: "The term *urban* in the following pages is used in particular sense. It refers to environments in which. . . ." The "which" is then followed by a description of the selected environmental characteristics. In effect, the essence of the definition of *urban* and other such terms resides in the specification of the aspects of the environment considered significant in this particular study.

Available Space

When the report of a study is issued as a master's degree thesis or doctoral dissertation, there are no space limitations. This is also the case with accounts of research prepared for funding agencies or for informal distribution among professional colleagues. In such outlets, the complete, detailed definition of *urban* should be published so that readers not only recognize how closely the setting of the investigation matches the settings with which they are acquainted, but also could replicate that research.

In contrast to outlets that offer unlimited space, articles in professional journals must conform to set space restrictions. The same is true of reports appearing in the popular press—magazines, newspapers, and radio or television broadcasts. In between these two extremes of unlimited and highly restricted space are short monographs and book chapters, which offer the opportunity for moderately detailed descriptions of a study. Consequently, a full operational definition of significant characteristics of education and of the environment should appear in outlets providing unlimited space. In contrast, in outlets that enforce stringent space restrictions, there may be room for only brief mention of the most potent educational and environmental features, so that detail and precision are sacrificed.

Nature of the Readership

Readers of professional journals usually have a store of specialized knowledge beyond that held by the general public. Therefore, a single word or brief phrase may suffice to inform the journal audience of some environmental feature or research procedure that would mean nothing to someone not well acquainted with the field. Examples of such items are *megalopolis, anova, systematic sampling,* and *Likert scale.* Such terms can be used in an article without the sort of accompanying explanation required by less knowledgeable readers. On the other hand, specialists in the field will often wish to know certain crucial technical details about a study that would be of no interest to the general reader. Such details are often needed in journal articles and extended research reports. Thus, the author of a research report can profitably consider the nature of the likely reading audience when deciding on how detailed the definition of *urban* and similar terms should be.

CONCLUSION

In this paper I have proposed that in research designed to explain how urban conditions affect aspects of education, investigators can profitably begin by defining in operational terms the aspect of the education system that will be viewed as the outcome variable. Then features of the urban environment that hypothetically contribute to the outcome variable are also defined operationally. This combination of education-aspect and urban-environment features becomes the definition of *urban* (or any similar term) for the purposes of the particular research project.

Furthermore, if the investigators choose to study the influence of some education aspect on the urban environment, then the selected education aspect becomes the imagined causal variable, and features of the environment that hypothetically are affected by that education aspect are defined operationally to form that study's definition of *urban.*

In summary, defining *urban* only in terms of population size and density is not sufficient. What is also needed is a specification of the particular characteristics of urban-ness that are thought to influence educational conditions or vice versa.

REFERENCES

Galster, G. C., & Keeney, W. M. (1988) Race, Residence, Discrimination, and Economic Opportunity. *Urban Affairs Quarterly 24* (1): pp. 87–117.

Gilbert, A., & Varley, A. (1990) The Mexican Landlord: Rental Housing in Guadalajara and Puebla. *Urban Studies 27* (1): pp. 23–44.

Nachtigal, P. M. (ed.) (1982) *Rural Education: In Search for a Better Way.* Boulder, CO: Westview Press.

1980 Census of Population. Characteristics of the Population: General Social and Economic Characteristics. (1983) Washington, DC: Bureau of the Census.

1990 Census of Population and Housing. Summary Population and Housing Characteristics—California. (1991) Washington, DC: Bureau of the Census.

Petersen, K. D., Deyhle, D., and Watkins, W. (1988) Evaluation that Accommodates Minority Teacher Contributions. *Urban Education 23* (2): pp. 133–149.

Rossell, C. H. (1990) The Carrot or the Stick for School Desegregation Policy? *Urban Affairs Quarterly 25* (3): pp. 474–499.

User's Guide: Part B. Glossary—1980 Census of Population and Housing. (1982) Washington, DC: Bureau of the Census.

2

Some Trends and Issues Affecting Education in the Urban Context

Nelly P. Stromquist

A frequent variable in many sociological and educational analyses is urban/ rural residence. Often the full meaning of this concept is left unspecified, as if *rural* and *urban* had identical meanings across cultures and as if the experience of being rural or urban affected equally all groups residing in those environments. Moreover, a common practice has been to treat urban/rural residence as a control variable, thus minimizing the fact that different territorial contexts have powerful interactions with other social forces and producing analyses that distort social phenomena through the use of inappropriate statistical assumptions.

A common characteristic of contemporary society is the increasing concentration of population in cities, as shown in Table 2.1. This increase in urbanization is occurring more intensely in developing countries. Of the twenty-one cities predicted to have more than ten million people in the early 1990s, seventeen are located in the Third World (World Bank, 1991). Another characteristic of this unstoppable urban growth is its tie to poverty, as most cities are not producing the necessary industrial and economic growth to accommodate their new inhabitants; an estimated 25 percent of the urban population is living in poverty (World Bank, 1991).

All social interaction takes place in space, and certain types of space produce relatively predictable outcomes. The Chicago School of social research comprised the first group of observers to pay systematic attention to factors such as density, size, and heterogeneity of population in the cities in the shaping of

Table 2.1
Projections of the Urban Population and Levels of Urbanization in the World (1980–2025)

	Urban Population 1980	2000 (in millions)	2025	Levels of Urbanization 1980	2000 (in percentages)	2025
Third World	905	1781	3621	38	36	42
Africa	106	288	609	24	35	38
Latin America	321	410	640	64	75	82
Asia (market economy)	356	745	1669	25	34	57
Asia (planned economy)	210	336	698	20	25	44
Developed countries	762	917	1067	65	66	71
Europe	321	363	393	66	71	75
USSR	161	214	262	61	66	71
North America	162	194	232	64	65	67
Japan	91	102	108	78	79	82

Source: Bairoch, 1988. (Copyright 1988. Permission granted by the University of Chicago Press and Mansell Publisher, UK.) The definition of *urban* varies by country.

social relations. Subsequent studies have linked the urban context to the scale of services and the relations between various institutions and state agencies. Today space is conceptualized not merely as an environment, but also as a factor itself in the creation of individual and collective identities and social inequalities. Space in the cities creates social hierarchies that are more structural than face-to-face in nature. These hierarchies are more intractable both to study and to modify.

Space is seen as structuring as well as being structured by individuals (Shilling, 1991). The contributions by Giddens (1984) have further helped us to conceptualize structures not only as external forces but also as a set of rules and resources which social actors draw upon in the process of social interaction. New research, such as that conducted by Garner in the United Kingdom (1988), has examined social effects at a higher level of aggregation than the family and at a more precise level than "urban" by identifying "neighborhood effects." This new level of aggregation involves sociospatial models that consider social, economic, and political processes in a local area and see the role of schooling (and other social institutions) as a mediating agency in these processes. This new level of analysis appears promising; its application, however, is still uncharted terrain.

Studies of urban education have been criticized on five counts: inadequate theorization of the urban; overemphasis on the cultural and underemphasis upon the structural as explanatory categories; domination of inquiry by various forms of abstract empiricism or by microinstitutional studies; inadequate sense of the historical in the understanding of social phenomena; and limited concepts of power and resources expressed in a narrow sense of the political (Grace,

1984, p. 17). It is not clear that these weaknesses have been satisfactorily redressed in developed countries. The dearth of articles dealing with the urban contexts in developing countries makes Grace's criticism academic for that region.

CHARACTERISTICS OF THE URBAN CONTEXT

Classical advocates of modernization (McClelland, 1961; Lerner, 1964; Inkeles and Smith, 1974) saw great promise in the city. They considered that through its concentration of individuals the city would give rise to economies of scale, which in turn would make possible widespread use of mass media and schooling, as well as enable the rise of efficient industries. Durkheim, an earlier observer, believed population growth increased "moral density" and that moral density raised both the level and scope of economic competition, causing individuals (especially those who fail in the competition) to explore new ways of making a living—and, one presumes, other innovations (Tuma and Hannan, 1984). For those who extol the virtues of city life, the city is the "cutting edge of society," as most changes and innovations appear first in the cities (Michelson and Levine, 1979; Bairoch, 1988). The city was also to foster social mobility by providing "the opportunity to move through innumerable sectors of urban economic life, both in industry and in services" (Bairoch, 1988, p. 341). The physical mobility it offered was to lead to different possibilities of employment: "Within a given sector or firm the chances of promotion are greater than in the country" (Bairoch, 1988, p. 342).

The city does provide advantages, but more so for the wealthy. Often the city's wealth does not heal the wounds of its poor but only salts them (McAdam, 1988). Most cities are characterized by significant internal differentiation. For those who are wealthy and live in cities, many advantages accrue: access to public services, to diverse and new forms of art, to modern technologies and comfort. For the rich, obstacles of space and distance are attenuated by easy transportation and communication facilities. For the poor, access to jobs and public facilities is difficult and the bigger the city, the greater the difficulties. In balance, however, cities are better off than the rural areas in terms of proximity to social services. Yet, this convenience comes at a high cost: Urban people are more vulnerable to unemployment, since they depend on their wages to survive. It has been found that urban households have worse nutritional status than rural households, and that there is a significant female disadvantage in nutrition, health care, and mortality (World Bank, 1991, p. 51).

While the poor are more bound to their physical environment, the proximity between the rich and the poor quickly develops an awareness of the gap between them. Katznelson captures this effectively when he states that "cities have always been condensations of their civilizations. If their density distorts, so it also reveals" (1992, p. ix). This gap sometimes creates social and racial tensions; most often it leads to segregated residential patterns and thus to differentiated access to social services, including education. On the other hand, the concentration of people in neighborhoods facilitates their organization, and their proximity to those in power guarantees attention to their demands and sometimes consideration of them. As social relations become fixed in space, these spaces acquire distinct and separate identities. Often one or more specific settings or buildings within these spaces become focal points for consciousness and interest formation and aggregation. Gradually a church, a marketplace, or a transportation center generates "a focus, a hub of activity, an identity, and a boundary" (Katznelson, 1992, p. 20).

The mobilization promoted by high social density has not been a universal phenomenon. As Schmidt-Kallert (1992) notes, the poor in Southeast Asian cities have not organized politically to the same extent as the poor in Brazil. It appears that under conditions of extreme hardship, all energies are devoted to daily survival. Nonetheless, several cities have experienced the emergence of popular movements whose demands have obtained significant response by the state. Castells (1983, p. xviii) notes that successful protest movements have emerged mainly in the city and that they have emerged around three major themes: demands focused on the collective consumption of goods and services; defense of cultural identity associated with a specific territory; and political mobilization, usually emphasizing the role of local government. Cities have also been the terrain for large mobilizations in favor of schools. Two recent cases are Zona Leste in São Paulo (Brazil) and Villa El Salvador (Peru), where the communities demanded and obtained more schools from government authorities and in some cases used community self-help to acquire classrooms and schools at primary and secondary levels. The urban context thus constitutes a crucial factor through which to analyze outside pressures upon the school system and how it responds to them.

Negative features of city life are multiple: residential and educational segregation, crowded and unhealthy housing conditions, polluted and congested roads, racial tensions, visible unemployment—the list could go on and on—most linked to economic differentiation. Among the poor, despite the density of the population and the physical proximity of people with similar strategic interests, there is much isolation. For example, the illiterate poor, unable to decipher printed messages on streets and buses, lead very circumscribed lives. Slum dwellers, even those located in the "inner city," living in cramped housing conditions, are isolated—both from others who live there and from those who live outside it. Their sense of community is reduced by the constant crime that poverty produces, and their poverty does not allow them to use financial resources to explore city features beyond their immediate neighborhood. For poor women, the low quality of services such as water, sewerage, and accessible transportation results in heavy domestic work loads.

Three broad patterns of spatial concentration and inequality have been identified: the economic and social differences between urban and rural areas, the economic and social disparities between different regions of a country, and the degree to which one city dominates the national urban structure (Gilbert and Gugler, 1982). The systematic impact of these patterns on the provision of public social services, particularly education, remains to be fully analyzed.

The functional density that was expected in cities has long given way to what is now recognized as hyperurbanization. Large cities place increasingly greater demands on rural agricultural production while simultaneously depriving the countryside of its most capable workers. Hyperurbanization has been identified as one of the main probable causes of the increasing food deficit in the Third World. Shantytowns have been a growing worldwide phenomenon since the 1960s, and it appears that they will continue to exist for a long time. The average proportion of urban populations living in shantytowns in the world is 44 percent; predictions are that it will continue to grow in the next decades. In many cities the proportion of people living in shantytowns exceeds 70 percent, including Addis Ababa (90 percent), Yaounde (90), Ibadan (75), and Santo Domingo (72) (Bairoch, 1988, p. 473, citing data from the UN World Housing Survey, 1976).

THE DOMINANT MODEL OF DEVELOPMENT

The dominant model of national development is predicated today on industrialization and free trade. Pricing and marketing policies consistently promote urban and industrial growth; they also rely on the exploitation of peasant labor (Martínez, 1990). The modernization model strongly favors cities over rural areas; hence cities accumulate much of the financial and intellectual resources of the nation and attract people from all regions of the country. The city has indeed its rewards; those who live in the country typically earn 25 to 50 percent less than those in the towns and cities (UNDP, 1991, p. 26). The relative wealth of the cities—to be sure, concentrated in the hands of a few—is often reflected in the high rates of urban consumption and characterized by investment in real estate rather than by redistribution in other regions of the country.

Those who migrate to the cities are those with more education than those who stay. "One of the most consistent findings of rural-urban migration studies is the positive correlation between educational attainment and migration" (Todaro, 1985, p. 256; see also Bairoch, 1988). One of the main reasons rural inhabitants move into urban areas is the belief (often a fact) that they will get jobs and that those jobs will pay better than any they could get back home. Migrations increase the growth rate of urban job seekers relative to overall urban population growth; urban areas always have surplus labor.

Even if the poor urban residents have low levels of formal political participation (that is, in electoral politics), their sheer number makes it difficult for decision makers to ignore the cities. In satisfying city demands, however, intranational disparities increase and so a vicious circle, by which the city draws in rural people and gives its growing urban populations increasingly more attention, is solidified.

The educational model, through its content and organization, establishes city life and norms as a standard for the nation. Observers have noted the widespread reluctance of individuals to live in rural areas after three or four years of schooling. Because the city serves both the rich and the poor, it ends up designing programs for its most powerful clientele, the middle and upper classes. This often translates into providing academic knowledge for eventual transition into the university. In consequence the public school curriculum contains very limited skills training, least of all those pertinent to rural activities.

Encounters with the use of the city's services and facilities give rise to the acquisition of city skills. Urban residents learn to use resources such as transportation, child care services, and schools; their exposure to mass media and other modern stimuli further enhances their awareness of social life. There is scant research on the differential effects of city and rural environments upon cognitive growth. Longitudinal research conducted in three different areas of Peru shows that children in a major urban area (Lima) obtained the highest scores in literacy and cognitive ability, while in a small rural community (Lamas), where both parents worked away from home and thus left their children unattended, children of similar ages and years of schooling obtained the lowest cognitive scores (Stevenson, Chen, and Booth, 1990). It would appear, therefore, that the city has a positive effect through its "informal" learning systems.

But city life produces negative consequences also at the personal level. Those who have acquired city skills tend to be city-bound. They see their lives as happening mainly in the cities and do not want to accept jobs elsewhere. Moreover, for the poor the "unhappy coincidence of home and neighborhood characteristics" (Garner, 1988) produces deleterious effects on formal schooling. There is some evidence that neighborhood characteristics affect educational achievement, even though methodologically speaking it is difficult to separate this influence from those of the home and the school. One study, by Garner (1988), based on a sample of 3,000 adults in Glasgow, found that "neighborhood deprivation" effects (independent of home effects) had a lowering impact of almost 40 percent of a standard deviation on educational attainment. Garner measured "neighborhood deprivation" by aggregating measures of employment, youth unemployment, and single-parent families.

THE COLONIAL INHERITANCE

In the colonized countries, the city was the instrument of conquest. In most cases, urbanization was a consequence of colonization. In Latin America new cities were established and each urban area given jurisdiction over a large tract of rural land and its subjugated population. Cities were located throughout the colonial empire on the basis of their geographical suitability for exports (Gilbert and Gugler, 1982). Following independence, urban and regional centers continued in the locations used by the colonial governments. Cities often became parasitic, owing to the loss of power suffered by traditional rural elites, who came to live in the city, and to the fact that colonization often involved partial or total prohibition of industrial production, favoring instead the exploitation of raw materials. In addition, the increased exports of nonstaple agricultural production brought excessive specialization in the production of these commodities and deteriorating productivity for food crops in the rural areas.

Colonization introduced new patterns both in social life and in the sexual division of labor, processes that became more intensive in the cities through schools and through less structured settings such as the *foyers sociaux* (the latter emphasized the training of women as Westernized housewives; see Hunt, 1990). Urbanization made women more dependent on men as men left agricultural subsistence to work in jobs in the cities (Duley and Edwards, 1986), which had the double consequence of depriving women of direct access to cash and making them work harder than before to support their families.

In Third World regions with older education systems derived from long-term colonial rule, such as those of over 300 years in Latin America, the educational system has over time undergone a process of bifurcation into private schooling—traditionally catering to the elites—and public—increasingly for low-income people. In newer nation-states, particularly those in Africa, private schools are not readily identified with elite or better education, since there they tended to emerge to satisfy unmet governmental supply. Nonetheless, there are signs that the educational system in these countries is also undergoing a process of bifurcation. This process is manifested in the educational gaps between rural and urban areas and within urban areas in the coexistence of elite private and low–social class public schools.

The current manner by which international agencies give support to developing nation-states so that they may continue their access to credits reduces the leverage that rural areas can exert on the government. Villagers can be ignored thanks to the available international credit; unattended by the state, these villagers become further alienated, a situation particularly evident in sub-Saharan Africa (Sandbrook, 1986).

PARTICULARITIES OF ADVANCED INDUSTRIAL COUNTRIES

For some time social crises in developed countries have been described as a crisis of the inner city. In the United States, these problems have been those of children without childhood, family disruption, noise, pollution, unemployment, drugs, and crime (Wilson, 1987). In this country, the phenomenon of decaying cities, caused by the concentration of the poor in inner cities, has lead to the identification of the "truly disadvantaged" (Wilson, 1987). This population has often been localized primarily in the "black ghetto," which developed from declines in the manufacturing sector and the rise of technological innovations that both diminished the demand for unskilled labor and relocated the skilled workers in the suburbs. In the United States between 1970 and 1980 the overall population in the fifty largest cities declined by about 5 percent, but the number of poor people in them increased by about 12 percent. In addition, the number of poor people living in "poverty areas" (defined as those with more than 20 percent poor residents) increased by 31 percent and the number of those living in "high poverty areas" (greater than 40 percent poor) increased by 66 percent. The growth of these areas has occurred primarily among people of color. It has been observed that "because schools in high poverty areas are likely to have greater proportions of [academically] poor students . . . the concentration of poverty in central cities has disturbing implications for achievement trends in urban schools in general and among African American and Hispanic American students in particular" (CPRE, 1991).

Most of the immigrants to the United States and other countries go to live in cities, thereby continually increasing the degree of cultural and linguistic diversity. In cities such as Los Angeles and New York there is a constant influx of non-English-speaking immigrants, which brings to the fore the issue of language policies in the school—usually suppressed with less vocal or visible populations. It appears that migration, especially among the Latin Americans in the United States, is characterized by high levels of family separation, for both men and women (Chinchilla and Hamilton, 1991). And among those from Central America, children usually arrive with traumatic war experiences. These immigrant children often find themselves in educational settings which do not recognize their cultural and psychological adjustment problems.

Large cities in the United States generate de facto racial segregation caused by residential patterns which legal measures such as busing have not been able to erase. In fact, there are trends toward increased segregation. Empirical evidence shows a general lack of equal educational opportunity at the elementary and secondary levels. (For a recent account of these disparities see Kozol, 1991.) Desegregation as a solution has been defective and has also shown unintended effects. In the absence of widespread acceptance, desegregation has had some negative consequences on urban life and the schools. A study of desegregation in the St. Louis metropolitan area (by R. Crain, quoted in *The Spencer Foundation Newsletter,* June 1991) found that it had lowered the morale of inner-city teachers, who felt desegregation took away the high-achieving and highly motivated students. Desegregation orders have also fueled much of the expansion of private schooling going on in U.S. cities today.

In major urban centers in the United States minorities have either become or are about to become the majority in institutions of postsecondary education, a proportion that will continue to rise as a result of immigration, comparatively high birth rates, and the aging of the minority youth already in school (Western Interstate Commission for Higher Education, 1987). On the other hand, the evidence also indicates only minor progress at the university level, since the proportion of minority students who transfer from community colleges—where those who continue past the secondary level tend to concentrate—to four-year institutions is extremely small.

The urban context brings people into close contact with each other and thus unleashes deeper discussions about the norms society must share to keep its coherence and those that can be allowed to vary with no loss of collective sense. In this respect, an understanding of the urban context in developed countries may provide insights into the challenges to schools in maintaining old values and creating new ones.

PARTICULARITIES OF THE URBAN CONTEXT IN DEVELOPING COUNTRIES

Third World urban space manifests itself in positive and negative ways. On the positive side, life in the city means proximity to the nation's center of political and economic power, greater exposure to racial and ethnic diversity, greater access to education and other social services, and more frequent exposure to the media and other forms of knowledge diffusion. Studies from the Latin American context show that geographical differences are often more powerful than social differences. Revealing data from Venezuela and Brazil indicate that school attendance rates of children from the poorest 20 percent of the population in urban centers were similar to or even higher than those of children from the second richest 20 percent of the population in rural zones. In both countries access to preschool was twice as great in cities and the absentee rate in primary school one-third of that in rural sectors (ECLAC-UNESCO, 1992, p. 83). Similar findings about the powerful impact of location have been found in China, where despite an explicit policy of educational equality, a study based on 1982 census data found that while some 75 percent of women in rural areas received only primary education, over 72 percent of the urban women had more than high school education (Fraser, 1991).

On the negative side in the city, one finds higher levels of disorganized growth, which poses a threat to close-knit communities, a sizable physical distance between areas of different economic power, tensions in the relationship between family life and urban work/survival, and constant racial tension and incidents.

Educational efforts in developing countries have been much more intensive in urban than in rural areas. Following independence, the educational offerings in the cities expanded and improved even further. The capital cities of former colonies are almost always overwhelming centers of power. Unlike the advanced industrialized nations, developing countries tend to have one major city (the "primate" city) dominating the national urban structure. Moreover, cities in the Third World tend to be not only centers of power but also centers of knowledge.

Also unlike the situation in the advanced industrialized countries, the crisis of urbanization is more pervasive throughout the city; it does not affect only the "inner city." As more and more destitute people come to the city, they occupy lands illegally and create environments where there is a lack of basic facilities such as water, electricity, sewerage, public transportation, and medical services. This influx of rural immigrants and the overextended and grossly inadequate services of the cities permanently change the urban profile of these population clusters.

It is characteristic of relatively new countries that although the majority of their populations still live in rural areas, the rate of urban growth is extremely high. Such is the case of Mali, which is undergoing a dramatic process of urban transformation even though the country as a whole is only 19 percent urban. Moreover, as Tounkara (1991) observes the "new urbanites" differ from the "real ones" in that the latter are committed to Western values while the former are very traditional. The migrant parents rely on their children's help to support the family, thereby creating sporadic school attendance in urban settings. Schmidt-Kallert (1992) echoes Tounkara's observation, holding that many newcomers to the city do not automatically become "town folks." Many of them, in fact, do not even stop farming. In many squatter areas of Asia and in various urban areas of Africa, growing vegetables and raising animals are integral parts of their survival practices (see also Mlozi, Chapter 6, this volume). Further complicating the picture is that many urban migrants do not necessarily sever ties with the countryside but rather combine rural and urban survival production, a phenomenon detected in several cities, including Manila and Jakarta. It is believed, for instance, that over the course of a year the population of Jakarta—which nobody knows exactly and which probably lies between 6 and 9 million—fluctuates by more than a million (Schmidt-Kallert, 1992).

Two contradictory trends can be observed in several developing countries, particularly in Africa. The still strong value attached to education creates a heavy demand on the educational infrastructure, creating the phenomenon of the high pupil/teacher ratios clearly observable in urban areas. In contrast, in some countries there is a noticeable decrease in the number of those enrolled in school. This trend has been linked to a changing perception of the value of education due to increased unemployment of school graduates in urban areas. It might also be linked to the fact that the informal sector of the economy is the main source of employment, and as such the credentials of formal education are less important. It is estimated that the informal sector involves as many as 75 percent of the urban employed in sub-Saharan Africa and as many as 85 percent in Pakistan (World Bank, 1991, p. 48).

WOMEN IN THE CITY

Even though cities are relatively resource-rich environments, they are still affected by inequalities of gender, ethnicity, and class. No matter what disadvantaged group they come from, women constitute a population that is further disadvantaged. The diversity of city life provides women a wide array of nontraditional role models, which facilitates their psychological receptivity to new social arrangements. But this diversity of social models, in the case of low-income women, contradicts their material possibilities. Poor women lead intensely local lives and in the final instance their choices are circumscribed by what is possible only in their immediate surroundings. The demands attached to domestic work, though not as intense as in the rural areas, persist. These constraints are evident in the lives of low-income women in Third World countries, mainly those in inner-city tenements or in slums, who must walk long distances to obtain water from trucks or from pipes down the hill and who depend on transportation to secure food and social services. Women in urban areas escape some of the subordination prevalent in the patriarchal rural household. But while they are less subordinate in the household they cannot escape subordination in the marketplace. The obstacles created by physical distance make women more vulnerable than men. These obstacles in turn affect the social construction of work, the notions of femininity and masculinity that evolve, and the values of social justice that are both constructed and mediated by the school.

When women are not permitted to go to the city, as still occurs in several African, Middle East, and Asian countries, they have suffered adverse effects, since they cannot gain access to advanced positions even in fields that have been traditionally dominated by them, such as education.

For poor women, residence in the city does not necessarily mean access to services. For instance, there is evidence that after living in the city for many years, many low-income women who immigrated as illiterates remain illiterate, and face an existence extremely restricted to the home (Stromquist, 1992). In the United States, similar effects have been detected among low-income women and foreign immigrants (Rockhill, 1987; Pratt, 1991). Although women change jobs constantly, they are still physically segregated to a few occupations and certain geographic areas (Chinchilla and Hamilton, 1991; Pratt, 1991). In both developed and developing countries, women represent the majority of those in the informal sector of the economy, thus occupying the worst-paying and most unstable jobs.

URBAN CHALLENGES TO EDUCATIONAL DEVELOPMENT

Educational phenomena that can be analyzed within an urban context are numerous. They include the schools' responses to multicultural diversity, the growth of adult education (increasingly concentrated in urban areas), the emergence of innovations, recent attempts at decentralization, the question of privatization of schools, and the attention to gender issues in urban schools. Below, a few specific issues are further developed.

• Schools in cities may have diverse characteristics. In some cases the student body consists primarily of children of longtime residents; in other cases it consists mainly of immigrants, and in other cases it reflects a combination of the two. This student diversity creates a difficult task for the schools, since they have to enculturate some students to familiar modern ways while trying at the same time to acculturate and "modernize" others. How do school systems face this diversity without boring or alienating one of the groups?

• Urban groups can force the state to listen and respond to their demands. What explains the generic and specific levels of state response? Under what conditions do urban features such as density and housing segregation facilitate the formation of social movements concerned with education? To what extent has education figured in the agenda of grass-roots groups? What educational changes have been produced so far by urban social movements?

• As cities attract large numbers of immigrants, not only from rural areas but in some cases from neighboring countries, to what extent have educational systems responded by setting up programs to address the needs of the newly arrived children? Or do school offerings continue to serve a type of student who no longer fits the profile of the majority of those attending public schools in urban areas? Are the adjustments by schools a product of their own administration or are these changes brought about by social pressure or mobilization?

• Given the relatively good supply and quality of schools in the city, the dense network of transportation and the decreased domestic burden, what has been the impact of urbanization on such educational features as attendance and retention? Do these patterns show differential impacts across gender and ethnic groups? How are the tensions between availability of schools and better infrastructure on the one hand and economic survival on the other resolved to reflect particular rates of school attendance and completion?

• As cities are centers of power, knowledge, and creativity, to what extent are they the site for the development of new ideas in educational administration, instructional methods, and content? What educational innovations in the Third World have urban origins? To the extent that urban origins prevail, which urban features shape the nature of the solutions/alternatives proposed? What consequences has this had on the processes of implementation and institutionalization of the innovations?

• With the informal sector of the economy growing and becoming permanent in many Third World cities, what reaction has this evoked from the educational system? In what ways has the school recognized the existence of the informal sector and made arrangements for the new economic conditions facing the urban student? What skills and knowledge need to be considered for the new labor force in the informal sector?

• The large-scale school systems made necessary by cities give rise to large bureaucracies. These structures tend to rely more on established policy for ordinary decision making and thus to be less flexible vis-à-vis particular demands. At the same time, since cities operate as magnets for a large population, this generates a need for educational bureaucracies to adapt readily. How is this basic contradiction between conformity to policy and flexible response resolved in the city?

• Some countries, notably the United States, have attempted desegregation either through busing or through the creation of magnet schools to correct racially imbalanced residential patterns. To what extent have legal and logistic measures by the school or government been able to counter dominant societal trends regarding housing and related forms of class segregation?

• The city absorbs most of the national social services as a function of its political mobilization and proximity to power sources. As urban areas receive more money, what forces become activated for gaining access to these resources and which social groups in the end prevail in having their demands satisfied? To what extent do factors such as location, density, and space play a role in the increased access to educational resources?

• What funding mechanisms have been tried to foster an equitable distribution of resources across the nation? In centralized educational systems, how can resources be allocated so that cities reduce their monopoly over the distribution of funds? What funding formulas (involving property taxes, income taxes, and so on) have been particularly appropriate to increase educational resources in rural areas?

Features of the urban context give rise to and intersect with important educational issues. In developed countries, many of these features have been seen as forms of aberrant manifestations of otherwise well-ordered functions and structures. Therefore, the responses have been seen in terms of policies to correct discrete and rather localized negative situations. In developing countries, the conditions of urban living concomitant with and subsequent to education are too pervasive to be considered deviant manifestations; they affect the majority of the individuals in the educational system and are conditions likely to endure despite educational policies focusing on them. A deeper knowledge of the set of urban agents and forces that create the dynamics that account for the recurrence and persistence of crucial educational conditions will help to understand not only what goes on in the cities but also how to regain a sense of what needs to be done for rural education.

REFERENCES

Bairoch, Paul. (1988) *Cities and Economic Development: From the Dawn of History to the Present.* Chicago, IL: University of Chicago Press.

Castells, Manuel. (1983) *The City and the Grassroots.* Berkeley, CA: University of California Press.

Chinchilla, Norma, and Nora Hamilton. (March 1991) Negotiating Women's Space: Latino Workers in Los Angeles. Paper presented at the Conference on Women in Urban Space, University of Southern California.

CPRE. (June 1991) *Policy Briefs.* RB-07-6/91. New Brunswick, NJ: The State University of New Jersey.

Duley, Margot, and Mary Edwards (eds.). (1986) *The Cross-Cultural Study of Women.* New York: Feminist Press.

ECLAC-UNESCO. (1992) *Education and Knowledge: Basic Pillars of Changing Production Patterns with Social Equity.* Santiago: Economic Commission for Latin America and the Caribbean—UNESCO.

Fraser, Stewart. (1991) The Impact of Education on Fertility. Bundoora, Australia: La Trobe University, mimeo.

Garner, Catherine. (1988) Educational Attainment in Glasgow: The Role of Neighborhood Deprivation. In Liz Bondi and M. Mathews (eds.), *Education and Society:*

Studies in the Politics, Sociology and Geography of Education. London, UK: Routledge.

Giddens, Anthony. (1984) *The Construction of Society: Outline of the Theory of Structuration.* Berkeley, CA: University of California Press.

Gilbert, Alan, and Josef Gugler. (1982) *Cities, Poverty, and Development: Urbanization in the Third World.* Oxford, UK: Oxford University Press.

Grace, Gerald. (1984) Urban Education: Policy Science or Critical Scholarship? In Gerald Grace (ed.), *Education and the City: Theory, History and Contemporary Practice.* London, UK: Routledge and Kegan Paul.

Hunt, Nancy. (1990) Domesticity and Colonialism in Belgian Africa. In Jean O'Barr, Deborah Pope, and Mary Wyer (eds.), *Ties That Bind: Essays on Mothering and Patriarchy.* Chicago, IL: University of Chicago Press.

Inkeles, Alex, and David Smith. (1974) *Becoming Modern.* London, UK: Heinemann Education Books.

Katznelson, Ira. (1992) *Marxism and the City.* Oxford, UK: Clarendon Press.

Kozol, Jonathan. (1991) *Savage Inequalities: Children in America's Schools.* New York: Crown Publishers.

Lerner, Daniel. (1964) *The Passing of Traditional Society: Modernizing the Middle East.* New York: Free Press.

Martínez, Hector. (1990) Las Relaciones Campo-Ciudad en el Perú: Pasado, Presente y Perspectivas. In AMIDEP (eds.), *Problemas Poblacionales Peruanos III.* Lima, Peru: Asociación Multidisciplinaria de Investigación y Docencia en Población, pp. 13–47.

McAdam, Doug. (1988) *Freedom Summer.* New York: Oxford University Press.

McClelland, David. (1961) *The Achieving Society.* New York: Free Press.

Michelson, William, and Saul Levine. (1979) Introduction. In William Michelson, Saul Levine, and Anna-Rosa Spina (eds.), *The Child in the City: Changes and Challenges.* Toronto, Canada: University of Toronto Press.

Pratt, Geraldine. (March 1991) Work and Gender in the Urban Space. Paper presented at the Conference on Women in Urban Space, University of Southern California.

Rockhill, Kathleen. (1987) Gender, Language, and the Politics of Literacy, *British Journal of Sociology of Education 8,* 2: pp. 153–167.

Sandbrook, Richard. (1986) The State and Economic Stagnation in Tropical Africa, *World Development 14,* 3: pp. 319–332.

Schmidt-Kallert, Einhard. (1992) Surviving in Asia's Megacities, *Development & Cooperation,* no. 4, pp. 23–25.

Shilling, Chris. (1991) Social Space, Gender Inequalities and Educational Differentiation, *British Journal of Sociology of Education 23,* 1: pp. 23–44.

Spencer Foundation. (June 1991) *The Spencer Foundation Newsletter 6,* 2.

Stevenson, Harold, Chuansheng Chen, and James Booth. (1990) Influences of Schooling and Urban-Rural Residence on Gender Differences in Cognitive Abilities and Academic Achievement, *Sex Roles 23,* 9/10: pp. 535–575.

Stromquist, Nelly P. (1992) The Interplay of Gender and Social Marginality in Adult Literacy: Becoming Literate in São Paulo. Report to EDUCARE. Los Angeles: University of Southern California, mimeo.

Todaro, Michael. (1985) *Economic Development in the Third World* (third edition). White Plains, NY: Longman.

Tounkara, Alhamdou. (March 1991) Challenges to the Expansion of Education in the

Developing World. A Case Study of Mali Focusing on Urban and Rural Areas. Paper presented at the CIES meeting, Pittsburgh, PA.

Tuma, Nancy, and Michael Hannan. (1984) *Social Dynamics: Models and Methods.* Orlando, FL: Academic Press.

UNDP. (1991) *Human Development Report 1991.* New York: Oxford University Press.

Western Interstate Commission for Higher Education. (1987) *From Minority to Majority: Education and the Future of the Southwest.* Boulder, CO.

Wilson, W. Julius. (1987) *The Truly Disadvantaged.* Chicago, IL: University of Chicago Press.

World Bank. (1991) *Urban Policy and Economic Development: An Agenda for the 1990s.* Washington, DC: The World Bank.

3

Urban Education and the Culture of Contentment: The Politics, Culture, and Economics of Inner-City Schooling

Gerald Grace

Urban education study is, among other things, a systematic attempt to understand and to improve the education of the urban poor. The urban poor, however they are constituted in ethnic, gender, or class terms in various societies, and wherever they are located, are a challenge to established institutions. They challenge central and local government agencies with a potential for social and political disorder or uprising. They challenge the legitimacy and credibility of democratic rhetoric (where it exists) about the dignity, rights, and empowerment of all citizens. Where equality of opportunity is a dominant principle of political discourse, the urban poor become a crucial indicator of its practical reality in health, employment, housing, and education. Where churches proclaim the importance of "faith in the city" or make an "option for the poor," then the current state of the urban poor must be a continuing challenge to religious organizations and faiths of all types.[1] If the world of corporate enterprise claims to take seriously the notion of "human capital" then it cannot stand by and watch the underdevelopment of the human capital resources of the urban poor. The urban poor are a challenge to capitalist ideology, to socialist ideology, and to the social commitments of humanism and of religion. They are a challenge to all forms of utopia, and they should be a challenge to all cultures of contentment.

J. K. Galbraith (1992) has suggested that all forms of political, economic, and social policy in many societies are now powerfully affected by the existence of sociopolitical cultures of contentment:

In past times, the economically and socially fortunate were, as we know, a small minority—characteristically, a dominant and ruling handful. They are now a majority . . . not of all citizens, but of those who actually vote . . . they will be called . . . the Contented Electoral Majority or, more spaciously, the Culture of Contentment. . . . They rule under the rich cloak of democracy, a democracy in which the less fortunate do not participate. (p. 15)

Galbraith argues that the constituency of contentment is socially and occupationally heterogeneous but united by articulate defense of its own relative privileges. As a sociopolitical constituency it is marked by strong self-interest, a belief that merit receives its just reward, a view of the state and of redistributive taxation systems as burdens to be resisted, and a relative unwillingness to look at longer-term social, economic, or environmental planning if these threaten present contentment. It is, in short, an influential and powerful group of citizens whose attitudes to the challenge of the urban poor in any society is likely to have a crucial effect upon what is done and what is not done in urban education policy.

Urban education study is just one part of the response of established cultural institutions to the challenge of the urban poor, whether they are located in inner cities, outer-ring working-class developments, ghettos, or shanty towns. Such study attempts, by theoretical and historical analysis and by contemporary research and empirical data collection, to illuminate the education of the urban poor, its problems and its possibilities, in different economic and political settings. The literature of urban education is dominated by two concepts, that of "crisis" and that of "improvement." At certain times the language of crisis in education is dominant, with its associations of failing students, failing schools, and failing communities, and its implicit or explicit predictions of social and political disorder. At other times, the language of improvement becomes salient, with emphasis upon effective schools and school leaders, progressive intervention programs and school reforms, influential community-business alliances, and powerful urban coalitions. There is, in other words, a contradiction in the literature about the education of the urban poor between analyses which suggest growing or incipient crisis and reports which document and exemplify school reform and progress. This can be confusing to students and teachers in the urban education field, who assume that once the causes of crisis have been identified and once examples of good educational practice have been closely studied there will be some sustained and linear improvement in urban education systems.

There are two problems with this view, which may be called a policy science perspective. The first, as I have argued elsewhere,[2] is that it is too schooling-system and school-focused in its analytical framework. Whatever may be said in the contextual rhetoric of this position about the influence of wider structural relations, the substantive emphasis of the literature remains focused upon what schools, teachers, and communities are doing or not doing. There is here a powerful and hegemonic idea that much of what is called the crisis of urban schools arises within the schools of the urban poor and can be solved by action taken within those sites or at least in the immediate school system or local community. This is an oversimplification. A second problem is that such a view is too present-time focused and has no developed sense of the conflicting forces which have shaped and reshaped urban school systems since their inception. Without this crucial sense of the historical struggles in and around urban schools and of the constant dialectic of crisis and improvement in each historical period, it can become difficult to make sense of an educational situation in which sustained linear improvement is hoped for and expected.

It is easy to see the attractiveness and appeal of this particular perspective in urban education despite the weaknesses mentioned. By oversimplifying the causes of urban crisis and of urban schooling crisis, this perspective can suggest apparently straightforward and effective courses of social, educational, and political action which will resolve urban schooling problems. It also celebrates the potential of all citizens, teachers, school leaders, and community groups to make the necessary improvements in urban schooling, and it holds up examples of good practice to be emulated. Its appeal arises, therefore, because it is accessible and focused in its diagnosis of the problems in urban schooling and it is apparently empowering and psychologically enhancing for those who work in urban education settings. The hegemonic power of this view of urban education arises precisely from its straightforward system-dysfunction analysis of problems in urban schooling and from its celebration of the importance of individual and local agency in the construction of solutions for those problems. It is, in short, a doctrine of simplicity and hope in the study of the education of the urban poor, and as such its appeal to educators, citizens, and politicians is immediate and considerable. Who does not prefer simplicity to complexity in theoretical analysis? Who does not prefer hope to pessimistic determinism in the policy field?

Attractive though this view is, it has intellectual limitations which have to be faced even at the price of some loss in simplicity and of some change in the nature of hope. I have already mentioned the confusions which this perspective can produce when crises reemerge or when school improvements and intervention programs appear to fail. What explanation does this paradigm have for such phenomena? Having located the main source of the problem in the schools or communities of the urban poor and having celebrated the potential of local citizens and professionals to solve ''their'' problems, the only credible explanation is that they have not tried hard enough. Despite being given urban aid, specialist advisers, models of good practice, and media attention, the students, teachers, school leaders, and community members have failed to sustain progress and the situation is reverting again to its familiar crisis.[3] Criticisms may more comprehensively take in the incompetence and mismanagement of city and local state government and bureaucracy, but in essence the analysis suggests that deficiencies and weaknesses in personal and local agency are responsible for the new crisis emerging in urban schooling. We have once again the modern version of the nineteenth-century practice of blaming the urban poor for their own condition, although in more implicit and apparently scientific terms.

If the field of urban education study is to move beyond the limitations of policy science analysis, which leads to these sorts of conclusions about the recurrent crises of urban schooling, it must develop more comprehensive theoretical frameworks to understand the problems it addresses. One consequence of this may be a movement from simple linear analysis to complex dialectical analysis and a movement from simple hope to complex hope[4] in urban education policy and practice. This paper will attempt to make some contribution to the development of a more comprehensive theoretical framework for the understanding of urban education problems.[5] In doing so it will attempt to follow the classic injunction of C. Wright Mills as originally set out in *The Sociological Imagination:*

First, one tries to get it straight, to make an adequate statement—if it is gloomy, too bad; if it leads to hope, fine. In the meantime to cry for "the constructive program" and "the hopeful note" is often a sign of incapacity to face facts as they are, even when they are decidedly unpleasant—and it is irrelevant to truth or falsity and to judgments of proper work in social science. (Mills, 1973, p. 9)

FACING THE FACTS (1): ON THE NEED TO RELATE STRUCTURE AND AGENCY IN THE STUDY OF URBAN EDUCATION

The intellectual and political challenge for those working in urban educational studies, wherever they are carried on, is to attempt to relate structure and agency and their dialectical relationships within urban schooling. By *structure*, I refer to the power relations associated with class, race, and gender divisions in all societies. These most fundamental power relations are manifested in their effects upon urban schooling systems throughout the world, although the particular patterning of effects may vary from one society to another. To these must be added the power relations associated with national and local states, party and bureaucracy, corporate business interests, the organized labor movement, formal religious organizations, and a variety of organized ideological movements. The starting point for all urban educational studies must be the realization that urban schooling systems have been historically shaped by the interplay of social and economic power relations. It must also be appreciated that urban schooling systems are being reshaped in the contemporary setting by new developments in the balance of these power relations.

Urban educational study cannot, however, become solely preoccupied with the structuring effects of power relations in the wider society, important though these are. To do so can result in a form of structural determinism which leads to feelings of powerlessness and which denies the significance of agency and of resistance in the shaping of urban school experience and practice. By *agency* here, I refer to a variety of forms of individual initiative, institutional and community developments, and wider forms of oppositional social action against what appear to be the inevitable outcomes of existing political and economic relations in particular societies. Such action may be pursued by exceptional individuals, by small community or citizen groups, by local entrepreneurs, or by informal groupings of women, workers, religious believers, or concerned environmentalists. In the urban context, and in its most developed form, such agency may express itself as an urban social movement where the participants have an explicit consciousness of the power relations which they are attempting to change.

It is in the study of agency and/or urban social movements that much may be learned from Third World countries. In South America, for instance, social movements supported by heterogeneous communities, organized women, and the church witness to the power of oppositional social action. Stromquist (in this volume) reports successful large mobilizations in support of improved schooling for the urban poor in São Paulo (Brazil) and in Villa El Salvador (Peru). More studies of this kind are needed to demonstrate both the potential of such movements and the structural forces which they have to overcome. Urban education study in Third World contexts has been relatively neglected, and yet it promises to be a fruitful source for the greater understanding of the potential of agency even in the starkest structural and political conditions.

The study of agency in urban educational systems is an important counterbalance to any possible tendencies toward structural determinism or pessimism. Empirical research studies and case studies in a variety of urban settings in a range of societies can exemplify and illuminate the effectiveness of such action. The detailed scholarship of urban education is rich with examples of how academic, social, cultural, and moral improvements can be made in specific schools and communities against the grain of external political, social, and economic conditions.[6] There are studies which show what can be accomplished in the improvement of urban schooling by the action of inspired school leadership, the work of dedicated professionals, the alliance of community and business interests, the implementation of progressive school reforms, the influence of women's groups, race and ethnic groups, and religious groups, and resource inputs by committed politicians and bureaucrats in the local state agencies.[7]

The nature and quality of the education of the urban poor is always the outcome of a complex and changing historical interplay between "external" power relations and "internal" forms of social agency.[8] Whether the education of the urban poor is in a state of crisis or of improvement at particular times and in particular societies can only be explained within an analytical framework which recognizes this dialectic and its constantly changing nature. This situation has a number of consequences for scholarship, research, and policy in urban education study and practice. There is a need to chart how particular changes in the wider structuring of power relations are affecting, or have the

potential to affect, urban school systems. There is an equivalent need to analyze the effectiveness of social agency (as defined here) in making and sus-
taining improvements in urban schooling systems in the face of changing ideological, cultural, political, and economic conditions. C. Wright Mills again
warns us of the potential dangers here of becoming lost in forms of abstracted
empiricism—"a scatter of requests for scattered information, statistical or otherwise, about a scatter of individuals and their scattered milieu" (Mills, 1973,
p. 77). In order to avoid that danger, which is particularly great in the case of
comparative studies, urban education inquiry must attempt to be relational in
approach and to locate its studies of "scattered milieu" within coherent theoretical and historical frameworks. The attempt in all situations to make links between structure and agency in urban schooling is basic to the emergence of any
critical scholarship of urban education, as opposed to a series of fragmented
policy science case studies. At the same time, a relational form of urban education study must lead to understandings and insights which can inform critical
policy and action. Hard-pressed politicians, community and school leaders,
teachers and parents, and the urban poor themselves rightly expect that urban
education scholarship and research will be productive of practical courses of
action which can be effective in the sustained improvement of schooling in the
inner city and in other deprived urban locations. In another classic contribution
to the literature of the urban question, David Harvey warns us that research
can be used as a substitute for action: "Mapping even more evidence of man's
patent inhumanity to man [sic] is counter-revolutionary in the sense that it
allows the bleeding-heart liberal in us to pretend that we are contributing to a
solution when in fact we are not" (Harvey, 1973, p. 144).

Urban education must be both a systematic attempt to understand the education of the urban poor and a generative source of policies and action to improve
that education.

FACING THE FACTS (2): ON THE NEED TO UNDERSTAND
THE CHANGING POLITICAL ECONOMY
OF URBAN SCHOOLING

By the *political economy of urban schooling* I mean not simply the specifics
of financial allocations and resource distributions within urban school systems
but, more significantly, wider changes in the political economy of various societies which powerfully shape those educational systems. The notion of political
economy is used here in its historical and comprehensive sense to refer to
interrelated networks of economic, political, ideological, and cultural relations
which account for the policy and the economy of particular societies. Two
important recent attempts to explain changes in the nature of those networks
deserve the attention of all students of urban education. From different theoretical positions, Manuel Castells in *The Informational City* (1989) and J. K. Galbraith in *The Culture of Contentment* (1992) have provided analyses rich in

scholarship and insight. Moreover, the trends they identify have far-reaching implications across a wide range of social formations for the future of urban schooling.

The essence of Castells' argument is that we are witnessing profound changes in the political economy of many cities and societies on a scale comparable with earlier industrial revolutions but of a radically different nature. These changes involve a new relation between information technology, economic restructuring, and the urban-regional process. Castells argues that a new informational economy based upon "high technology" is emerging. A key structuring feature of societies will become therefore not simply a relation to the means of production (in general) but a specific relation to information and knowledge-based means of production, in short, a relation to new forms of information technology and their applications. With the major transformation most apparent in the political economy of the United States (but with worldwide implications), processes of polarization and segmentation of populations and spatial areas take place: "A new type of labor demand determined by a new occupational structure is creating new types of jobs, characterized by a bifurcated distribution in which the bulk of the new jobs pay low wages and enjoy less social protection than in recent historical experience" (Castells, 1989, p. 202).

The duality which arises here results in greater polarization of occupational structures, with implications both for race relations and for gender relations, as women have entered the labor market mostly in low paid and semi-clerical jobs, while ethnic minorities and immigrants increasingly fill equally low paid jobs in service and manufacturing.

As with earlier major transformations of political economy the consequences of these trends are seen most dramatically and most visibly in the large metropolitan cities with the rise of a new form of the dual city.

If we continue to follow the injunction of C. Wright Mills that we have to face the facts "even when they are decidedly unpleasant," then those working in urban education settings have to consider the social, cultural, and educational implications of such major economic and urban restructuring for the operation of urban schooling systems. Castells describes the

mismatching of skills determined by inequality in the educational systems, itself a result of spatial segregation by class and race. Public schools in the largest inner cities receive proportionately fewer resources than those in the suburbs and cater to the poorest sectors of the population, with an overwhelming proportion of ethnic minorities with the greatest educational need to overcome a cultural disadvantage in their family background. The majority of the resident population of inner cities cannot match the skill requirements of the new labor market because of the inefficiency and segregated nature of the public school systems. (Castells, 1989, p. 204)

The question is, How can the schools of the urban poor respond to changes in the wider political economy of this magnitude when they start from a position of structural and cultural disadvantage? While individual communities and schools, and innovations such as magnet schools, may provide some much-publicized sectional response to this challenge, the need is clearly for whole system restructuring and improvement. While the achievements of individual and local agency in improving urban schools are impressive, it cannot be expected that the whole system of urban schooling can be transformed by these means alone. Major structural transformation in the wider society requires major structural transformation in the political economy of urban schooling. This must imply a strategy of intervention by major social institutions acting in a nationwide coalition to improve the organization, process, resourcing, and ethos of urban schooling. The agencies of central and local government acting in alliance with corporate enterprise, the labor movement, voluntary agencies, and religious organizations could, if the political, social, and moral will were manifest, transform the experience of urban schooling. Adequate human and material resources are fundamental to the renaissance of effectiveness and of hope in urban education.[9] Only those who have not taught in the inner city assert otherwise. With such resources the capacity of urban schools to respond to the new informational economy and its consequences could be greatly enhanced. The children, youth, and adults of the inner city and of other deprived urban locations could realize the skill and knowledge capacities which they undoubtedly have. In other words, the contradictions which Castells so sharply illustrates could be partly overcome by educational resourcing which would help to liberate potential in inner-city populations.

Such a prescription for improvement and for transformation is hardly new. It has been repeated in various forms throughout the history of urban education. In some historical periods and in various locations, significant urban education interventions have been made. These interventions have often been the result of fears of urban disorder or loss of social control. On other occasions they have resulted from organized social and community action expressed by urban social movements. Sometimes religious, philanthropic, and voluntary agencies have played a key role in such interventions, supplemented by short-lived manifestations of central or local government's declared commitments to equality of opportunity, social justice, and the empowerment of all citizens. In all cases they have been dependent upon a manifest political, social, or moral will that something should be done to improve the schooling of the urban poor. There has been historically an influential social and political constituency which has worked in various ways to support urban schooling in the face of many challenges. A full understanding of the changing political economy of urban schools requires some examination of how this constituency may itself be undergoing a process of transformation.

In 1979 Diane Ravitch, in the United States, commented upon a significant change in the social and political constituency working against the interests of urban schools. This change, in Ravitch's view, involved both a weakening of the formal and institutionalized political power of large cities and a growing indifference to the fate of the schools of the urban poor in the wider society:

The dilemma facing urban schools today and for the foreseeable future is that their objective needs grow larger as their financial capacity diminishes. The middle class exodus from the city reduces the city's tax base and its ability to generate revenues for the schools and other public purposes. . . . When the big cities turn to the state government for aid, they tend to get an unsympathetic response from legislatures dominated by a suburban and rural majority with little interest in paying more taxes to subsidize city schools. The political power of the cities is impaired by their loss of population, by the rising proportion of politically inactive people in the cities as well as by the city's inability to create coalitions with non-urban interests thus leaving the cities as politically isolated claimants for more state aid. The fact that city schools are perceived as non-white enclaves that are inefficient, poorly disciplined and infinitely capable of consuming tax money without producing tangible results merely confirms the predisposition of state legislatures not to provide additional subsidies. Even in the Congress, the political strength of the urban bloc has waned. . . . (Ravitch, 1979, pp. 76–77)

If Ravitch's analysis is correct and generalizable to other social and educational contexts, then both the formal and the informal political constituencies in support of the schools of the urban poor are becoming increasingly disempowered precisely at the time when they require to be empowered. While reductions in formal power relations have very serious consequences for the resourcing of urban schools, the more fundamental disempowering of the schools arises from the growth of either indifference or hostility in the informal constituency, that is, from citizens who might have been expected, through the democratic process, to support urban school transformation.

In a number of societies this trend is becoming apparent. It may be broadly described as a change in sociopolitical climate from a culture of commitment to relative public good to a culture of defense of relative private interest. Relative public good involves some degree of commitment to a set of wider social principles. In a political culture of relative public good, a significant sector of citizens accept the legitimacy (and even desirability) of political action taken in support of disadvantaged citizens as a practical expression of commitment to ideas of social justice, equality of opportunity, and equity in a given society. In a political culture of relative private interest a growing number of citizens reject the legitimacy of action in support of the disadvantaged (who are seen to be responsible for their own problems) and support policies designed to enhance their own interests or those of their families and their immediate local community. If such citizens are particularly active in the democratic process, then their influence upon both central and local government can be considerable. The consequences of these latter developments for the future of the schools of the urban poor are quite obvious.

But is the culture of relative private interest in the ascendant to the extent implied by Ravitch's analysis of 1979? A powerful argument that in fact it is has been provided by J. K. Galbraith in his much-discussed book *The Culture of Contentment*. Galbraith perceives a rise in the ascendancy of the culture of relative private interest in many societies. While self-interest has always been present in the political cultures of the past, Galbraith argues that it has found a new legitimacy and a new controlling power through the mechanisms of existing democracies:

What is new in the so-called capitalist countries—and this is a vital point—is that the controlling contentment and resulting belief is now that of the many, not just of the few. It operates under the compelling cover of democracy, albeit a democracy not of all citizens but of those who, in defense of their social and economic advantage, actually go to the polls. The result is government that is accommodated not to reality or common need but to the beliefs of the contented who are now the majority of those who vote. (Galbraith, 1992, p. 10)

In continuing his investigation of "the political economy of contentment" Galbraith notes that the comfortable and contented majority (of those politically active) are increasingly opposed to government or state intervention in the provision of public services unless those services are of particular value to the contented. Thus:

Social expenditure favorable to the fortunate, financial rescue, military spending and of course, interest payments—these constitute by far the largest part of the federal budget and that which in recent times has shown by far the greatest increase. What remains— expenditures for welfare, low-cost housing, health care for the otherwise unprotected, public education and the diverse needs of the great urban slums, is what is now viewed as the burden of government. (Galbraith, 1992, pp. 25–26)

While Castells' analysis (1989) delineates powerfully the challenge for the schools of the urban poor arising from the transition to an informational economy and points to an urgent need for resource interventions on behalf of these schools, Galbraith's analysis (1992) presents starkly the actual political and cultural impediments to such interventions taking place in the United States or in other societies dominated by the culture of contentment. Galbraith observes that contemporary political discourse in the United States is high on rhetoric about education and low on proposals for action:

There has been much talk of educational reform; President George Bush has sought to have himself called the Educational President; absent only has been the willingness to appropriate and spend public funds, especially on the schools in the central cities. Without this willingness no significant educational improvement can be expected. (Galbraith, 1992, p. 181)

If Galbraith's analysis of the culture of contentment is taken to be valid and generalizable, it presents a major challenge to those who work for the improvement of the schools of the urban poor. In the past, public interventions drawing their dynamic from a culture of social concern in the wider population have been made on behalf of such schools. This social concern has had complex historical origins—concern about urban disorder (the social control imperative); concern about personal, spiritual, and moral degradation (the moral and ethical imperative); concern about the disadvantaged (the social justice imperative); concern about wasted talent (the human capital imperative); and concern about souls (the religious imperative). If as a result of contemporary economic, ideological, and social change these classic imperatives for intervention are either weakening or being seriously delimited in their application, then the political economy of urban schools will undergo a profound transformation in a negative direction.

Stark and compelling though this analysis is, structural and cultural determinism has to be resisted, and the constant dialectical interplay of structure and agency must be brought back into the analysis. In other words, while there may have to be pessimism of the intellect (arising from facing the facts) there should also be optimism of the will (arising from the potential of agency).

OPTIMISM OF THE WILL: ON THE POTENTIAL OF AGENCY IN URBAN EDUCATION

There are two senses in which the potential of agency in urban education may be examined. The first is at the level of attempting the transformation of the culture of contentment, which threatens the long-term effectiveness and improvement of urban schooling. The second is at the level of local and community initiatives in urban education, which demonstrate concretely what can be achieved in particular contexts as a result of positive effort and commitment. The first refers to the agency of the political will and the second to the agency of educational good practice despite external conditions.

But the question which has to be faced is, Can the culture of contentment and its associated political and social will be changed given that it represents that most powerful conjunction in history, that is, self-interest "democratically" in power?[10] For the content and the context of urban schooling Castells (1989) has pointed out that social protest, urban disorder or uprisings, and urban social movements have in the past and in the present had the potential to shatter complacency and contentment. While it is clear that forms of protest and resistance by the urban poor will continue to be a significant aspect of social agency in confronting institutionalized indifference to the fate of urban schooling, the capacity of urban social movements alone to bring about a lasting transformation of the culture of contentment seems limited. If Galbraith's analysis is correct, then the efforts of the urban poor on their own behalf evidently need to be supported by an alliance of other social institutions, agencies, and movements whose common purpose is to move the political and moral will of a particular society to concern about, and social commitment to, the improvement of urban schooling. This alliance could include corporate enterprise[11] (attempting to make the notion of welfare capitalism more than rhetoric), the labor movement[12] (recognizing the need for action beyond the workplace), the women's movement[13] (recognizing the immense political and cultural potential of organized and socially committed women), and churches and religious organizations[14] (recognizing that of all existing institutions they have the clearest mission to transform the culture of contentment).

In one sense, however, education itself has the greatest responsibility for attempting to change the culture of contentment and its practical effects in the world. Education, in its broadest sense, that is, including formal schooling, adult education, and the educative potential of mass media, has yet to achieve one of its most important contemporary functions, that of "making democracy work." Galbraith notes that at present only a limited version of democracy is in fact working in the United States, because of the active involvement of the contented in defense of their own interests. A new social and political alliance intent upon changing the situation will have to have as a top priority the development of educational programs and educational experiences which are capable of generating the active political participation of all citizens on the one hand and commitment to principles of social justice and equity on the other. In particular, teachers in all the schooling contexts in which the children and the youth of the controlling, contented constituency are educated would have both a professional challenge and a professional responsibility to be leading agents of these processes.[15] In this way, education could help to transform rather than simply to reproduce the culture of contentment.

Given the political, social, and moral will to transform urban schooling systems, there are many examples of the successful agency of good practice to be drawn upon and generalized to other settings. These examples have to be closely studied to establish in what particular ways a school's ethos and functioning can be improved, a whole school system revitalized, and effective local alliances created in support of urban schools. This evidence of success in the face of existing circumstances is a continuing source for optimism of the will in urban education. But its real significance lies in the recognition that if this is what can be accomplished in existing circumstances, what might be achieved if these circumstances were radically changed?

Existing circumstances in urban education will be radically changed only if the historical sources of the culture of social concern and of relative public good are renewed and strengthened to deal with present challenges. A decade of assault from New Right ideologies and agencies in various societies has weakened commitments to welfare, social justice, equity, and public good[16] and has sought to legitimate and sanctify private interest and the free operation of the market as the dominant concerns of public policy. One of the consequences of this can now be seen in the current state of and prospects for urban education wherever this ideology is in power.

If "democratic" government is incapable of providing principled and moral resistance to such assaults and if "democratic" political leadership cannot be looked to for the protection of the interest of the urban poor, then other major social institutions in conjunction with community and voluntary agencies will have to fill this moral vacuum.

NOTES

I received helpful comments on the first draft from J. K. Galbraith, Nelly Stromquist, Frank Coffield, David Galloway, and my wife, June Grace. I thank them for their trouble, which has improved this paper without making them responsible for the final version.

"Inner-city schooling" is used here as a shorthand form of reference to the education of the urban poor.

1. This challenge was recognized, for instance, by the Conference of the Latin American Bishops in 1968 at Medellín in Colombia, which issued a strong call to the Roman Catholic church to take up the case of the poor and oppressed, to adopt "a preferential option for the poor." Such ideas have subsequently been developed in the literature of liberation theology. See Gutierrez (1973). For the Church of England, see Sheppard (1983) and also, *Faith in the City: A Call for Action by Church and Nation* (Commission on Urban Priority Areas, 1985).

2. See Grace (1984a) for distinctions between policy science and critical scholarship in urban education.

3. There are strong parallels here between the recurring crises of the inner city and the recurring crises of so-called Third World societies. In both cases there is a powerful but implicit ideological message that despite having been given aid, the participants have failed again.

4. By "complex hope" I mean an optimism of the will that recognizes the historical and structural difficulties which have to be overcome in urban education.

5. I have already attempted to make one contribution to this in "Theorizing the Urban: Some Approaches for Students of Education," in Grace (1984a, pp. 94–112).

6. Representative examples of such studies are Rutter et al. (1979), Mortimore et al. (1988), and Louis and Miles (1990). For an important review of such studies for the United States, see Cibulka (1992).

7. The Inner London Education Authority (ILEA) was, for instance, an exemplar of both progressive educational policies and progressive educational resourcing on behalf of the urban poor in London until its abolition by a Conservative government in 1988. For one account of this and its consequences, see Jones (1992).

8. Despite their dialectical relationship, power relations are often perceived as "external" and agency as "internal" to educational systems. One of the most limiting ideas in education is precisely that power relations are perceived to be "external" and therefore either beyond the capacity of educators to transform or inappropriate as proper subjects for professional discussion.

9. In a recent authoritative world survey of urban education Coulby et al. (1992)

concluded that "most urban educational systems have serious problems in adequately resourcing their activities . . . issues of equity remain intractable in all the states analyzed here. . . ." (Preface).

10. The challenge cannot be underestimated. Castells notes the influence of those

who hold the strategic position of information producers in the new economy, enjoy a high cultural and educational level . . . and control the key to political decision-making in terms of their social influence and organizational capacity. . . . This new professional-managerial class that by and large is white dominated and male dominated . . . is not a ruling class in the traditional sense. It is a hegemonic social class that does not necessarily rule the state but fundamentally shapes civil society. (Castells, 1989, p. 228)

11. In documenting some of the existing relationships between corporate enterprise and urban schooling systems, Spring (1992) warns of the danger of business domination of urban school reform and of its associated research.

12. It seems important that the labor movement should understand in a more developed sense that the struggle for jobs takes place in education as well as directly in the workplace.

13. It is recognized that the women's movement is not a unitary formation but is itself segmented by race and class. Nevertheless there is much contemporary evidence that organized and socially committed women are prepared to challenge government's military establishments, churches, and major social institutions where structures of either oppression or indifference exist. In other words, socially committed women represent a potentially powerful agency in any struggle to transform the cultural of contentment.

14. As a major social institution having a strategic relation with whole populations of the urban poor in various societies, the Roman Catholic church and its associated schooling systems could be a leading agency in the transformation of urban education.

15. In this sense teachers would be expected to be "transformative intellectuals" at work in the schools of the contented and the privileged as well as in the schools of the urban poor. In this role it might be expected that teachers in schools of religious foundation would play an especially important part. For further discussion of teachers as transformative intellectuals, see Aronowitz and Giroux (1986), pp. 23–45.

16. For an example of this in New Zealand, see Grace (1991).

REFERENCES

Aronowitz, S., and H. Giroux. (1986) *Education under Siege: The Conservative, Liberal and Radical Debate over Schooling.* London, UK: Routledge and Kegan Paul.

Castells, M. (1989) *The Informational City: Information Technology, Economic Restructuring and the Urban-Regional Process.* Oxford, UK: Basil Blackwell.

Cibulka, James. (1992) Urban education as a field of study: problems of knowledge and power. In Cibulka, J., R. Reed, and K. Wong (eds.), *The Politics of Urban Education in the United States.* London, UK: Falmer Press.

Cibulka, J., R. Reed, and K. Wong (eds.) (1992) *The Politics of Urban Education in the United States.* London, UK: Falmer Press.

Commission on Urban Priority Areas. (1985) *Faith in the City: A Call for Action by Church and Nation.* London, UK: Church House Publishing.

Coulby, D., C. Jones, and D. Harris (eds.) (1992) *Urban Education: World Yearbook of Education 1992*. London, UK: Kogan Page.

Galbraith, J. K. (1992) *The Culture of Contentment*. London, UK: Sinclair-Stevenson.

Grace, Gerald (ed.) (1984a) *Education and the City: Theory, History and Contemporary Practice*. London, UK: Routledge and Kegan Paul.

Grace, Gerald. (1984b) Theorizing the urban: some approaches for students of education. In Grace, Gerald (ed.), *Education and the City: Theory, History and Contemporary Practice*. London, UK: Routledge and Kegan Paul.

Grace, Gerald. (1991) Welfare Labourism versus the New Right: The struggle in New Zealand's education policy, *International Studies in the Sociology of Education 1*, pp. 25–42.

Gutierrez, G. (1973) *A Theology of Liberation*. Maryknoll, NY: Orbis Books.

Harvey, D. (1973) *Social Justice and the City*. London, UK: Edward Arnold.

Jones, C. (1992) Dogma, equality and excellence: Education in London. In Coulby, D., C. Jones, and D. Harris (eds.), *Urban Education: World Yearbook of Education 1992*. London, UK: Kogan Page.

Louis, K., and M. Miles. (1990) *Improving the Urban High School: What Works and Why*. New York: Teachers College Press.

Mills, C. Wright. (1973) *The Sociological Imagination*. Harmondsworth: Penguin Books.

Mortimore, P., P. Sammons, L. Stoll, D. Lewis, and R. Ecob. (1988) *School Matters: The Junior Years*. Wells, UK: Open Books.

Ravitch, Diana. (1979) A bifurcated vision of urban education. In Newitt, J. (ed), *Future Trends in Education Policy*. Lexington, MA: D. C. Heath.

Rutter, M., B. Maughan, P. Mortimore, and J. Ouston. (1979) *Fifteen Thousand Hours: Secondary Schools and Their Effects on Children*. London, UK: Open Books.

Sheppard, D. (1983) *Bias to the Poor*. London, UK: Hodder and Stoughton.

Spring, J. (1992) Knowledge and power in research into the politics of urban education. In Cibulka, J., R. Reed, and K. Wong, *The Politics of Urban Education in the United States*. London, UK: Falmer Press.

PART II

BUREAUCRATIC DYNAMICS IN URBAN EDUCATIONAL SYSTEMS

4

Safety Net or Safety Valve: How Choice Is Constructed in an Urban Dropout Program

Deirdre M. Kelly

At a time when the very definition of *city* is debated, what characteristics set U.S. urban school districts apart from their rural and suburban counterparts? Three characteristically urban factors are: (1) cultural diversity, (2) competing agendas of large numbers of low-income families and the threat of affluent "flight," and (3) relatively rapid change in the makeup of their student populations due to immigration shifts and the volatility of city economies. Urban school administrators must manage tensions arising from these factors, which are not present in suburban and rural districts to the same degree.

In so doing, they are pressed to create alternative routes through their systems, programs that might be described as either safety nets for students or safety valves for the organizations. A safety net provides a program geared to meet the intellectual and social needs of those whom the mainstream schools cannot or will not help, a program that meets with some measure of success in reengaging students. A safety valve provides a mechanism to rid mainstream schools of failures and misfits without holding school administrators fully accountable for the consequences, a mechanism that reinforces students' disengagement from school. As students are shifted out of mainstream programs into these alternative ones, issues of choice—both real and illusory—arise. California's continuation education program provides an excellent illustration. One out of every ten high school students attends a continuation school. Although a safety net for some students, it is more often an arena for the final stage of dropping out. Statewide, 45 percent of those enrolled in continuation programs at some time during the 1986–87 school year left without graduating (28.5 percent transferred elsewhere, 16.5 percent dropped out, at least for the time being); 11 percent obtained a diploma or the equivalent (Calif. State Dept. of Education, 1988, pp. 21, 26). Although continuation school advocates interpret these numbers favorably, my case studies indicate far higher dropout rates, for reasons I will discuss later in this chapter. Comprehensive high schools can send disengaging students to continuation, thus masking their own true dropout and pushout rates. Using continuation programs as a safety valve, many districts continue to collect attendance monies for students even when they are barely hanging on in school.

In this chapter I will examine the ways in which choice has played out in three school districts' continuation high schools. Specifically, I will analyze the process whereby continuation programs became institutionalized, student perceptions of choice and coercion in entering and leaving these programs, and the lack of attention to the consequences of the choices made by and for students as they slip in and out of the schooling system. In the end, I will argue, the idea of choice in the continuation school context has been more a tool of urban school administrators to maintain the status quo, and less a means of allowing students and their families to increase their chances of survival and success in the public schooling system.

The three tensions arising from cultural diversity, the class gap, and rapid change aptly describe the now classic urban districts as well as the newer shape of large cities and their schools. The defining characteristics of cities no longer seem to be merely density, centers of job creation, or length of existence. By emphasizing rapid change and diversity in class, race, and ethnicity, my definition of *urban* can also capture what is distinctive about a more recent type of city. The familiar urban landscape of smokestacks and tenement housing, skyscrapers and waterfront piers now vies with low-lying sprawl crisscrossed by freeways, light industry, white-collar job centers, and low-income subdivisions, all making up a semisuburban patchwork.

This description of the modern city aptly fits the setting of my study, carried out in three districts located in a high-technology center in California during 1988–90. (To protect the anonymity of people who participated in the study, I will refer to the three districts and continuation high schools as Beacon, La Fuente, and Willows, and the setting as High Tech City.) The fast-growth economy has helped spawn housing developments and industrial parks where orchards stood twenty years ago. Jobs have attracted large numbers of immigrants, and an insufficient supply of housing to meet the needs of low- and middle-income families has created familiar urban problems. The once-promising high-technology economy, intertwined with and buffeted by volatile world markets, now seems increasingly polarized into the haves and have-nots.

Despite all that is new about High Tech City, students face familiar pressures to leave school without graduating. Before transferring to Beacon, La Fuente, and Willows, students typically have attended large, comprehensive high schools. There, the teachers have contact with as many as 150 different students daily, so they hardly remember their pupils' names. Students speak many different languages and come to school with diverse backgrounds and experiences. The comprehensive school provides few opportunities inside or outside the classroom for students to learn about each other; more often, they are pitted against each other for grades and scarce claims to status via participation in athletics and student government. These conditions lead to conflict, sometimes violent, and make affiliating with gangs more attractive. Those who bring problems to school find that counselors have either been eliminated or relegated to course scheduling and discipline. In such an anonymous, status-conscious, and alienating environment, some students turn to drug dealing and many to the "culture of cutting" classes (see Hess, Wells, Prindle, Liffman, & Kaplan, 1986) and "partying."

For those most disengaged from the schooling enterprise, one of two things happens. One, the student decides the comprehensive school is too uncaring, inflexible, violent, or anonymous and ceases to attend (such a student is conventionally termed a dropout). Or two, school administrators feel they need to remove nonconformists and troublemakers from the mainstream program; such students become pushouts. An array of "alternatives" and "options" have emerged over time for dropouts and pushouts in California and elsewhere in the United States. The oldest and largest is the continuation education program. Continuation schools have expanded in number from 13 before 1965 to 425 today. They serve over 115,000 students—nearly one tenth of California's high school student population and about one fifth of eleventh and twelfth graders (Calif. State Dept. of Education, 1987). A brief analysis of this program's history will show that it is one attempt to resolve enduring tensions in urban schooling.

HISTORY OF CALIFORNIA'S CONTINUATION EDUCATION PROGRAM

Continuation schools were first designed primarily by and for city school personnel as a response to (1) changes being brought about by industrial capitalism, (2) diverse students with special needs or those who did not or would not conform to the standard curriculum, both formal and hidden, and (3) a concern for "Americanizing" working-class immigrants (Kelly, 1991, Chap. 2; Calif. State Board of Education, 1926). At bottom, school administrators and school board members were responding to middle-class worries about juvenile delinquency and perceived threats to the social order, as well as administrative problems such as how to accommodate an increasingly diverse student body (immigrants, newcomers to the city, students with handicaps and health problems, school-age mothers, those who needed to work, truants, students on probation, students with discipline problems).

In its original form, continuation education took place largely in compulsory part-time schools designed to provide young workers with four hours of vocational tutoring per week. At the turn of this century, a coalition of professional educators allied with businesspeople, politicians, and social reformers grew increasingly concerned about the number of students dropping out after elementary school as well as the new entrants to the high schools, and began to push for vocational education. This was an early call for choice within the curriculum.

The changing forces of production fueled concern over dropouts. New technologies—high-speed machinery, telephones, cash registers, pneumatic tubes, and other devices—were eliminating many of the unskilled jobs held by young people (Tyack, 1978). Child labor and compulsory school attendance laws, backed by trade unions and social reformers, began to limit the participation of children in the labor market.

Vocational reformers disagreed on how the system should be organized, however. Alternatives ranged from differentiated tracks within the comprehensive high school to separate vocational schools divided by sex to continuation schools for young workers outside of the public schooling system. Many employers favored opening continuation schools inside factories, where young workers would alternate learning the general principles behind specific occupations with attending school (Kett, 1982). John Dewey and other humanitarian progressives argued, on the other hand, that vocational education should focus on general industrial knowledge and should not be administered separately from general public education. A dual school system would deny young people, particularly those from working-class backgrounds, an equal opportunity by forcing them to specialize in a trade too early. Trade unionists, too, argued against separate continuation schools, interpreting them as an attempt to sanction child labor, whose cheaper rates undercut the unions (Katznelson & Weir, 1985).

Some professional educators tended to gloss over the class interests inherent in the debate over continuation schooling. Argued one: "The continuation school is an institution typifying the real democracy of education. She has no aristocratic standards for admission" (McDonough, 1921, p. 255). This claim of nonelite admission standards was seriously misleading because continuation schools were originally designed for young workers, not children from more privileged backgrounds, who would hardly choose to attend them.

Allied to this attempt to construct a practice of schooling that appeared classless were progressive educators' plans for citizenship training, which found their way into federal and state legislation on continuation schools. Citizenship training would "assimilate foreigners" and introduce them to "our customs and to the ideals peculiar to America," according to a U.S. Bureau of Education bulletin (Jones, 1907, pp. 140–41). This assimilationist vision ignored existing ethnic and racial divisions deeply embedded in U.S. society and implied that an uncontested set of customs and ideals existed.

In California the compulsory Part-Time Education Act of 1919 required out-of-school youth aged sixteen to eighteen to attend general continuation classes for at least four hours per week; employed minors between the ages of fourteen and sixteen were also subject to this law. It further required people between the ages of eighteen and twenty-one who were not proficient in English to attend for instruction in citizenship. State officials advised school districts to provide continuation students "an opportunity to study trade, industrial or commercial subjects." In the absence of a vocational focus, they warned, these pupils "will constitute a problem which will be very difficult to handle" (Calif. State Dept. of Education, 1919, p. 4). These reformers feared juvenile delinquency among part-timers: "It is from this group that most criminals are recruited" (Calif. State Board of Education, 1923, p. 100).

Although educators and others left it unsaid, they had boys in mind when concerns about delinquency were expressed. Continuation girls were more apt to have violated middle-class norms of sexual behavior; these included pregnant girls, parenting or married teens, and runaways often assumed to have become prostitutes. Continuation classes were seen as an ideal place to teach middle-class moral values and household skills to immigrant and working-class girls. For example, the state Department of Education showcased a "citizen-home-makers" course offered to mainly Mexican immigrant girls in Bakersfield. The principal purpose of instruction was the transmission of middle-class norms of self-presentation, morality, and housekeeping (Calif. State Dept. of Education, 1920). Half the girls were working as maids in local homes, and their middle-class women employers telephoned the teachers to report on their work daily. During the sewing hours at school, "All kinds of weighty problems are discussed, salaries, good taste, husbands, preference of country, U.S. or Mexico, homelife, whether it is right to break an engagement of marriage, and the right age for marriage" (p. 19).

Continuation schools continued to grow in number throughout the United States until the Great Depression. Thereafter, they continued to exist only in the largest cities, less as schools for part-time workers and more as sites of what became known as "adjustment education" (see Shaffer, 1955). Other "options" had emerged within the comprehensive high schools like tracking, ability grouping, special education, and vocational programs such as school-work cooperation, work experience, and apprenticeship training. These programs superseded the original purpose of continuation education, and it was no longer funded through the Vocational Education Act passed by Congress in 1963.

Despite the many programs that had sprung up to meet the "special needs" of youth, many young people continued to drop out. Civil rights activists focused legislators' attention on the disproportionate number of African-American and Latino students who were being expelled in certain districts without recourse. Together with other youth advocates, the California Continuation Education Association (CCEA) and a half-time consultant within the Department of Education lobbied for recognition and increased funding of their program as the solution to the pushout problem.

Meanwhile, a California Assembly Legislative Reference Service study showed that "the long-term suspension mechanism has, at least in part, been substituted for the traditional and more formal [expulsion] process" (Calif. Legislature, Assembly Comm. on Educ., 1965, p. 10). Validating the claims of the CCEA that continuation education was a solution to the pushout problem, researchers found that 80 percent of long-term suspensions occurred in districts that did not operate continuation classes or schools (p. 8). This study persuaded the legislature to pass a law requiring all school systems to provide continuation education (or a transfer to a similar county-run school) for youths suspended ten days or more.

School districts that did not comply with this 1965 law faced having 10 percent of all state apportionments withheld annually (*Education Code* Section 7757, 1965). These were the teeth that continuation leaders had been fighting to put into the compulsory attendance laws; the effect was immediate. In four years, the number of continuation high schools in the state increased from 13 to 183 (Weber, 1972, p. 571). The *Education Code* of 1967 (Section 5950) identified a new purpose to be served by continuation schools: to meet the "special needs of pupils with behavior or severe attendance problems."

Despite the change in stated purpose, the composition of the continuation high school student body has remained relatively stable. Students continue to be defined as misfits within the conventional schooling system and have either dropped out or been pushed out. These misfits include disproportionate numbers of certain ethnic minorities, working-class or low-income students, and girls who, as explained above, have violated middle-class norms of sexual behavior.

Institutional convenience, framed by a larger conflict between advocates of equality and advocates of efficiency, best explains the origins and transformation of California's continuation program. In response to a changing, hierarchically structured economy and an influx of immigrants, professional educators were experimenting with ways to deal with students who could not or would not conform to the dominant culture and class standards. Social reformers argued that juvenile courts, detention homes, reformatories, jails, penitentiaries, sanitariums, and asylums already strained community coffers. They hailed continuation education as a humane, preventive response to these individuals' neglected needs. Yet by segregating rebels and failures from the mainstream high school, educators stigmatized them and the continuation program while easing their disciplinary load and scaring other students into relative conformity.

When policymakers and school administrators later looked for solutions to the problems of juvenile delinquency, pushouts, and teen pregnancy, the chameleonlike continuation program changed its colors to accommodate. Its expansion was boosted by the climate of the late 1960s, for example, when protest groups were demanding greater social justice in education, and continuation schools—recolored as alternative programs—were a ready solution. Victories for greater equality in schooling were being won, such as the recognition of the right to an education for girls regardless of pregnancy and the funding of small schools for them and other continuation students. As Carnoy and Levin (1985, pp. 232–33) argue, such victories were made possible partly by favorable economic conditions in the 1960s: high employment levels and economic growth. At the same time, comprehensive high schools did not have to adapt to students; rather, those who did not fit could transfer to separate, almost always devalued institutions.

SAFETY VALVE OR SAFETY NET: SOCIAL CONSTRUCTION OF CHOICE

Today 85 percent of continuation students transfer into the program voluntarily (Calif. State Dept. of Education, 1988). In the three programs I studied, all Beacon students attended voluntarily, while half of La Fuente and Willows students did so. These statistics tend to reflect a bureaucratic notion of choice: Before the actual transfer and after some counseling, did the student consent to attend the continuation school or not? To get a sense of whether the choice was real or illusory, one would need to know more about the counseling, the actual range of options offered, whether the program delivered on the claims made for it, and the degree of stigma perceived to be attached to the program.

With these aims in mind, I observed the transfer, screening, and subsequent progress of students at all three schools and conducted in-depth interviews with thirty-nine Beacon students (twenty-three girls, sixteen boys), forty-three La Fuente students (twenty-four girls, nineteen boys), and eighteen Willows students (eleven girls, seven boys). I conducted a pilot study at all three sites in spring 1988, intensive fieldwork at Beacon and La Fuente during school year 1988–89, and occasional follow-up visits during school year 1989–90. What I found was that the distinction between involuntary and voluntary transfers was not as clear-cut as administrative records would lead one to expect. Exploring how choice gets constructed is important because it tends to mediate how students react to the continuation school environment, which in turn builds that school's particular reputation as a safety net or safety valve. In this section, I will describe three processes that contributed to the ambiguity in the choice concept: (1) the role played by the continuation school in achieving comprehensive school discipline, (2) the construction and perception of choice by involuntary transfer students, and (3) the perception of coercion by voluntary transfer students, particularly pregnant girls.

The Continuation School as Disciplinary Threat

Any alternative program—in the context of a competitive struggle for, and hierarchical distribution of, status and resources—tends to get stigmatized almost by definition because it exists in opposition to the traditional program. Insofar as the continuation school acts as a dumping ground for students who pose a problem to the mainstream schools, it reinforces the idea that the problem rests with a minority who can and should be segregated.

Principals at Beacon, La Fuente, and Willows were all clear that their districts used the continuation school as "the ultimate scare tactic," as one put it, to maintain discipline at the comprehensive schools. They were equally forthright in saying, particularly in the two districts allowing involuntary transfers, that the continuation school serves to keep the mainstream high schools "pure": "[In this district], the philosophy is send everybody here, just get rid of them, dump 'em; it cleans out those kind of kids from the regular school and makes the regular school a better school. And it does that. It makes the regular school less impacted by resistant kids, truant kids, tardy kids, behavior problem kids" (principal, Willows). As La Fuente's principal argued, however, there then emerges a tradeoff between offering a safety net and serving as district safety valve: "I always felt that the biggest loophole in dropouts was in La Fuente. . . . But as soon as we plug that hole [by trying to reduce the high turnover rate in the continuation school], it creates other problems for the district's comprehensive high schools because it becomes a bottleneck [of at-risk students]" (principal, La Fuente).

Given these arguments of institutional convenience, continuation teachers had little or no say over which students ended up at their school. Indeed, they joked freely about the "dumping" cycle. The first dumping occurs at the beginning of November. The comprehensive schools routinely hold on to disengaging students until enrollment levels have been established for staffing purposes, and these are reported to the state at the end of October. The second dumping occurs late in the spring as comprehensive school principals rid themselves of disciplinary cases they do not want to deal with the following year.

Beacon, unlike La Fuente or Willows, held a "screening" every other week, in which all teachers and the principal would meet with comprehensive school vice principals, counselors, and a district psychologist to be briefed on incoming students. Theoretically, if Beacon's principal and teachers felt that a particular student recommended for transfer to their school by one of the comprehensive high schools would not benefit from the continuation program, they could veto the transfer. I attended every screening save one during 1988–89, however, and not a single student was screened out, despite several instances in which Beacon's teachers and principal expressed strong concern or doubt about the wisdom of a particular transfer. Further, I recorded four separate instances in which comprehensive high school vice principals explicitly stated that a particular student would not be allowed to return to their schools, thus suggesting that the transfer to Beacon was coerced by comprehensive school staff, despite an official policy to the contrary.

In summary, all three districts used their continuation schools, even Beacon, which billed itself as a "school of choice," as safety valves, and this fact often overshadowed their role as safety net and contributed significantly to their stigma. But students reacted differently to the program depending on their particular circumstances and the degree to which the program met their individual needs.

Much mainstream social science theory, as March and Olsen (1984, p. 737) argue, assumes that people's preferences are stable, unambiguous, and consistent, and precede a particular choice or decision in time. My data, however, call all three of these assumptions into question. Student preferences changed partly in response to what they were told and asked to consider by adults in positions of authority (and by family and friends), partly in response to their experience of the continuation program after transfer. For many students, the mode of recruitment might best be described as semivoluntary. Like military conscripts, they are "required to serve but are given much opportunity to feel that this service is a justifiable one required in their own ultimate interests" (Goffman, 1961, p. 118).

Students at Beacon, La Fuente, and Willows were asked several questions about the transfer process and whether they considered it their choice. I categorized their views by the number of options they said were available to them at the time of transfer and the value of the credential attached to each option. If students indicated that obtaining a traditional diploma was still open to them in a regular high school, they were classified as perceiving more choice. By this measure, 38 percent of boys and 66 percent of girls were voluntary transfers. Significantly more girls than boys—across ethnic groups and at all three schools—felt that they chose to come to the continuation school, reflecting in large measure the fact that boys more often were disciplinary placements, whereas girls came as counseling and pregnancy referrals.

Perception of Choice by Involuntary Transfers

For new arrivals at the continuation school, the line between voluntary and involuntary can blur depending on how administrators, parents, and particularly students construe the event. Continuation students—both voluntary and involuntary transfers—tend to be behind on credits. The major incentive that counselors and administrators at both the comprehensive and continuation schools hold out and stress is the chance to make up credits faster. Thus, students can perceive the continuation school as either an alternative route to a high school diploma or as a bridge back to the comprehensive school.

A number of involuntary transfers interpreted their presence in the continuation school as their choice once they discovered that they liked the new environment. For example, Rodney was "kicked out cuz of fighting," but says: "It was my choice. [The principal] said I could go back, but I don't want to go back. I like La Fuente. I want to graduate early, and I can from this school." Rosa was transferred out of a comprehensive high school for fighting: "I got kicked out because I got into a fight with a white girl cuz she was saying that Mexicans are stupid.'' Rosa said she was happier at Willows—where about half the students are of Mexican descent—and perceived it as her choice.

To the extent that continuation programs offer a better chance to students to be academically successful, they are more likely to be seen as true schools of choice—safety nets—by both voluntary and involuntary students. To varying degrees, all three schools in this study offered small school and class size, teachers who saw themselves less as subject-matter experts and more as educators of "the whole child," more counseling (including the brokerage of much-needed social services), increased access to extracurricular activities, more opportunities for students to work at their own pace and make up high school credit, and a greater sense of community through the reduction of competition and an elimination or opening up of traditional sources of status (for example, athletics, academic tracking, and student government). Interestingly, these features also tend to characterize a number of rural school programs in the United States (see DeYoung, 1987). The continuation schools I studied were less successful, however, in protecting students from the ills of urban poverty, notably high youth unemployment, the temptations of drug use and dealing, and violence.

Some students exercise another form of choice, one that is unofficial. They know how to behave in comprehensive high school so that they will be "involuntarily" transferred (Willows, La Fuente) or given priority (Beacon); this is necessary in schools that have waiting lists for voluntary transfers. According to one comprehensive school teacher I interviewed, "In some groups it's almost a status symbol to go to Beacon, and students will misbehave here in a traditional high school, hoping to get kicked out so they can go to the continuation school." In formal interviews, a boy and a girl said they purposely "messed up" to get into Beacon; others boasted of it informally. Like the high school students that Page (1987) studied, who deliberately dropped down into the lower track to get an easier schedule, continuation students sometimes feel they have outwitted the credential system: They can attend a "kickback" or "easy" school and still receive their diploma.

Others, usually those who had been involuntarily transferred or placed in the school by a probation officer, predominantly boys, were clear that attending the continuation school was not their choice. Sometimes these students claimed that they had been pushed into leaving, and one principal acknowledged that as a vice principal, he had been aware that a number of teachers "baited" students they perceived as problems until such students committed an act that warranted their removal, a practice he himself engaged in on occasion.

Perception of Coercion by Voluntary Transfers

Of the voluntary transfers I spoke with, some, for example pregnant or parenting girls, felt they were given little choice in reality. This finding is underscored by a recent Equality Center survey of twelve geographically and demographically diverse schools which revealed that nine of the schools may have been violating the rights of pregnant girls. A common violation was channeling pregnant and parenting girls into specific courses of study (cited in Snider, 1989). Title IX of the Educational Amendments Act of 1972 requires schools to allow pregnant students to stay in regular classes if they so desire.

Both La Fuente and Willows had on-site School Age Mothers (SAM) programs. I interviewed twelve girls at La Fuente and five girls at Willows who had participated in the SAM program. A few girls reported feeling coerced. According to Beverly, "My counselors was the people who were sort of pushing me over here [to La Fuente]. . . . They should talk to you and they should tell you your alternatives." Cindy said, "I would have liked to stay at [my old school] when I was pregnant, . . . but as soon as it came out of my mouth that I was pregnant, they said I had to leave [that] school."

More typically, SAM girls felt "strongly counseled" into the continuation school, as Willows' vice principal described the transfer process to me. In other words, most SAM participants felt that counselors and other school administrators had not presented options in an evenhanded way, although the girls quickly conceded that the SAM program supported them materially and emotionally in their choice to have a baby in an environment away from peers and teachers who might have ridiculed their pregnancy. Anna, a La Fuente student, explained that when she told administrators at her high school that she was one month pregnant: "They said, 'We don't want to take responsibility for you. We'll just withdraw you out of here and stick you at La Fuente.' . . . They didn't tell me I had a choice [but] . . . I probably would have said I want to try [the] SAM [program at La Fuente] first." According to Anita, the principal at her previous school "said it would be better if I came to Willows because I was pregnant. And I was having trouble with the other kids because of that." Unfortunately, this "strong counseling" can occur without the prior consent of parents, as I observed at Willows one day when a mother who spoke only Spanish called to complain.

At La Fuente, the young mother's program staff noted in a self-evaluation: "Curriculum and class scheduling at La Fuente provides problems for special ed or college prep students (often they cannot get the classes they need); many students feel stigma attending a continuation school only because they are pregnant." This problem was echoed by students like Molly, a college preparatory student, who felt she had no choice but to attend La Fuente because she had no money for day care: "We know that the education that we receive here is at least 50 percent less than what we would get at a regular school. . . . I don't think it's fair just because we have children that we should have any less of a chance than what we had before we got pregnant. Because what are we going to do?"

Other voluntary transfers also described their "choice" as heavily influenced by comprehensive school personnel. Given that most students who ended up at

Beacon, La Fuente, and Willows were from working-class families and that significant proportions at all three schools were ethnic minority (45 percent, 80 percent, and 57 percent, respectively), one must ask whether students and parents with less access to information and few independent resources can exercise meaningful or informed choices. For example, 4 percent of students interviewed at Beacon and La Fuente said their parents had been completely unaware of the continuation transfer or of its significance; in all cases, these were non-English-speaking, first-generation immigrant parents. At Willows and La Fuente, where court-mandated school desegregation was in effect, some students spoke of not understanding their options beforehand, of being bused long distances to predominantly white schools in wealthy neighborhoods, and subsequently seeking refuge from the ethnic conflict and academic competition in the continuation program.

Indeed, educational life histories done with a subset of Beacon and La Fuente interviewees revealed that a number of so-called voluntary transfers had already been preconditioned to exclusion from comprehensive schools by virtue of their ethnic and class background and previous schooling experiences, including suspension, detention, and placement in remedial, opportunity, and special education classes. A number of students discovered they were more comfortable in the continuation environment interacting with peers seen to be more like themselves. Mandy, a white working-class student at La Fuente, described feeling out of place at the comprehensive school, where "they're not rich but they're well-off, whether they're black, Mexican, or white. And here . . . we all don't have that much money and stuff. And I guess it's weird because it's so true, that if you don't have as much money, you're more laid back."

Some voluntary transfers tended to perceive coercion after participating in the continuation school for a while and then concluding that the promises made for it had been largely unfulfilled, namely accelerated credit earning and the ability to return to the regular program. All three schools operated under a variable credit system which did allow highly motivated, self-initiating students to succeed. The problem was that few students had been adequately prepared to work on their own. Complained Ingrid, a Beacon student, "A lot of the kids could be getting credit, they could be reading and writing something, but instead they just yak, yak, yak." A number of students described being socialized to actually put forth less effort than they were capable of making. David, another Beacon student, reported:

Like the first time you come to this school, you work hard cuz that's how you were doing at a normal high school, and then you look at other students: They're always kicking back, and you get irritated with that cuz they're not working. . . . Then the next year, you'll be slowly kind of slacking off. Then later on, you'll be talking the whole period, and you won't even recognize it.

Too late, these students realized they were not making up the credits they thought they would.

Trying to return to the comprehensive high school from the continuation school can, in some instances, be like trying to back a car up over the curved spikes designed to prevent drivers from reentering a parking lot. Many students said they were told they could return to their home school and quite a few said they still planned to do so, but in reality, few ever do (less than 5 percent at both Beacon and La Fuente during 1988–89). Continuation personnel often explained this by saying that students liked the alternative program and chose to stay. But this begs examination of how this choice gets constructed within the schooling system.

First, the few who did return tended to be the most successful. Teachers and administrators sometimes discouraged this group from leaving the continuation school, partly because they demonstrated to others through their attendance and academic performance that the continuation school was a place for serious students. "Our students definitely feel the stigma. They'll say, 'I need to get back to [the home school] to get the diploma'," said one Beacon teacher, who confided: "That presses some of my buttons, obviously, because I think this is the neatest place in the whole world to go. I would love to go here; I see all its value." In addition, the return of students to their home schools undercut teachers' efforts to lessen the stigma for those who liked the continuation school and planned to remain.

Second, the rules regulating return were left vague. A few La Fuente students whose petitions to return were signed by continuation personnel were denied by their home school principal. Others were persuaded that they would not be able to graduate if they left the continuation school. Still others saw so few of their classmates returning that they forgot or never realized that they had this option. According to Joan, a Beacon student:

I didn't realize that I could go back 'til a couple of months after I'd been here and I overheard this girl go, "Think I should go back to [Comprehensive High] for graduation?" I was, "Hmm." It does say it in the pamphlet [distributed at orientation], but I don't think many people read through the pamphlet. It doesn't really talk about it. It just says, "After completion of one . . . good semester, student can return to previous high school."

The pamphlet did not define a "good semester." This made it difficult for even the most successful to leave. Bob, a Latino with senior credits, had maintained "honors" status for the semester he was at Beacon, and although he was still shy a few credits, he wanted to return to his home school. Bob's counselor met with him several times and tried to discourage him. Privately, she told me that his return would "set him up for failure." Bob was able to return only after he publicized his concern and the entire faculty considered his case. He eventually graduated from his home school, making up the credit difference through a night class.

Third, comprehensive schools had no incentive to accept continuation students back. When they did so and the students had problems adjusting, comprehensive school personnel marshaled this as evidence that continuation education was inferior and only succeeded to the extent that academic and behavior standards were lowered. No transition programs existed to support students as they reentered the more rigid environment.

Many continuation students "choose" not to return. But that such an overwhelming number of students remain in what many perceive as a stigmatized organization cannot be explained simply by reference to individual choice. This choice is shaped by the organizational context in which it is constructed.

MAINTAINING THE CREDENTIAL HIERARCHY BY PUSHING SOME STUDENTS OUT

In trying to persuade students to reengage, teachers and administrators throughout the educational system often use negative motivations as a last resort. Unwittingly, they reinforce a hierarchy of stigmatized organizations in the students' minds. Many comprehensive staff members cast the continuation school in a negative light in the hopes of scaring misbehaving or truant students into changing their behavior. Students who ended up in the continuation school anyway sometimes repeated the horrors they had been told, to the dismay of the staff. Ironically, when continuation staff members' bag of tricks to motivate disengaged students approached empty, they reached for the same "dirty" trick: They disparaged the educational alternatives that remained open, usually adult education, the GED, or independent studies—even the continuation school's own afternoon shift in the case of Willows.

The continuation schools had ways of pushing out, or disengaging from, students seen as "troublemakers" or "nonstudents"—including girls but more often boys. Students who did not demonstrate a certain amount of success—measured formally at Beacon and informally at La Fuente and Willows by attendance, productivity, and punctuality—were routinely transferred to other alternative programs one rung down the credential ladder. At Beacon, truant or nonproductive students were routinely enrolled in the district's adult education program, which in turn was not required to report them as dropouts if they subsequently left. Of the seventy eventual dropouts who were enrolled at Beacon during 1988–89, Beacon referred 64 percent to adult ed after several months, and most of these students—78 percent of such referrals—never actually enrolled. Three fifths of these adult education no-shows were male, two fifths female. Explained one teacher-counselor at Beacon: "There is no monitoring once they are at adult ed. It's really the end. They leave saying they'll make it there, but 99 percent won't. We say, 'Yeah, good luck'—sending them out feeling good. But we know they won't make it."

At La Fuente, the independent study program (ISP) served a similar purpose. Out of 350 dropouts from La Fuente high school, 16 percent had transferred to ISP; almost a third of those were considered no-shows, while the rest stayed a couple of weeks or longer before leaving the schooling system altogether.

Increasing gang and drug-dealing activities and the large demand by its feeder comprehensive schools—with a combined enrollment of over 20,000 students—to enroll their misfits put La Fuente under pressure to withdraw students who were especially truant, disruptive, or reluctant to work. School staff employed several means of implementing this unstated mandate. First, incoming students had to attend a half-day orientation class for one to three weeks. Among other things, they were told what was expected of a good student. If after the first day they came to orientation class late or without a notebook, the teacher, selected for the job because she was well liked by most students, motivating yet demanding, routinely sent them home.

Barry appeared at the door around 10:00 saying he'd overslept. Ms. Wilson told him to go home. Barry: "At least I made the effort to come." Lance added: "Yeah, if you keep kicking us out, how are we gonna get an education?" Ms. Wilson explained that Barry had to take responsibility for being tardy, and Barry left. (Field notes, 10 May 1989)

If students were frequently absent or reluctant to complete in-class assignments or participate in discussion, they often had to repeat the class for another three weeks. These policies did discourage the most disengaged students: 18 percent of all eventual dropouts left after six weeks or less at La Fuente during 1988–89. Wrote one such student in his journal: "I just got some desturbing [*sic*] news that I might have to repeat the window. . . . I'm not going to go to the class. I will just get into the GED program." He did not do so while I was at La Fuente.

Another means of disengaging from students deemed marginal was referrals to what was euphemistically called the Responsibility Center. About half the teachers routinely sent tardy and disruptive students there, where they had to copy rules from the student handbook. In interviews, students and some teachers complained that the man in charge treated them harshly. He repeated his philosophy to me several times: "I tell the kids [who come to the Responsibility Center], 'It's like cancer and garbage. You cut one out, and the other you throw out'." More often than not, girls reported being shocked, upset, and inclined to skip future detention, whereas boys were prone to swear, flee, or challenge the disciplinarian to a fight. As one teacher explained: "The kids [especially boys] who get sent to Mr. Zuniga are at risk of suspension because they're just not as equipped as adults to deal with his abrasive personality. They end up fighting him over piddling offenses like being tardy."

Other teachers and the counselor fully supported Mr. Zuniga's approach and encouraged each other to deal with chronic absenteeism and other discipline problems through the referral system because this created an official record. At a certain point, students who had built up poor reputations were withdrawn under the code "other"—the largest but least explanatory category of dropouts/ pushouts. Sitting in the office on numerous occasions, I witnessed students being quietly withdrawn under the "other" code for smoking marijuana, chronic absenteeism and failing grades, and fighting.

One teacher referred a Latina to the office for chronic tardiness, saying she was "not a serious student" and "taking up space in the class." The counselor withdrew her from school that day. I then overheard the girl asking a secretary if she could appeal to the principal—apparently unaware that La Fuente had no principal at that time. A similar pushout practice was observed at Beacon for a Mexican-American boy considered "too disruptive." His teacher-counselor asked that he not be sent registration information, and he was withdrawn under the code "over 18—not reenrolled."

Some teachers at both schools told me they were unhappy with these school-initiated, exclusionary practices. At La Fuente, a group of teachers formally complained to the acting principal that students were being withdrawn before they even knew the students were in trouble. But they hesitated to push strongly for due process unless they felt a particular student had academic potential, was pleasant if unmotivated, and/or had participated in school activities.

IN SEARCH OF A RELIABLE DROPOUT/PUSHOUT RATE

Throughout the year of intensive fieldwork at Beacon and La Fuente, significant numbers of continuation students dropped out or were pushed out. Over half (52 percent) of those enrolled some time during 1988–89 at La Fuente left the educational system without graduating, while about one third did so at Beacon. These dropout/pushout figures are higher than the annual rates reported to the state because I was able to verify that certain students who had supposedly transferred to adult ed or independent study programs either had never actually enrolled or had dropped out after a short time.

Fewer students graduated. Ten percent of all students enrolled during 1988–89 obtained a diploma or the equivalent from La Fuente and one fifth received a diploma from Beacon. These graduation rates were lower than those of nearby comprehensive high schools, as expected given the "at risk" status of their student bodies, particularly the low credit standing of most pupils as they enter. The lack of close correspondence between a student's age and his or her grade level, as well as the open entry/open exit feature of the program (students enroll or leave throughout the school year), further complicates measurement and interpretation of graduation and dropout rates.

To clarify this, I examined the transcripts of students who entered Beacon (because its smaller size made the task more manageable) from September 1986 through May 1989 and selected those who had entered the ninth grade in

1985–86. The resulting 131 students (58 girls, 73 boys), who had ever enrolled at Beacon, comprised the should-be class of 1989. I tracked these students through to the end of their fifth high school year, after which time few continue. My extensive search shows no similar research tracking a cohort through continuation school to dropout or diploma.

By July 1990, 58 percent had dropped out (two thirds from Beacon directly, another third from other schools, mainly adult ed), 30 percent had graduated, 11 percent had been last enrolled in another school (current status unknown); only one remained at Beacon. Because Beacon has, historically, been more successful at graduating students than either La Fuente or Willows, one can only conclude that a similar longitudinal analysis would reveal these schools to have even lower graduation rates and higher dropout rates than Beacon.

POLICY IMPLICATIONS

With large numbers of students, urban districts can capitalize on economies of scale and specialized staffs that can pursue discretionary funds to create more options. In California "education options" at the secondary level have grown dramatically over the last ten years. Besides continuation high schools, these options include educational clinics, alternative education and work centers, county community schools, concurrent enrollment in adult education, independent study programs, teenage parenting and pregnancy programs, and partnership academies.

Most represent a dual response: (1) to students' need for flexibility and personalization with the stated aim of "dropout prevention and recovery," and (2) to mainstream comprehensive high schools' need for mechanisms to isolate students identified as discipline problems and to provide specialized services efficiently. In a society stratified by class, ethnicity, and gender, however, these second-chance programs sometimes turn out to be second-rate.

People interested in reforming urban high schools to incorporate the positive aspects of educational options—flexible scheduling, personalized attention, brokerage of social services—argue that once these reforms are implemented, the need for options outside of the comprehensive high schools will be reduced. But there are reasons to be skeptical. Foremost is the imbalance of power and resources that shape the politics of schooling, particularly in large urban districts that draw on a dwindling property and industry tax base for funding. In times of fiscal constraint, dropout programs—which sometimes redirect resources to help those most in need—are among the first items to be cut.

Another problem is that options within a single setting tend to pit various groups against each other over academic and behavior standards, a dynamic which has led administrators to establish alternatives apart from the mainstream. As the various options proliferate, however, problems of communication, coordination, and accountability increase and so, therefore, do the possibilities that students will slip between the cracks.

As an examination of the history of continuation education shows, offering options without major reforms both inside and outside the educational system (for example, job programs, more and better funding for child care, funded access to contraception and abortion services, balanced housing development, social and health services) can simply mean replicating the sorting process pioneered in traditional educational settings. Continuation personnel throughout California are under pressure to demonstrate results or face elimination, and consequently some have begun to screen out the most disengaged students, relegating them to other optional programs further down the credential hierarchy. In Ontario, for example, continuation administrators have argued: "Many students referred to the program have no positive academic intentions and are simply attempting to continue 'game-playing' and take up space in the program." As a solution, the district has begun a precontinuation independent study program, which administrators feel has "enhanced" the continuation program because "non-attenders" and "non-productive" students are "redirected without enrollment," thus improving average daily attendance figures and the "academic setting" (Bratta, 1990, p. 8). In Milpitas, the continuation school requires students to improve their attendance at the comprehensive school as a condition of enrollment. Not coincidentally, its district uses temporary placement on independent study as a disciplinary threat, reserving the continuation school as a "privilege." I have not surveyed the over 400 continuation programs in California and therefore can make no claim that these instances are representative. However, both were publicized through the California Continuation Education Association, one in the CCEA newsletter (Ontario) and the other at a regional CCEA meeting I attended (Milpitas), which suggests a possible trend in the making.

In the short run, the state could increase accountability for retaining and engaging students throughout the educational system by requiring schools to track individuals from entry into kindergarten through to age eighteen or high school graduation and to calculate longitudinal dropout rates by ethnic group and sex. Currently, California requires schools to report an annual dropout rate; this estimates the number of students who drop out or are pushed out during the school year. A longitudinal rate provides a more accurate and complete picture by estimating the percentage of students in a particular class who drop out or are pushed out between the time they enter and graduation.

The longitudinal rate, and monitoring system needed to calculate it, would help administrators prevent students from slipping through the cracks. At present, students who drop out between school years or in transition from one school or program to another, even within the same district, are sometimes not counted as dropouts. Or if they are counted, it is often by alternative programs such as continuation or adult education rather than the students' neighborhood comprehensive school; this accounting practice makes the mainstream school's record of retaining and engaging students seem better than it actually is.

Both the comprehensive high school and the options connected to it should

borhood of the city (Sit, 1980, pp. 233–34). Because of the existence of such specificities of Asian cities, it is necessary to take into consideration what is specific to the Asian context when looking into urban education in Asian countries.

This chapter studies some of the educational issues in a socialist Chinese city—Guangzhou (Canton). Studying Guangzhou is of particular interest and significance. It is the administrative, economic, and cultural center of Guangdong Province, and is the biggest city of the Pearl River Delta. It was the first of the fourteen coastal cities of China open to the outside world, serving as China's window on the world. Situated on the northern part of the Pearl River (Zhujiang) Delta and bordered on the south by the South China Sea, it has long been a center of Chinese trade, and of communications in south China. Moreover, it is close to two capitalist cities, Hong Kong and Macau, and is near other cities in Southeast Asia. Because Guangzhou is the southern gate of China, and because of China's open door policy and the city's physical proximity to the outside world, Guangzhou is the socialist city most subject to Western influences. Therefore, looking into urban education in Guangzhou requires a consideration of all possible factors, that is, characteristics of both socialist and capitalist cities, and features of both Eastern and Western cities.

CONCEPTS OF URBAN AREAS IN CHINA

Changes in Definitions of Urban Areas

Defining *urban* in China is difficult, since ways of counting urban populations vary, involving a mixture of both administrative and functional criteria (Lo, 1987, 1989; Hsu, 1987). Moreover, official definitions of urban areas have changed three times since 1949 (in 1955, 1963, and 1984). The 1955 definition was based on Soviet models. Urban areas were referred to as: (1) regions in which a municipal people's committee or people's committee of the county *(xian)* level or higher is established, (2) regions with a permanent resident population of 2,000 persons or more, of which the nonagricultural population comprises 50 percent or more, or (3) centers of commerce, industry, mining, or transportation, and locations with schools and scientific research organizations.

Because of economic difficulties, the 1963 definition of urban areas was narrowed considerably, in order to "shrink" the existing cities and towns. Urban areas were then referred to as regions with: (1) a permanent resident population of 3,000 persons or more, of which 70 percent or more was nonagricultural, or (2) a permanent resident population of 2,500 to 3,000, of which 85 percent or more was nonagricultural.

However, with the adoption of the open door policy, in 1984, the government regarded the city as a center of economic development, and in order to boost the country's economic growth, the government loosened the criteria for defining urban areas to create more economic centers. First, all locations with county-level government organizations had to establish themselves as officially designated towns. Second, population criteria for officially designated towns were eased considerably. For example, village areas *(xiang)* with total populations of 20,000 or less, but with nonagricultural populations of over 2,000 near the village government offices, were also designated as towns. Moreover, minority areas, hinterland areas with sparse populations, mountain regions, small industrial or mining centers, small harbors, sight-seeing areas, border towns, etc. were officially designated as towns even when having nonagricultural populations of less than 2,000. Third, compared with the 1963 definition, the towns were given jurisdiction over rural areas, as opposed to the old system under which the rural areas had jurisdiction over the towns (Kojima, 1987, pp. 4–6). And this has changed the traditional single-city planning into urban-regional planning or "urban-borough planning" (Hu, 1990, p. 5).

Hence, studies of urban development in China have to take into account these changes in definitions of urban areas. Moreover, studying changes in urban population have to consider the so-called "mechanical growth," which is a combination of natural growth and growth due to changes in boundaries of municipalities as a result of the redefinition of urban areas.

Spatial Organization of the Chinese City

The Chinese "city" is in fact an urban region covering both municipality *(shi)* and rural counties *(xian)* under its jurisdiction. According to the State Statistical Bureau, city regions *(diqu)* are classified into three divisions: city *(chengqu)*, suburb *(jiaoqu)* and counties under city's jurisdiction *(shixiaxian)* (State Statistical Bureau, 1990, p. 753). However, even within the municipality, a considerable rural suburban district is found. Sometimes, the suburb is developed into a new city region, as in the case of Guangzhou's new city. With a consideration of both the administrative and functional criteria, the spatial organization of the Chinese city region can be a combination of the central city plus suburban districts, the new city developed from the suburb, and counties *(xian)* under the city's jurisdiction.

URBAN POLICIES IN CHINA

China's urban strategy has been greatly influenced by the socialist city planning principles of standardization of housing or living space, city size limitation, desegregation (that is, a classless society), dividing the city into uniformly self-contained units, and reducing the rural-urban contradictions. This was particularly so during Mao's period (Lo, 1987, p. 454). To achieve these aims, the Chinese government has taken a number of measures, for example, (1) transforming existing "consumer cities" into "producer cities," that is, cities supplying producer goods rather than consumer goods; (2) limiting the growth of big cities by controlled movement of labor, planned allocation of investment, including the investment in large- and medium-scale capital construction to secure regular high yields from the land, and giving priority to industries that provide direct inputs to agriculture; (3) creating neighborhood units in order to divide the city into uniformly self-contained units; and (4) reducing the social and economic status attached to city locations, such as those having institutions of higher education or government offices (Lo, 1987, p. 444; Chiu, 1980, pp. 92–93). Obviously, urban strategy in China was generally characterized by a strong sense of centralized control in terms of city planning, urban population control, and definitions of urban areas, although a certain extent of flexibility and decentralization did exist.

With the inception of the Four Modernizations in the post-Mao period, there were obvious changes in China's urban policy. For example, with the adoption of the open door policy, and also as a result of the Third Plenary Session of the Twelfth Party Central Committee in October 1984, China's urban reform policy designated the city as the economic center of the next stage of development. This led to the opening up of new enterprises, and the permission for a certain degree of free market operation in the cities, especially the open cities and the "Special Economic Zones" (SEZ), in order to attract foreign investments (Kwok, 1985, pp. 2, 23). Another significant policy change in recent years was the agricultural reform, which virtually abolished the commune system established in 1958. An aspect of this reform was the introduction of the agricultural production responsibility system in 1978. Under this system, the decision-making power of production was returned to the farmers in order to promote their incentives for higher and better production for improving their own standards of living (Lo, 1987, p. 443). In cities, the structure of ownership was readjusted, and the collective and private economies in the cities and towns were developed. At the same time, the policy of openness to the outside world was further carried out to attract foreign funds and investments (Wu, 1990, p. 9).

However, despite recent policy changes toward local decentralization and an allowance for a limited degree of capitalism, the Chinese cities and urban systems continue to exhibit the socialist ideal of the city, including standardization and equality, especially between the rural and urban areas (Lo, 1987, p. 455). Moreover, strictly controlling the development of cities is still a practice of China. Despite many political changes, "strictly controlling the size of the large cities, rationally developing medium-sized cities, and actively developing small cities" has remained the guiding principle of urban development throughout the 1980s (Hu, 1990, p. 4). As a result, although China possesses the largest urban population in the world, its level of urbanization is rather low by world standards.

GUANGZHOU CITY

Guangzhou is the biggest city in southern China, and is the capital of Guangdong Province. According to the 1990 figures, Guangzhou covers an area of

7,434.4 square kilometers, with a population of 5.943 million (*Guangzhou Yearbook,* 1991, p. 617). With its size of population, the whole city region is classified as an "extra-large city as center of big economic region."

The spatial organization of the city has changed many times since 1949, as a result of regional developments and changes in definitions of *city* (see *Guangzhou Yearbook,* 1984, p. 71; 1986, p. 60; 1987, p. 476; 1988, p. 478). At present, the whole city region can be organized into three major divisions: the central city, the new city, and counties under its jurisdiction. The central city is actually the oldest part of the whole city region. It is comprised of four districts: Dongshan, Yuexiu, Liwan, and Haizhu. The new city is really developed from the suburbs, and is comprised of another four districts: Baiyun, Fangcun, Tianhe, and Huangpu. There are four counties *(xian)* under the city's jurisdiction: Hua, Conghua, Zengcheng, and Panyu. The spatial organization of the whole city region is illustrated in Figure 5.1.

As is typical of a Chinese city, the city region exemplifies a single-core concentric pattern of development, interrupted by radial developments of industrial and residential areas along the main arteries of communication, with neighborhood workshops widespread; this spatial pattern is different from the usual arrangement in Western industrial cities (Lo, Pannell, & Welch, 1977, pp. 281–83; Sit, 1980, p. 245). Since 1949, the Chinese government has been making efforts to convert Guangzhou into a socialist city that will play a producing role, in part, by introducing new industrial and service activities. This can be illustrated by the development of Haizhu District. Once a crime-infested slum, Haizhu is now predominantly an industrial, administrative, and residential area (with large hotels), befitting the center of a socialist city. However, Guangzhou's historical significance as a trade center and its trade links with foreign countries allow it to retain certain characteristics of a "consumer city." This at the same time manifests an aspect of flexibility in China's urban policy (Lo, Pannell, & Welch, 1977, pp. 280–81).

In Guangzhou, reforms are being implemented to incorporate elements of free market operation (Li, 1986, p. 36). With the adoption of the open door policy, Guangzhou has been classified as *danlie chengshi,* that is, a city being specifically considered by the central government in its overall economic planning, instead of being subsumed under the provincial level's economic planning. The main purpose of this policy is to speed up the city's economic reform. As a result, Guangzhou's economic development has been fast and impressive. The city now ranks third among Chinese cities in the total value of retail sales, and fourth in export trade. Guangzhou surpasses many other cities in China in terms of economic growth. For example, between 1980 and 1986, Guangzhou achieved an average annual GNP growth of 13.38 percent, not only surpassing the country's average annual growth of 9.9 percent, but also surpassing all other cities in China. Between 1982 and 1989, the average annual income of a worker in the central city rose from 1,236 yuan to 3,272 yuan, and that of a farmer in the counties rose from 752 yuan to 1,543 yuan (Zibiao & Lee, 1991, p. 3). Because of its historical significance, Guangzhou is also a

Figure 5.1
Spatial Organization of Guangzhou City (1992)

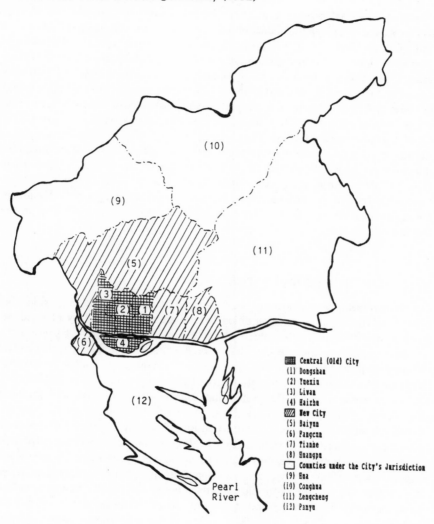

Central (Old) City
(1) Dongshan
(2) Yuexiu
(3) Liwan
(4) Haizhu
New City
(5) Baiyun
(6) Fangcun
(7) Tianhe
(8) Huangpu
Counties under the City's Jurisdiction
(9) Hua
(10) Conghua
(11) Zengcheng
(12) Panyu

Pearl River

cultural center in the south, being the venue of twenty tertiary institutions and 300 research organizations where 180,000 professionals work (Ma et al. 1985, p. 52).

RECENT EDUCATIONAL DEVELOPMENT IN GUANGZHOU

China has regarded the development of education as a key strategy for the country's Four Modernizations, and has therefore made efforts to improve and expand the education system since 1978. To support the Four Modernizations, the municipal government of Guangzhou has also taken a series of actions to expand educational provision and improve its quality. As a result, Guangzhou has experienced substantial educational expansion over the past decade and a half (Xiong, 1988). By 1984, primary education was in general universalized, which provided a good foundation for the implementation of the Law on [nine-year] Compulsory Education, promulgated in 1986. From 1986 to 1990, the city raised the enrollment ratio at the junior secondary level to 95 percent, and the municipal government is making efforts to further raise the enrollment ratio to 98 percent by 1993. The municipal government has passed ordinances to enforce compulsory education, held meetings regularly to evaluate progress, expanded projects of teacher training and school construction, raised funds by imposing an "education-added tax" (and others) and by collecting donations from people in Hong Kong and Macau, and also initiated a series of educational reforms (Zibiao & Lee, 1991, pp. 4–5). Hence Guangzhou's dynamism and expansion are manifested not only in the economic arena but also in the education sector.

REGIONAL DISPARITIES IN EDUCATION

Urban development naturally leads toward imbalances and disparities between regions, even in socialist cities, which are characterized by planned development or centralization justified on egalitarian principles. Examining a number of Soviet cities, Bater (1980, p. 132) observed that despite several decades of promoting egalitarian principles of spatial organization, disparities persisted in respect to the general quality of life, both within cities and between cities in various regions. Dangschat and Blasius (1987, p. 190) looked at the housing situation of different education groups in Warsaw, Poland. They observed regional disparities similar to those of Warsaw's Western European counterparts. There are certain factors leading to the occurrence of disparities and imbalances between regions. The first is the tension between efficiency and equality, a problem always faced by socialist city planners (Bater, 1980, p. 165), especially at a time of rapid growth in population and economic development. In the case of Guangzhou, the rapid growth of the economy since 1978 is unprecedented. This has resulted in changes in many facets of the city, such as the development of new districts, the attraction of migrants to the city, new demands for educational provisions, and so on. In the face of sudden and rapid changes, it is not surprising at all that imbalances and disparities between regions emerge in many respects.

A second factor leading to regional disparities is diverse patterns of historical development. In Guangzhou, the differences between the central city and the larger city region, that is, the new city and the counties, can be traced back to their historical roots. For example, because of its historical significance, the central city enjoys a high concentration of offices, shops, and cultural establishments (Yeh, Xu, & Hu, 1989, p. 25). Dongshan is a concentrated area of provincial offices of the army, the Communist Party, and the administration and the location of institutes of higher education, cultural and community organizations, and hospitals. It has been an area of the intelligentsia, high-ranking cadres, and overseas Chinese. Yuexiu used to be Guangzhou's old city core and is presently a most important commercial center, with a high concentration of offices, shops, recreational establishments, schools, and medical and health centers. Liwan is also an old urban district and another established commercial area, though not as densely populated as Yuexiu. Haizhu is relatively newly developed, with a growing concentration of industry. In 1985, there were 500 factories and 246 "neighborhood street factories." However, it is also the location of two important higher institutions, Zhongshan University and Guangzhou College of Arts (Zhang & Zhang, 1985, pp. 101–2). Students residing in the central city no doubt benefit from the cluster of social and cultural facilities, such as museums, art galleries, libraries, bookshops, publishers, research institutes, and youth centers.

The new city, which is actually developed from the suburbs, is, on the other hand, developed into an industrial region. Shipbuilding and ship-repairing industries are well established in Huangpu. As an officially designated economic and technological development district, it is also an important site for oil refining, chemical, and other engineering industries. Steel industries and pharmaceuticals are found in Fangcun. Situated at the junction of the Guangzhou central city, Fushan city, and Zhuhai city, Fangcun is also an important transportation center. Textiles, flour, and paper-making industries are found in Tianhe. It is planned that the district will also be developed into a new education and R & D center. Baiyun retains its agricultural characteristics, as it is an important district for growing vegetables and rice, and producing milk. The counties are no doubt mainly agricultural areas (see *Guangzhou Yearbook,* 1983, p. 32; 1985, p. 685; 1990, p. 46; 1991, pp. 395, 553). This suggests that the government has indeed made efforts to upgrade the fringe areas, but because of its historical significance as an administrative and commercial center, the central city has advantages over the other regions that persist despite efforts to bring about standardization and equality.

Disparities in educational provisions between the central city and the other parts of Guangzhou are manifested in a few areas. First, schools in different regions, such as city, county, and town, are funded by their particular levels of government. Because there is a difference in financial conditions between different levels of government, this subsequently leads to disparities in educational financing between regions. The provincial government, and even the city-level government, may allocate extra funds to those counties which experience special financial difficulties for particular programs, such as school-building projects for speeding up the universalization of compulsory education. However, generally speaking, educational development in different regions is reliant on the level of government. Differences in educational financing between regions can be illustrated by statistics on per-capita educational expenditure. According to the 1989 figures, the annual per capita educational expenditure in the primary and secondary schools was 1,053.45 yuan in the central city, whereas it was only 796.97 in the new city, and only 397 yuan in the counties (*GEBS*, 1989). Moreover, with rapid economic and industrial development in the central city, the annual average net income of a worker in the central city has become much higher than that of a farmer (3,504 yuan versus 1,539 yuan) in the counties (*Guangzhou Yearbook*, 1991, p. 615). As a result, students in the central city generally enjoy better financial support than their counterparts in the counties.

Second, despite the existence of a system of planned employment or job assignments, the central city and the new city together tend to enjoy a larger proportion of qualified teachers, as in many cities in the capitalist world. For example, in 1989, the proportion of qualified teachers (postsecondary qualifications at the junior secondary level and university degree qualifications at the senior secondary level) stood at 95.4 percent in the senior secondary schools and 83.1 percent in the junior secondary schools in the central city. In the counties, while the senior secondary schools enjoyed a slightly higher proportion of qualified teachers (96.1 percent), there was obviously a lower proportion of qualified teachers in the junior secondary schools (62.9 percent) (*GEBS*, 1989). The existence of such a discrepancy in teachers' qualifications was mainly due to three reasons: (1) There is a need for allocating better-qualified teachers to keypoint schools in order to maintain the keypoint school system, which was reinstated in 1978; (2) schools in the central city can apply to be allocated certain teachers from the counties to fill certain justifiable positions; and (3) teachers in the counties can also apply for moving into the city because of nonteaching/nonfinancial reasons, such as family reunion.

Third, because of historical factors, and also as a matter of government policy, secondary schools in Guangzhou can be classified into five categories, which are listed as follows in descending order of quality: (1) keypoint schools in the central city, (2) keypoint schools in the local districts, (3) prestigious comprehensive schools, (4) ordinary comprehensive schools, and (5) schools for the low achievers. Schools in higher categories usually enjoy better facilities and also better teachers, which is especially typical of the policy for the keypoint schools. However, prestigious schools, even though not classified as keypoint schools, do have their own ways of drawing extra funds and facilities. Being prestigious schools, they have already established very good networks with various associations of the society, and can attract donations from parents, alumni associations, and even industries. All this reinforces the advantages that these schools already possess, and there is a clear difference in student performance in these different categories of schools. For example, in the "category one schools," nearly 100 percent of junior secondary graduates can proceed to the senior secondary level of education, and 80–98 percent of the senior secondary graduates can proceed to higher education. By contrast, in the "categories four and five schools," only about 60–75 percent of the junior secondary graduates can proceed to the senior secondary level of education, and only a small proportion of the senior secondary graduates can enter higher institutions. For some schools, there is not even a single graduate admitted to a higher institution.

As a policy of population control, students residing in districts outside the central city (except Tianhe and Fangcun) cannot be admitted to the "category one schools." The best schools they can aspire to are therefore the local keypoint schools. Apart from the "category one schools," there are also some other schools open only to the residents of the central city. For example, while a limited number of specialized secondary schools admit students from districts outside the central city, the rest do not. This reveals that under a model of planned development, there are students being excluded from the best chances they may deserve on merit.

Fourth, maybe as a summation of all the above factors, coupled with a difference in attitude toward education between people in the central city and the counties, there are obvious differences in student performance between regions. For example, in respect to the rate of primary students graduating to the junior secondary schools in 1984 it was 95 percent in the central city, but only 84 percent in the new city, and about 60 percent in the counties. It was not until 1990 that these other two regions could raise the promotion rate to 95 percent (Zibiao & Lee, 1991).

The above analysis suggests that there exist disparities between regions in terms of educational opportunities, resources and school facilities, teacher qualifications, and school achievements. Factors leading to these differences vary, and are probably a combination of historical factors, regional development factors, and the government policy of differential regional development. Egalitarian principles may not be easily carried out in the face of other needs of the country, such as the need to develop certain keypoint schools. The idea of keypoint schools is hardly egalitarian, in the sense of deliberately concentrating the best facilities and teachers in a few schools. The policy has thereby been decried and criticized since its implementation (Pepper, 1980, 1982). However, this is considered necessary by the government in order to speed up the country's development (Qiang & Huang, 1987, p. 95). City population control is a conspicuous factor depriving the bright students of the fringe areas of the opportunity of studying in the best schools in the central city. Further, the differences in average annual income between workers in the central city and workers in the counties, resulting from rapid economic development in the city, may well lead to educational inequalities based on families' socioeconomic backgrounds.

THE PRESSURE OF DEMOGRAPHIC CHANGES
ON EDUCATION

Population Growth and Educational Expansion

In 1949, Guangzhou had a population of 1.04 million. It had risen to 1.97 million by 1960—an 89 percent increase in eleven years. Between 1961 and 1976, the municipal government adopted a policy of controlling the city's population by sending rural-urban migrants back to their original villages, and Guangzhou's population had dropped to 1.62 million by 1976 (Zhang & Zhang, 1985, p. 105). Notwithstanding the adoption of a policy of "strictly controlling the size of the city," Guangzhou city has experienced considerable population growth since the adoption of the open door policy, owing to the relaxation of the definition of *city*, the return of those "sent-down youth" of the Cultural Revolution period, the migration of rich farmers (those who benefited from the introduction of the responsibility system) to the city, and the transfer of people to the city because of job assignments.

Between 1985 and 1990, Guangzhou's natural population growth was between 6.75 and 9.26 per 10,000 (*Guangzhou Yearbook*, 1991, p. 72). Between 1983 and 1986, its annual "mechanical growth" amounted to 28,750 people, that is, an addition of 115,000 people in four years (*Guangzhou Yearbook*, 1987, p. 95). In the central city and the new city, between 1972 and 1982, there was an annual increase of 98,346 people, that is, a total increase of 786,914 people in ten years. In the central city alone, there was an annual increase of 33,780 people, that is, a total increase of 270,242 people (*Guangzhou Yearbook*, 1991, p. 101). In 1990, the population of Guangzhou totaled 5.936 million.

This rapid growth of population was followed by a rapid growth in the student population. Between 1950 and 1986, the number of students, schools, and staff grew 15.7 times, 37.2 times, and 26.9 times, respectively (Huang & Peng, 1988, p. 73). It is estimated that there will be an annual increase of 5,500 (that is, a total increase of 22,000) students within the central city from 1991 to 1994. Accommodating these additional students will require seven more schools in four years. This future increase is not particularly impressive. However, as the city is making an effort to materialize the implementation of nine-year compulsory education by 1993, further increases simply imply additional difficulties.

Population Mobility and Educational Problems

Guangzhou has a sizable "floating population" of people who reside in the city on a temporary basis. The existence of this large pool is closely associated with the expansion of the economy. Because of its booming economy, the city attracts a number of illegal immigrants from the counties and even from poorer cities in China who migrate to the city to seek their fortune. The country's system of direct control of population movement implies that without official approval for their migration, such people are unlikely to be granted residence registration and will therefore be excluded from any social welfare and services of the city. However, this disadvantage has not discouraged these immigrants from continuing to come to the city. At times, the city has to face a sudden, massive "blind influx" of immigrants; a recent such event took place in February 1992. In case of massive "blind influx," the municipal government will certainly take immediate action to transport people back to their places of origin. However, normally it is difficult and indeed burdensome for the government to detect these illegal immigrants and deport them. Moreover, with a real demand for additional labor resulting from the expansion of the economy, the existence of such a floating population does help to alleviate shortages in the labor force. Moreover, many enterprises prefer these immigrant workers employed from elsewhere to local workers, since, in order to stay longer in the city, they are more hardworking and are willing to accept lower wages. It was estimated that in Guangzhou there was on average a floating population of 1.2 million per day in 1988. In 1989, the figure grew to 1.5 million, of whom 95.42 percent were actually in the central city (840,000 in Liwan and 202,000 in Yuexiu) (Ma, 1989, p. 52).

With such a supply of floating population and a real demand for additional labor, the municipal government has no good alternative to allowing these immigrants to register as "temporary residents" in the city. Moreover, channels have been created for them to seek employment in Guangzhou. For example, under the administration of the Labor Bureau, labor services companies have been established in almost every district to employ temporary labor and to recruit rural labor (ibid.). In 1989, about 420,000 people registered as temporary residents in Guangzhou, of whom 330,000 resided in the central city (*Guangzhou Yearbook,* 1990, p. 443). Of these temporary residents, most of the men were employed as construction workers and porters. And most of the women were employed in textile and manufacturing industries, domestic services, the service sector, and individual enterprises.

A consequence of the increase of temporary labor is the increase of "temporary students," who are the children of these temporary residents. In 1989, 1,038 children entered Primary 1 as temporary students in the central city. With continued economic growth and consequent increasing need for migrant workers, it is anticipated that the number of temporary students will continue to grow. This creates further problems for the municipal government in providing additional school places in the process of implementing the universalization of primary and junior secondary education. However, those who suffer most are the temporary students themselves. A survey of 494 such students in primary and junior secondary schools found that 70 percent of them were "not interested in study," "did not concentrate in class," and were being classified as "low achievers" (Tan & Zhang, 1988). It is not difficult to understand why these temporary students lack incentives in their studies, since, residing in the city on a temporary basis, they do not know how long they are going to stay in the school. Moreover, they are believed to be from generally unfavorable family backgrounds, since their parents are receiving lower wages, and migrants are not eligible for social welfare and services (Ma, 1989, p. 101).

Pressure for Educational Provision in a Densely Populated City

In Guangzhou, city development and construction are under centralized planning. However, this is not always successful in bringing about balanced development. First, at a time of emphasizing production rather than consumption in city development, infrastructural investments have been neglected. As a consequence, there is very little new housing, and the existing houses are allowed to become dilapidated. And overcrowding has become a perennial problem in the city, although the intensity of land use is not high (Li, 1986, pp. 13–15). Second, while planning is centralized in the structure, at the implementation level it is necessary to permit departments to take independent action and make decisions in order to get things done. In some cases, the possibility of production units having exclusive use of the land on which they are located has created difficulties for the implementation of resettlement projects (ibid.).

The Guangzhou central city is one of the most densely populated areas in the world, with an overall population density of 34,217 persons per square kilometer (1990 figures). This density is much higher than that of the metropolitan area of Hong Kong (Hong Kong Island, New Kowloon, and Tsuen Wan), which is only 20,300 persons per square kilometer (*Hong Kong 1991,* p. 373). Including the new city, the population density is as high as 18,200 persons per square kilometer (*Guangzhou Yearbook,* 1991, p. 101). Population growth in the city is the major cause of the growth of population density in Guangzhou. With an increase in population density, there is also an increase in the density of student population. According to the Guangzhou Education Bureau Statistics, between 1988 and 1989 the number of primary students in the central city increased by 7,072. This is equivalent to the student population of nine schools (each with eighteen classes and forty-five pupils per class). Between 1989 and 1990, the size of the primary student population further increased by 8,427, equivalent to the student population of eleven schools (Guo, 1990). At present, there is already a clear difference in teacher/class ratio between regions. In primary schools, the ratio is 1:2.1 in the central city, 1:1.9 in the new city, and 1:1.7 in the counties. In junior secondary schools, the ratio is 1:2.8 in the central and new cities and 1:2.5 in the counties (Guangzhou Board of Education, 1991, p. 19).

To accommodate the increasing number of students without adversely affecting the quality of schooling, especially in terms of staff/student ratio and school facilities, it is necessary either to expand existing schools or to construct new ones. However, either of these attempts faces severe difficulties in a city of extremely high population density. Not only are existing schools already surrounded by buildings, but it is difficult to find extra space for new school buildings in the central city. What is more, prices of land and construction are comparatively high in the central city, with resulting financial implications for school construction projects. An alternative is to arrange resettlement in the fringe areas, but given that students residing outside the central city are deprived of access to the best schools of the city, and that people are reluctant to move from where they habitually live, it is difficult to resettle people. In fact, even when new industries are planned for the new city, many residents of the central city who are allocated to work there prefer traveling for a long distance daily to moving outside the region. In 1985, 150,000 persons worked in the new city or suburban areas but resided in the central city. It was said that even if one to two thirds of these people and their families would resettle in their area of work, it could contribute a lot to ease off the problem of density in the central city (Zhang & Zhang, 1985, p. 109).

EDUCATIONAL OPPORTUNITIES FOR FEMALES IN THE CITY

Since 1949, China has made explicit effort to promote sexual equality in the country. Article 48 of the Constitution stipulates that women in China enjoy equal rights with men in all political, economic, cultural, and social aspects as well as in the family. This of course covers educational opportunity, and Article 46 states that all Chinese citizens have the right and obligation to be educated, and that the country has the responsibility to provide education for all children.

Generally speaking, the status of women has been raised considerably. According to a 1986 survey, the educational levels of female workers were very impressive; the proportion of female workers with a secondary level of education amounted to 81.81 percent, which was even higher than that of male workers (72.98 percent) (Xing, 1990, pp. 38–40). As a result of the improvement in status, women's aspirations have changed. In a survey of female workers in Guangzhou, 31 percent of the respondents stated that their happiness came from success in a career, while 17 percent said that their happiness came from satisfaction with family (ibid., p. 41).

However, despite this general improvement in the educational level of women, they seem to face considerable difficulties in advancing higher up the social and educational ladder. While the proportion of female workers with secondary education was slightly higher than men's, the proportion of female workers with higher education was only 6.92 percent, which was much lower than that of male workers (11.38 percent) (ibid., p. 38). In 1988, the Sixth National Women's Congress expressed concern for the problems that women faced in China. Discussing the role of women in the country's recent reform and reviewing their participation in jobs, politics, and education, the congress reported that the sexual equality mandated by law was difficult to attain. Discrimination in employment was reported, and there was concern about the decline in the proportion of women leaders in the party and government departments and the lack of women in top leadership. In respect to education, it was also reported that 80 percent of the school dropouts were girls (Zhao & Guan, 1989, pp. 11–12). Moreover, females' illiteracy was higher than that of males. According to the 1987 figures, of those aged twelve to nineteen, the illiteracy rate was about 4 percent for males but 10.9 percent for females (Wang, 1991). In Guangzhou, the Education Bureau observes that there is a certain degree of sexual discrimination in the school admission process, as some schools prefer admitting boys to girls, and also raise the admission requirements for the girls only (Central Educational Research Science Institute, 1991).

REDUCING DISPARITIES

As Bray (1991, p. 371) remarks, regional disparities exist almost everywhere; they will never be eliminated but can be reduced. In the face of regional disparities, whether due to regional development or unbalanced population growth, the municipal government of Guangzhou has taken certain measures to reduce existing disparities in education. The municipal government adopts the principle of "assisting, promoting independence, emphasizing moral development, and reforming" to foster educational development in the less advantaged regions. To achieve this, the policy of "positive discrimination" is adopted in the first place. This is manifested in the allocation of a large proportion of "education-added tax" (for example, 81.8 percent of a total of 1.7 billion yuan collected during 1985–90) to the new city and counties (Zibiao & Lee, 1991) and extra school administration funds (for example, 5 yuan per student in contrast to an average of 1.5 yuan) to schools in these regions, in order to speed up the universalization of primary and junior secondary education. As a result of deliberate efforts to improve educational conditions in relatively disadvantaged regions, and to provide the type of education relevant to local needs, the enrollment ratio has been substantially raised in some regions. For example, in the county of Conghua, which is regarded as a poor county, only 62.66 percent of primary graduates could be promoted to junior secondary schools in 1986. However, the promotion rate increased to over 99 percent in 1989, and the enrollment rate in junior secondary schools reached 95 percent in 1988. Second, the government adopts a policy of localization. For example, in the county of Conghua, the government particularly focuses on developing vocational and technical training in schools and provides the type of skill training that is relevant to the needs of the region. Moreover, the government provides special training for local school administrators and teachers in the new city and counties, in order to improve the quality of school administration and strengthen the teaching force in the regions. Third, to enhance further the standards of schools in the new city and counties, the government encourages the keypoint schools to build up close relationships with ordinary schools by running joint seminars and sending teachers from the keypoint schools to take up responsible positions in ordinary schools, hoping that the keypoint schools may stimulate improvement in the latter schools.

At a time of rapid expansion of the educational system to implement the policy of nine-year compulsory education, increasing numbers of children who may not adapt to the academic tradition of education are required to attend schools. Although academically these students are low achievers, they may still have other potentials to develop. To cater to the needs of these students, the government has also attempted to establish certain specialized schools, such as those specializing in music and in arts, so that these students may have a chance to develop according to their personal dispositions.

CONCLUSION

Examination of the case of Guangzhou suggests that the nature of the socialist Chinese city is different from that of the Western capitalist city in some fundamental ways. However, the city is not therefore immune from such fundamental urban problems as regional disparities and social inequalities. On the one hand, this is due to uncontrolled factors in the course of rapid economic development, and flexibility in the implementation process. Bakken points out that these are fundamental causes for the occurrence of regional brain drains, whereby good teachers in the counties are reallocated or attracted to the central city (Bakken, 1988, p. 145). On the other hand, as Szelenyi (1983, pp. 10–15) remarks, the nature of centralized allocation itself can become a factor for the occurrence of disparities.

First, looking into the case of centralized planning and control, this policy has been regarded as necessary in socialist China in order to uphold the principles of standardization and equality in the process of urban development. It is manifested not only in land use and industrial development, but also in resource allocation and educational development. For example, to allocate extra resources to more disadvantaged regions and to enforce the policy of localization, centralized planning and control is indeed necessary and desirable. However, despite its egalitarian claims, centralized allocation may also lead to certain disparities in the face of other needs. For example, to meet the need of developing keypoint schools, better resources are allocated to these schools, resulting in a certain degree of discrimination in resource allocation. Moreover, to apply a policy of direct population control, people living in the fringe areas are being deprived of the opportunity of studying in the best schools in the central city.

Second, even though the socialist Chinese city is characterized by centralized planning, the designation of Guangzhou as an open city allows a considerable extent of flexibility in regional development, and the existence of private enterprises. It is because of this that there exists a large floating population in the central city, and this further creates tensions in the provision of education in the city, which is already densely populated. Even though there have been efforts to promote equality in the city and between regions of the city, disparities have existed owing partly to historical factors, such as the concentration of resources in the central city, partly to reasons inherent in the nature of the system, such as the deliberate allocation of better resources to the keypoint schools and the funding of schools in different regions by different levels of government, and partly to uncontrolled factors, such as rapid population growth and economic development.

Third, the different concept of the Chinese city has made possible the division of the city into the central (old) city and the new city. However, the central city is different from the inner city in the West. As a result of the reluctance of people to move from the city center to the suburbs, the central city remains a multifunctioning city center, with heterogeneity in social and economic status. The central city therefore remains a center of development, with a concentration of offices and good schools. A high population density creates tension in educational provision within the central city, and a high concentration of facilities in the central city becomes an initial cause for regional disparities.

Measures have been taken by the municipal government to reduce regional disparities and to help those educationally disadvantaged. There are obvious improvements in some regions, such as the county of Conghua, but the effects of these measures in all other areas remain to be seen. The measures to reduce disparities display certain centralization characteristics, but there is also allowance for some nongovernmental participation in the sense that the government has encouraged local donations to improve school facilities.

NOTE

The authors would like to express thanks to Mark Bray, G. A. Postiglione, and Nelly P. Stromquist for their useful comments on the draft of this chapter.

REFERENCES

Bakken, B. (1988) Backwards Reform in Chinese Education, *Australian Journal of Chinese Affairs 19/20:* pp. 127–163.

Bash, Leslie. (1987) Introduction. In Leslie Bash (ed.), *Comparative Urban Education: Towards an Agenda* pp. i–iii. London, UK: Department of International and Comparative Education, University of London Institute of Education.

Bater, James H. (1980) *The Soviet City.* London, UK: Edward Arnold.

Bray, Mark. (1991) Centralization versus Decentralization in Educational Administration: Regional Issues, *Educational Policy, 5,* 4: pp. 371–385.

Central Educational Research Science Institute [Zhongyang Jiaoyu Kexue Yanjiusuo] (ed.). (1991) *References to Education Information [Jiaoyu Qingbao Cankao],* no. 36.

Chiu, T. N. (1980) Urbanization Processes and National Development. In C. K. Leung and Norton Ginsburg (eds.), *China: Urbanization and National Development* pp. 89–107, Research Paper No. 196. Chicago, IL: Department of Geography, University of Chicago.

Cowen, Robert. (1987) Social Space, the Japanese City and Schooling. In Leslie Bash (ed.), *Comparative Urban Education: Towards an Agenda*, pp. 12–26. London, UK: Department of International and Comparative Education, University of London Institute of Education.

Dangschat, J., & Blasius, J. (1987) Social and Spatial Disparities in Warsaw in 1978: An Application of Correspondence Analysis to a "Socialist" City, *Urban Studies 24*, pp. 173–191.

French, R.A., and Hamilton, F. E. Ian. (1979) Is There a Socialist City? In R. A. French and F. E. Ian Hamilton (eds.), *The Socialist City: Spatial Structure and Urban Policy*, pp. 1–21. New York: John Wiley and Sons.

Grace, Gerald. (1984) Urban Education: Policy Science or Critical Scholarship? In Gerald Grace (ed.), *Education and the City: Theory, History and Contemporary Practice*, pp. 3–59. London: Routledge and Kegan Paul.

Guangzhou Board of Education. (1991) The Needs for Teachers in Primary and Secondary Schools in Guangzhou and Solutions [Guangzhoushi Zhongxiaoxue Jiaoshi Xuqiu Qingkuang Ji Qi Duice], *Guangzhou Education [Guangzhou Jiaoyu]*, nos. 8 and 9: pp. 18–22.

Guangzhou Education Bureau Statistics (GEBS) [Guangzhou Jiaoyuju Tongji Ziliao]. (Various years). Guangzhou: The Bureau.

Guangzhou Yearbook [Guangzhou Nianjian] (Various years). Guangzhou: Guangzhou Cultural Press.

Guo, Qiaozhi. (1990) The Problems of Primary School Admissions in the Central City Require Immediate Solutions [Jiejue Shiqu Xiaoxue Ruxue Wenti Keburonghuan]. Paper presented at the Guangzhou Primary School Planning Conference, October 5, Guangzhou.

Hong Kong 1991: A Review of 1990. (1991) Hong Kong: Government Printer.

Hsu, Mei-ling. (1987) Chinese Cities: Controlled Growth and Employment Problems, *Urban Geography 8*, 5: pp. 336–369.

Hu, Xuwei. (1990) New Trends of Urban and Regional Planning in China, *The Journal of Chinese Geography 1*, 1: pp. 2–12.

Huang, Chao, and Peng, Dezhao. (1988) The Evolution of Guangzhou's Secondary Education Administrative System. In Li Zibiao et al. (eds.), *Studies of the Development of General Secondary Education in Guangzhou [Guangzhoushi Putong Zhongdeng Jiaoyu Fazhan Yanjiu]*, pp. 70–75. Guangzhou: Guangdong Education Press.

Jones, Crispin. (1987) Urban Centers, Space and Education: A Comparative Perspective. In Leslie Bash (ed.), *Comparative Urban Education: Towards an Agenda*, pp. 1–10. London, UK: Department of International and Comparative Education, University of London Institute of Education.

Kojima, Reeitsu. (1987) *Urbanization and Urban Problems in China.* Tokyo, Japan: Institute of Developing Economies.

Kwok, R. Y. (1985) *Recent Urban Regional Development in China.* Hong Kong: Center of Urban Studies and Urban Planning, University of Hong Kong.

Li, Si-ming. (1986) *A Comparative Study of the Urban Land Use Patterns in Guang-*

zhou and Hong Kong. Hong Kong: University of Hong Kong Department of Economics Discussion Paper 79.

Lo, Chor Pang. (1987) Socialist Ideology and Urban Strategies in China, *Urban Geography 8*, 5: pp. 440–458.

Lo, Chor Pang. (1989) Population Change and Urban Development in the Pearl River Delta: Spatial Policy Implications, *Asian Geographer 8*, 1 and 2: pp. 11–33.

Lo, Chor Pang, Pannell, Clifton W., and Welch, Roy. (1977) Land Use Changes and City Planning in Shenyang and Canton, *Geographical Review 67:* pp. 268–283.

Ma, Chui Fun. (1989) *An Inquiry into the Life Situation of Female Migrant Workers in Guangzhou*. Hong Kong: M.S.W. Dissertation, Department of Social Work and Social Administration, University of Hong Kong.

Ma, Junrong, et al. (eds.). (1985) *Guangzhou's New Look in the Programme of Reform and Opening to the Outside World*. Guangzhou: Red Flag Publishing House.

O'Connor, J. (1973) The Fiscal Crisis of the State. *Socialist Revolution 1:* 40–47 and 73–82.

Pepper, S. (1980) Chinese Education after Mao: Two Steps Forward, Two Steps Back and Begin Again? *China Quarterly*, no. 81.

Pepper, S. (1982) Quality vs. Quantity: China's Education Debate, *Asian Wall Street Journal*, Thursday, April 22.

Qiang, Jingfang, & Huang, Kexiao. (1987) On the Contemporary Reform of Secondary Education in the Eighties (trans. Shi Weiping), *Canadian and International Education 16*, 1: 86–102.

Rowies, S. T. & Scott, A. J. (1981) The Urban Land Question. In M. Dear & A. J. Scott (eds.), *Urbanization and Urban Planning in Capitalist Society* pp. 159–178. London: Methuen.

Sit, Victor F. S. (1980) Urban Neighborhood Workshops. In C. K. Leung & Norton Ginsburg (eds.), *China: Urbanization and National Development*, Research Paper No. 196, pp. 233–255. Chicago, IL: Department of Geography, University of Chicago.

Sit, Victor F. S. (1985) *Chinese Cities: The Growth of the Metropolis since 1949*. Hong Kong: Oxford University Press.

Smith, H. D. (1979) Tokyo and London: Comparative Conceptions of the City. In A. M. Craig (ed.), *Japan: A Comparative View*, pp. 49–99. Princeton, NJ: Princeton University Press.

State Statistical Bureau. (1990) *Statistical Yearbook of Chinese Cities [Zhongguo Chengshi Tongji Nianjian]*. Beijing: China Statistics Press.

Szelenyi, I. (1983) *Urban Inequalities under State Socialism*. Oxford, UK: Oxford University Press.

Tan, Yuan & Zhang, Jianguan. (1988) A Study of the Educational Problems of Students without Household Registration [Guangzhou Wu Huji Xuesheng Jiaoyu Wentin De Yanjiu]. Paper presented at the Symposium on Reviving Guangzhou's Education [Zhenxing Guangzhou Jiaoyu Yantaohui], Guangzhou.

Wang, Xinxin. (1991) An Analysis of the Educational Standards of the Chinese, *Population Studies [Renkou Yanjiu]*, no. 3.

Wu, Chuanjun. (1990) The Urban Development in China, *The Journal of Chinese Geography 1*, 2: pp. 1–11.

Xing, Hua. (1990) Female Workers in Reform—A Survey and analysis of the Current State of Female Employees. In *Women and Education in China, Hong Kong and*

Taiwan, pp. 36–46. Special Studies in Comparative Education, no. 26 (Chinese Education Translation Project). New York: Comparative Education Center, State University of New York at Buffalo.

Xiong, Shaoyan. (1988) An Outline of the Secondary Education Policies in the Last Decade [Shinian Putong Zhongdeng Jiaoyu Zhengce Gaiyao]. In Li Zibiao, et al. (eds.), *Studies of the Development of General Secondary Education in Guangzhou [Guangzhoushi Putong Zhongdeng Jiaoyu Fazhan Yanjiu]*, pp. 56–69. Guangzhou: Guangdong Education Press.

Yeh, Anthony G. O., Xu, Xueqiang, & Hu, Huaying. (1989) *Social Spatial Structure of Guangzhou*. Hong Kong: Center of Urban Studies and Urban Planning, University of Hong Kong.

Zhang, Guixia & Zhang, Yingqi. (1985) Urban Housing Construction in Guangzhou. *Asian Geographer 4*, 2: pp. 99–111.

Zhao, Ning & Guan, Xing. (1989) Reform: A Mutual Benefit, *Women of China*, January, pp. 11–12.

Zibiao, Li, and Lee, W. O. (1991) Compulsory Education in Guangzhou and Hong Kong [Suigang Liandi De Yiwu Jiaoyu]. Paper presented at the Hong Kong Educational Research Association Eighth Annual Conference, 23–24 November, Hong Kong Baptist College, Hong Kong.

6

Inequitable Agricultural Extension Services in the Urban Context: The Case of Tanzania

Malongo R. S. Mlozi

This chapter begins with a global overview of urban agriculture. It then offers some compelling reasons for the undertaking of urban agriculture in Africa. The genesis of urban agriculture in Tanzania, especially in Dar es Salaam, is discussed. The focus is on Agriculture and Livestock Extension Services (ALES), an agency which offers nonformal education administered under the Ministry of Agriculture, Livestock and Cooperative Development (MALCD). For further understanding of this nonformal education, a description of the characteristics of urban agriculturalists is provided. The study examines the conditions which led to an inequitable provision of the nonformal education offered by ALES staff. Finally, the study makes recommendations for improving the provision of NFE efforts by ALES change agents in Dar es Salaam.

URBAN AGRICULTURE: AN OVERVIEW

Urban agriculture involves the growing of food crops and the raising of animals in towns and cities. This might seem like a nightmare to people in the West accustomed to well-trimmed lawns and tidy backyards. However, to the Tanzanian elite, it has become an essential source of income, an arena for sociotechnological innovation and the source of a new form of confidence. Urban agricultural plots have existed in towns and cities from time immemorial, when they were referred to as "urban gardens" and were mainly for aesthetic purposes; hence the "gardens of pleasure" (*Encyclopaedia Britannica,*

1979, pp. 893–900). In 1400 B.C. there were the Egyptian gardens, and in the fifth–fourth centuries B.C. there existed the famous Byzantine gardens of Greece. The *Encyclopaedia Britannica* also mentions the Renaissance gardens of Italy during the thirteenth–fifteenth centuries, which later gave rise to the twentieth-century gardens, the *giardini segreti* of Italy and the *compartiments de broderie* of France. These gardens then gave rise to *le jardin anglais,* which culminated in the small town gardens of Europe, later introduced to the colonies. Similar gardens existed in China, India, and Japan (the *saiho-ji*). Urban agriculture is, thus, not a new undertaking in towns and cities around the world, except that it has changed its purposes and form.

Several countries are engaged in urban agriculture, with varying degrees of success. For example, in Katmandu (Nepal) almost one third of the fruit and vegetable needs of the city are met by household production (Wade, 1980, p. 499). In China, 85 percent of the vegetables eaten by the urbanites are produced within the six large municipalities (Skinner, 1974, p. 215). In South America, urban agriculture is becoming a solution to the problems of the beleaguered urban poor. In Brazil several cities have started urban agriculture projects; the same is happening in the shantytowns of Santiago (Chile) and elsewhere in Latin America (Sachs, 1985, p. 5). In Poland, Kleer (1987) reported that about 46 percent of vegetables and potatoes consumed in cities are produced in urban areas. In the West, there is considerable concern about the extent to which "hobby farms" are consuming land for food and fiber production near cities. D. Berry (1978) and Luzar (1988) and many others are investigating strategies for preventing this land from being taken over by cities. Furthermore, urban agriculture in the United States was encouraged through the "greenbelt towns" of 1935–38 (Christensen, 1986), based on Ebenezer Howard's "garden city" idea of 1898 (Osborn, 1965). The 1960s "back to the land" movement in the United States saw "hippies" starting gardens around cities. However, many gardens in cities and greenbelt movements failed because of socioeconomic, cultural/political, and managerial factors.

Most towns and cities in sub-Saharan Africa undertake urban agriculture in varying degrees and forms. Its various undertakings have been studied in Nairobi, Kenya (Lado, 1990; Freeman, 1991); in Dar es Salaam and Morogoro (Mlozi, Lupanga, and Mvena, 1989), and four cities and two towns, Tanzania (Mvena, Lupanga, and Mlozi, 1991); and in Lusaka, Zambia (Jeager, 1985; Sanyal, 1985; and Rakodi, 1988). Elsewhere in tropical Africa, urban agriculture studies have been conducted in Ouagadougou, Burkina Faso (Skinner, 1974); in Harare, Zimbabwe (Mazambani, 1982); in Ibadan (Gbadegesin, 1991) and Zaria, Nigeria (Schwerdtfeger, 1982); and in Kisangani, Zaire (Streiffeler, 1987), to name but a few. All these studies suggest that urban agriculture is an important source of food and income.

REASONS FOR PRACTICING URBAN AGRICULTURE IN AFRICA

Urban agriculture in most African towns and cities is done for a combination of reasons which are inherent in the socioeconomic, political, and cultural backdrop of the African countries. In most African countries, food production from the traditional rural hinterland has not kept pace with the food requirements of the people in the urban areas. Moreover, there have been problems associated with transportation of food items from the hinterland to the urban centers; shortages of vehicles, fuel, and spare parts; poor roads; and the formidable intermittent droughts which have undermined farmers' food production capacities, as most depend on the natural rain.

Urban agriculture is carried on predominantly to feed the increased numbers of people resulting from high rates of internal population increase in towns and cities and from the influx of rural-to-urban migrants. Increased urban food demands have been largely triggered by increased education levels and food catering services such as for hotels, restaurants, army barracks, schools, hospitals, colleges and universities, and kiosks.

Most African countries implicitly condone urban agriculture in their towns and cities to reduce food shortages. Urban dwellers strive to supplement their food and generate some income from urban agriculture. As will be seen later, in most countries this has had a big impact among poor urban residents (the underclass), who constitute the majority in many African towns and cities. In some countries, Tanzania for example, members of the elite have also become prominently involved in urban agriculture "projects." These activities appear to play a major role in the urban agricultural economy, in most African countries, especially in boosting food supply and income generation. For example, Gbadegesin's (1991) study in Ibadan, Nigeria, revealed that farming in the urban environment was guided by the logic of survival. Most of the farmers surveyed who were engaged in urban cultivation were low-income earners and they farmed mainly to reduce their expenditures on food and to supplement their families' incomes. Similarly, Freeman's (1991) study in Nairobi, Kenya, reported that the most important motives for urban agriculture were: first, to use the entire amount harvested to feed the farmers' own families or dependents; second, to grow vegetables as a diet supplement; third, to use urban produce for cash sale; fourth, to free up scarce cash that would otherwise be spent on purchases of food, but which, as a consequence of subsistence cultivation, could then be devoted to other pressing family needs.

URBAN AGRICULTURE IN TANZANIA: RESEARCH ISSUES

In Tanzania's case, urban agriculture could be considered unique because it was practiced mainly by members of the elite. The elite were also found in managerial positions in the urban councils or as authorities who were empowered to enforce regulations and/or bylaws which were meant to control urban agriculture in most towns and cities. City "fathers" in Dar es Salaam and officials of the ministries concerned kept mute in collaboration as if urban agriculture were developing according to plan. The elite who practiced urban agriculture had a great impact on policies which concerned the control of this practice in the city. In most African countries, too, those with high social status were the bureaucrats and government policymakers. These elite members usually influenced policies of ministries responsible for agricultural and livestock education which were to be provided to the urbanites. When urban agriculture was practiced by the elite stratum in a given country, regulations and bylaws were relaxed and often violated by the elite with impunity; Tanzania can be cited as a case in point.

In these agricultural efforts, was any education provided to help those urban farmers? If so, how was it provided to the elite and the underclass and to those in between? Who designed those educational programs, who made the decisions about them, and who benefited most? Were members of the underclass considered legitimate clients by the agricultural and livestock education agencies, including the extension workers? In many African countries these questions have not been adequately addressed. We will attempt to answer them using Tanzania as a reference.

Data for this study came from one city (Dar es Salaam) out of a pilot research project conducted in four cities (Dar es Salaam, Dodoma, Mbeya, and Morogoro) and two towns (Kilosa and Makambako) in Tanzania from 1986 to 1991. Interviews and observations were the central method of data collection. The researcher talked to urban agriculturalists, members of the elite and underclass, and agricultural and livestock extension agents.

URBAN AGRICULTURE IN TANZANIA: HISTORY

In mid-1988, Tanzania had an estimated population of 24.0 million. Most of the population are Africans, although people of Indian and Pakistani ancestry make up a significant part of the urban population (L. Berry, 1990). The backbone of the economy is agriculture and fishing, which account for over 90 percent of domestic and foreign economic activities. About 80 percent of Tanzanians live in rural areas and depend on subsistence agriculture. Agriculture alone makes up about 50 percent of the country's gross domestic product, with the main exports being coffee, cotton, cloves, and cashew nuts. However, the persistent decline of world market prices for these crops has eroded foreign reserves, decreased national income, and contributed to a slump in the industrial and agricultural sectors and a consequent inability to support other vital services. Tanzania is one of the least urbanized countries of Africa; only 7.8 percent now live in urban areas. With an annual population growth rate of 2.8 percent, Tanzania's population will reach about 30 million by the year 2000. The main cities and their populations in 1988 were: Dar es Salaam (1,300,000),

Zanzibar (270,000), Mwanza (171,000), Dodoma (the capital, 160,000), Tanga (143,000), and Arusha (88,000) (Carroll, 1990).

In the mid-1980s, various restructuring programs, such as trade liberalization and economic adjustment, were introduced. The country has moved toward economic pragmatism with a drastic shift from a state-controlled to a market-based economy, and a shift from the predominant political rhetoric of socialism to "pragmatism." Private enterprises and individual initiative, once neglected, have been promoted, favoring the development of the informal sector in the city, including urban agriculture. Urban agriculture can be defined as the rearing of animals and the growing of crops in areas designated urban by the United Republic of Tanzania Local Government (Urban Authorities) Act Number 8 of 1982, Section 80. Animals reared include dairy cattle, poultry, pigs, and goats. Vegetables grown include African spinach (mchicha), cabbages, tomatoes, eggplants, and carrots. Field crops include maize, cassava, sweet potatoes, pineapples, pawpaws, legumes, and plantains.

Urban agriculture in many towns and cities in Tanzania is an old phenomenon, but the current activities, which began in the 1970s, had a form and purposes far different from those of the earlier subsistence agriculture. In the 1970s the ruling party, Tanganyika African National Union (TANU), which later merged with Zanzibar Afro-Shiraz Party to form the Chama cha Mapinduzi (CCM, The Tanzanian Revolutionary Party), encouraged urban agriculture. The new mode of urban agriculture developed partly because the CCM and the government wished to encourage urban dwellers to become self-sufficient in food production to offset skyrocketing prices of food items and other goods in towns and cities. Urban agriculture was also considered a solution to the continued dependency of the urban workers on a poor rural community for cheap subsidized food. Although urban agriculture was supposed to benefit the majority of the population of low-income earners, most urban agriculture in Tanzanian towns and cities was being practiced by the elite. However, to carry on viable urban agriculture "projects," urbanites had to look for specialized skills and knowledge offered by a government educational agency, ALES, which provided nonformal training.

URBAN AGRICULTURE IN DAR ES SALAAM CITY

The first master plan for Dar es Salaam was developed by the London-based consultancy of Sir Alexander Gibb and Partners in 1949. It set residential areas and land uses according to the differing "needs" of three social groups—the Europeans, Asians, and Africans (Armstrong, 1987). Low-density zones, with one-acre plots located in salubrious seaside localities, were primarily for the Europeans. In the adjoining medium-density zones, plots from one-sixth to one-half acre were established for Asian residents. These are now domiciles for the medium-level African elite (the middle class). The high-density zones, with land, water, electricity, roads, and other services, were exclusively allocated to Africans, and continue today to be inhabited by the nonelite. But, significantly, urban agriculture is practiced by the senior- and medium-level elite.

As the city of Dar es Salaam has been growing, so also has urban agriculture. To decrease the primacy of Dar es Salaam, the ruling party and the government decided in 1973 to shift the capital of Tanzania from Dar es Salaam to Dodoma in the center of the country. Despite this change, Dar es Salaam remains the largest seaport and the industrial, commercial, and communication center of Tanzania. As Sawers (1989) contends, "Tanzania has been largely unsuccessful in preventing or even slowing the growth of Dar es Salaam. Indeed, by some measures of primacy in Tanzania, urban hierarchy has increased since the anti-primacy policies were first implemented" (p. 81). Peil and Sada (1984) maintain that the primacy of certain cities and the distribution of population within them are affected by government policies or elite interests, which encourage or discourage urban growth. They further assert that there is an interrelationship among four elements: the population, organization of people, environment, and technology. These elements influence urban agriculture as practiced in Dar es Salaam. Specifically, they led to an intensification of agriculture in the city, which covers an area of 1,100 square kilometers. However, the proliferation of urban agriculture in Dar es Salaam, particularly involving dairy cattle and poultry keeping, was in part due to the initial failure of the government, through the Dar es Salaam city council, to enforce bylaws meant to control animal increase.

Also of interest for urban agriculture was the increasing expropriation by the elite of land owned by the poor farmers residing in the outskirts of Dar es Salaam city. Gradually, prime land was bought by plutocratic urban agriculturalists whose incomes were derived mostly from their previous urban agriculture investments, or "projects." Acquired farms ranged from five to fifty hectares grown with perennial crops (palm tree, citrus) and annuals (corn, cassava, plantains, pulses, and pineapples). In a rural-like economy without salaried jobs to rely on, a little cash from the sale of a piece of land or farm was a blessing to the whole family. However, the cash thus received could not stretch too far, and sooner or later most families ran out of money and were then impelled to provide wage labor to the elite's farms and often resorted to squatting. Casual observations suggested that the "bought-out farmers" became squatters on the elite's farms, providing labor at low rates because they had few alternatives to survive. Areas most affected in Dar es Salaam city were: Goba, Mwanambaya, Tuangoma, Kwembe, and Kiluvya. Others included Kigamboni, Mbezi, Mbweni, and Mbagala, to name but a few.

Urban Agriculture Projects

Most members of the elite relied on the urban ALES staff's expertise to plan, organize, and plant crops. Strolling through urban areas of Dar es Salaam city, one would likely see government and institutional workers, political party officials, university staff, members of the business elite, and members of the underclass engaged in the following urban agriculture activities: One family might be keeping chickens, dairy cows, and goats, and growing African spinach; another might be growing African spinach and keeping pigs and dairy cows; yet another might be keeping chickens and growing a variety of field crops including cassava, pulses, plantains, and maize; still others would be growing African spinach as a monocrop beside the roads, in backyards, and in city creeks. The combination of activities depended on the availability of infrastructure such as a house, open space or land, water, electricity, and roads; capital; area of residence; the socioeconomic and political status of the urbanite; and land ownership.

Typology of Urban Agriculture

The situation of urban agriculture can be succinctly portrayed by contrasting two types of agriculture, which vary according to the city's zoning regulations, historical background, urbanite characteristics, presence of infrastructure, type of enterprise, and problems faced.

Type I Agriculture. Type I involves urban agriculture done on government quarters, some inherited from the colonial era. The rectangular plots range from the medium-density areas of 30 by 40 meters (1,200 square meters), up to low-density areas with plot sizes of 40 by 50 meters (2,000 square meters). Quarters in low- and medium-density areas were provided with "big gardens," and sometimes a servant annex, running tap water, electricity, and an elaborate road network. During the colonial era (1885 to 1961), Europeans resided in these areas and were known as *uzunguni* in Swahili. Since independence (in 1961) some privately owned houses have been built in the medium-density areas. Animals feature prominently here, especially dairy cattle, and are kept in the existing government houses or in temporary animal sheds. Open spaces between houses, along roads and fences, on old golf courses, and along beaches, hedges, and streams provide pasture for animals. Poultry, for production of both eggs and broiler meat, is also an important component of this type of agriculture.

Type II Agriculture. Type II agriculture occurs mainly on privately owned plots. Some of these include the "workman's home" houses built by the petty bourgeoisie on planned and unplanned high-density areas and have plot sizes of 15 meters by 30 meters (450 square meters). Most houses here are rented out, and the population deals with an infrastructure which is poorly planned and inadequate. This is the home of the underclass. Crops are common here and include African spinach and a variety of vegetables, such as tomatoes, okra, and eggplants. Other crops include cassava, rice, maize, cow peas, bananas, pineapples, coconuts, and oranges. These crops are raised mainly in the backyards, on pavements, and along roadsides. Few keep chickens, and if so no more than about 100, for broiler and egg production. Owing to scarcity of space, dairy cattle are rarely kept.

Type II urban agriculture includes the itinerant elite from the city who commute to farms located on the city periphery, the elite who have moved and reside there permanently, and the underclass who had been living in those areas before the city expansion. These areas, according to Burgess (1923), represent the "commuter zone." Here the elite bought big plots (70 by 70 meters and over) from the underclass and now practice modern agriculture. They keep pigs, dairy cows, chickens, and goats, and grow field crops. It is also common to see pockets of "traditional farmers" practicing subsistence agriculture. Problems here arise from the poor infrastructure and theft of animals and crops.

In both types explained above, the type of agricultural production undertaken is dictated by the size of the plot; availability of infrastructure such as water, electricity, roads, and houses; and labor. How many animals to keep? How big should the plant garden be? In Dar es Salaam, however, as one moves from low-density to high-density areas and finally to the city periphery, urban agriculture "projects" become less intensive. Also, among the elite, the number of houses is growing, especially in the newly opened-up low-density areas such as those in Kunduchi, Msasani, Mbezi, Mikocheni, and Ukonga. These areas are adequately supplied with infrastructure that attracted the elite to engage in urban agriculture, and the elite here are more likely to have intensive contacts with ALES agents.

THEORETICAL PERSPECTIVES ON URBAN AGRICULTURE

Theories and concepts which help explain the growth of urban agriculture and subsequent nonformal education endeavors in Tanzanian towns and cities are rare. We can extrapolate from those of a socioeconomic nature developed for industrial societies, although most of them are not directly relevant to the African perspective (Okpala, 1987; Hyden, 1983). These theories and concepts, developed largely by Western academicians, provide us with heuristic devices for understanding the motives of the urban agriculturalists. The hypothesis of the research discussed in this chapter was that nonformal education about urban agriculture offered by ALES staff to urbanites was positively related to elitism. From the point of view of education, Brookfield's work (1986) is pertinent in this case. Brookfield argues that practitioners of adult education usually accept the institution mission statement as their philosophy and judge effectiveness by what works. He advocates the use of critical theory (see Habermas, 1971, 1974; Freire, 1972) in formulating a philosophy of practice. This theory could be pertinent to ALES practice in Dar es Salaam.

Viewing the urban agricultural activities carried on, one could explain them by a number of theories which seem to support both intensity theory and the urban industrial hypothesis. The intensity theory, developed by von Thuenen (Kellerman, 1983), predicts that there is more intensity of input use in agricultural areas located closer to market centers. Support for this theory lies in the fact that urban agriculture is encouraged by the presence of inputs such as animal feed stores, animal medicaments, day-old chick-hatching units, and low-density areas with large plots. The urban industrial hypothesis (for example, Shultz, 1953) holds that the degree of economic organization near the center of the matrix of economic development offers opportunities which tend to enhance agricultural production possibilities. Another theory states that economic analysis of the relationship between population concentration and agricultural productivity emphasizes locational advantages of access to urban markets (Hayami and Ruttan, 1985). Losch's (1954) central-place theory is also relevant. It states that, for any given good, the number of production centers will be determined in a manner that minimizes total unit production costs and access costs to consumers. All these theories are based on the ready availability of markets for urban agricultural products. These products include milk, eggs, broiler meat, and vegetables.

As discussed above, urban agriculture practiced by the elite seems to be buttressed by several theoretical perspectives. For example, the availability of markets for urban agricultural products further reinforces urban agriculture practices. Moreover, such practices perpetuate inequalities between the elite and the underclass, which are in turn enhanced by nonformal education provided by ALES agents to the elite. Mutlu (1989) summarizes this argument by saying,"It is the high income groups and the other elites in the city who are at the same time the chief beneficiaries of the public-provided physical and social infrastructure and the disbursers of public funds" (p. 615). To what extent, therefore, do nonformal education efforts provided by ALES support any of those theoretical perspectives? Who made decisions about nonformal education and who were the main clients of ALES? These questions are explored in the next section.

ORGANIZATION OF ALES AS NONFORMAL EDUCATION

Nonformal education is "any organized, systematic, educational activity carried on outside the framework of the formal system to provide selected types of learning to particular subgroups in the population, adults as well as children" (Coombs and Ahmed, 1974, p. 8). In the Tanzanian context this education is offered by both government and nongovernment sources. Through an individual's lifetime, maintains La Belle (1982), he or she comes in contact with different modes of education or learning. For example, a prominent source of information about urban agriculture among the underclass originates from nongovernmental sources, such as neighbors, friends, and family members. As Coombs notes, "Similarly nonformal education is not a system in the true sense. It is simply a convenient generic name for the motley family of organized educational activities outside the formal system, intended to serve particular learning needs of particular subgroups in the population" (1989, p. 58).

ALES, in this context, is an organized government function which deliberately imparts modern skills and knowledge concerning crops and livestock to urbanites so that they will increase production. "So if adult education [particularly nonformal] is to contribute to development, it must be part of life. It is not something which can be put into a box and taken out for certain periods of the day or week—or certain periods of a life" (Nyerere, 1976, p. 10). To understand how ALES provides nonformal education to urbanites, it is necessary to understand the hierarchical organization of the Tanzanian government.

At the top of the hierarchy is the government seat which oversees all ministries' operations, including those of the Ministry of Agriculture, Livestock and Cooperative Development (MALCD). The government issues specific directives through MALCD concerning the country's overall agricultural development, which includes the production of food crops, livestock, and the proper functioning and development of cooperatives. MALCD also has the mandate for planning, organizing, and administering the nonformal educational endeavors through the division of agricultural and livestock extension services. As shown in Figure 6.1, nonformal educational endeavors were offered through ALES to two main groups: the elite and the underclass.

The elite, mostly high officials in government offices, quasi-governmental institutions, the armed forces, and private companies, and businesspeople, receive most of the nonformal education offered by ALES in the city. The same elite includes decision makers in several levels of the agencies linked to the government who, together with those in MALCD, influence in their favor nonformal education policies provided by ALES. Most members of the elite operate profitable urban agriculture enterprises, referred to as *miradi* in Tanzania. They monopolize the urban market for urban commodities and from those sales they attain superior social status and economic well-being.

Most members of the elite practicing urban agriculture have access to urban infrastructure (such as houses, roads, piped water, and electricity), loans from government financial institutions which enable them to purchase animals such as cows and day-old chicks, government and/or institutional vehicles, and other inputs. Also, because of their high social status they circumvent city bylaws meant to control urban agriculture. All these combined intensify the elite's urban agricultural "projects." Here the nonformal education provided by ALES plays a substantial role in the increase of urban agriculture. For example, the nonformal education thus provided to the elite has caused a rise in the numbers of dairy cattle in Dar es Salaam, with consequent environmental degradation.

CHARACTERISTICS OF THE ELITE AND UNDERCLASS

Several characteristics of urban agriculturalists in Dar es Salaam provide a heuristic device for comprehending why nonformal education has been provided inequitably by ALES. These characteristics include their geographical distribution in the city relative to the Central Business District (CBD); their modes of production, which to a large extent are dictated by the city infrastructure, such as roads, water, electricity, sewerage, and open spaces at their disposal; and their socioeconomic status, which has an impact on the form and magnitude of urban agricultural "projects."

The Elite

Katz (1980) defines the African elite as comprising "the business [people], bureaucrats, large landowners, and the urban middle class" (p. 11). Mitchel and Epstein's (1959) study in Zambia concluded that African townspeople were differentiated according to their wealth, skill, education, and living standards. Shivji (1976) identifies six distinct social classes in Tanzania: the metropolitan bourgeoisie, commercial bourgeoisie, petty bourgeoisie, kulaks (a member of a well-to-do class of peasants), workers, and peasantry. State technocrats who manage and plan commodity production for a market, or figure critically in accumulating or allocating state financial resources, may also be defined as state capitalists who fall under the conspicuous rubric of the African elite (Lubeck, 1987, p. 3).

The elite in this study are defined as indigenous Africans falling into three groups: first, the senior elite individuals who hold high positions in the CCM, government, quasi-governmental organizations, and state institutions such as the university, hospitals, and the armed forces; second, the middle-rank elite (or middle class) who hold middle-rank positions in the above-named offices and institutions; third, those who hold high positions in privately owned companies or businesses, and retired individuals from high positions in any of the first-mentioned offices or institutions.

In Dar es Salaam the elite and underclass coexist in distinct contrasting conditions such as: their socioeconomic strata—the "rich" and the "poor"; their political and power control levels—the "powerful" and the "powerless"; their occupations—"officials" and "workers"; and their areas of residence—in "low/medium-" and in "high-" density areas. These conditions determine to a great extent who receives the most nonformal education provided by ALES, and they can also be used to account for the reproduction of inequality. Some of these conditions are captured in Table 6.1 below, which identifies urban agriculturalists' attributes that influence the educational services provided by ALES.

Characteristics of the Senior Elite

Members of the senior elite were found to comprise about 10 percent of the urbanites involved in urban agriculture. They reside in low-density areas of Dar es Salaam, within two to seven kilometers from the CBD, though this sometimes varies. Most own cars and have access to office or institutional vehicles

Table 6.1
Urban Agriculturalists' Attributes Influencing the Provision of Agricultural Extension Services

CATEGORY	OCCUPATION	RELATIVE DISTANCE FROM CBD	AREA OF RESIDENCE	TYPE OF RESIDENCE	AGRICULTURAL ACTIVITIES	MODE OF TRANSPORT	CONTACT WITH AGRIC. EXTENSION WORKERS
CORE CITY							
1. ELITE	Senior officers in: Ruling Party--CCM, Government, Quasi- Govt. institutions, Private companies, Private businesses, and Armed Forces	Near to CBD (from 2 to 7 km)	Low density, e.g. Osterbay, Msasani, Bunge area, Upangaown and S/Bridge	Party, government institution, or company houses, or own	Dairy cattle, poultry, mchicha	Client's office or own car	Most intensive contact
2. ELITE	Middle officers in: Ruling Party--CCM, Government, Quasi- Govt. institutions, Private companies, Private businesses, and Armed Forces	Some distance from CBD (from 8 to 15 km)	A few live in low density, majority in medium areas, e.g. Msasani, Mikocheni, Upanga Sinza, and Chuo Kikuu	Party, government institutions, or company houses, or own	Few dairy cattle, mostly poultry, few pigs, mchicha, and goats in medium areas	Client's office or own car	Intensive contact
3. UNDERCLASS	Office/industrial/ company workers in: Government, Quasi- Govt. institutions, in private, individual Armed Forces and businesses	Farther from CBD (from 15 to 25 km)	Mostly in high density areas, e.g. Magomeni, Tabata, Ubungo, Mabibo, Keko, Buguruni, Manzese, etc	Majority renting in privately built houses; e.g. in Govt. quarters, Quasi-Govt. institutions, e.g. NHC, THB, Banks, etc.	Unemployed youth grow mchicha. Others grow pulses, mchicha and a few field crops	Office cars, (seldom used), mostly bicycles and walking	Little contact, if any
CITY PERIPHERY							
1. ELITE	Officers as in the first and/or second group. Some retired officers	Far away from CBD (from 25 to 40 km)	Farm-like; low density (own farm 10 to 20 hectares) areas of: Kimara Mbezi, Kiluvya, Toangoma, Mwanambaya, Kigamboni, Kwemba, etc.	Live in own houses built on land bought from farmers	Dairy cattle, poultry, pigs, citrus, field crops, some vegetables	Client's office or own car	Intensive contact
2. UNDERCLASS	Traditional subsistence farmers annexed due to city expansion	Very far (from 25 to 70+ km), live on city's periphery	Low density farms in villages, e.g. Goba, Toangoma, Kwemba, etc.	Live in own houses	Variety of field crops, e.g. cassava, palm tree, pulses; citrus; keep goats and local fowls	Extensive use of public transport; few use bicycles	Very little if any

which are likely to be used for urban agriculture "project" chores. Most have high levels of education, with baccalaureate degrees and above, and are aged forty-five and over. The senior elite are more likely to receive loans from the national banking institutions and have an average family size of five people. They are also more likely to have built "modern" houses within Dar es Salaam and/or up-country, and most have bought farms outside the city.

As depicted in Table 6.1 above, most members of the senior elite are characterized as being more likely to receive nonformal education provided by ALES. They keep an average of four milking dairy cows and six yearlings, 600 broiler chickens and 300 laying hens, and grow some African spinach. This group also encompasses the elite who reside on the city periphery about twenty-five to forty kilometers away from Dar es Salaam's CBD. However, these latter elite are distinct from the city-dwelling senior elite in terms of areas of residence, type of residence, agricultural "projects," and means of transport. Typically this group, though shown here, comprises few of the senior elite, as most who have farms on the periphery live in the city. Farms belonging to the senior elite who live in the city, are managed by a relative, usually brought in from an up-country region, and/or a laborer or squatter employed for a wage.

Characteristics of the Middle-Rank Elite

The middle-rank elite comprise about 20 percent of the total urban agriculturalists. However, they are younger than the senior elite described above and hold middle-rank positions in the above-named offices or institutions. Most reside in medium-density areas and are likely to receive less nonformal education provided by ALES than are the senior elite. They are also less likely to get loans, and so their urban agricultural enterprises are less intensive compared to those of the senior elite. Their average family size is smaller (about four) and their age range is thirty-five to forty-five. Most middle-rank elite urban agriculturalists have higher education levels, above form six (above high school).

Characteristics of the Underclass

The underclass can be defined as the low-income earners of the working class who work in government offices, institutions, quasi-governmental institutions (parastatals), the university, hospitals, the armed forces, privately owned businesses, and those with small businesses or employment which earn them some income. This definition excludes those individuals who reside in the city periphery as shown in Table 6.1, because they had been in those areas engaged mostly in farming before they were "artificially" incorporated into the city boundaries owing to its expansion.

The underclass are a majority comprising about 50 percent of the total urban agriculturalists. Their enterprises are small, and are located in high-density areas with poor infrastructures of roads, piped water, electricity, and telephone facilities. The distance from the CBD varies, but most live between fifteen and twenty-five kilometers away. They hold low-level occupations in the above-named offices and institutions, and their family sizes are large, averaging about seven people. Most have levels of education below primary education, and their ages vary from eighteen to seventy-five. Nonformal education provided by ALES is minimal. Most members of the underclass grow African spinach and a variety of vegetables, including tomatoes, eggplants, and okra. Other crops grown include cassava, rice, maize, pawpaws, sweet potatoes, cow peas, bananas, pineapples, coconuts, and oranges. These crops are raised mainly in the backyards, along roadsides, in fields away from residences, and sometimes outside the city boundaries. A few members of the underclass keep chickens for broiler and egg production, but seldom more than 100. Owing to scarcity of space, dairy cattle are rarely kept.

The senior elite, because of their high social status and positions, carry on more intensive "projects" than the underclass. Nonformal education provided by ALES addresses agricultural features of the elites, thus perpetuating inequalities between them and the underclass. From the educational view, one can argue that there are factors contributing to ALES agents' preference for working with the elite, and this can further be confirmed by reviewing urban women's involvement in urban agriculture in Dar es Salaam. The next section, therefore, looks at their role and how ALES has served them.

URBAN WOMEN AND URBAN AGRICULTURE

The role played by women in urban agriculture in Dar es Salaam is undoubtedly paramount. As in most African countries, women in Tanzania dominate the production process, particularly in the agricultural sector. At the same time, they have continued to occupy a subordinate position in society to such an extent that they are limited in their gainful involvement in economic activities. Africa is the region of female farming compared with other regions of the world (Boserup, 1970). Women in Tanzania's largest city, Dar es Salaam, used to be described as "relatively inactive" as regards paid work or self-employment (Bryceson and Swantz, 1985). The situation could not have been more different in the late 1980s, with as many as 66 percent of women in Dar es Salaam being self-employed (Tripp, 1989). The self-employed figures have risen substantially since 1985 owing to Tanzania's shift in policy to revitalize the battered economy. In Dar es Salaam, employed women have gradually opted out of salaried jobs to take up high income–generating projects, including urban agriculture. This situation started in the 1970s and lasted through the 1980s during the economic crisis in Tanzania, when a dramatic decline in urban family incomes made most urban wage earners seek alternative ways of earning money.

Most women urban agriculturalists interviewed indicated that, when a decision was made to start an urban agricultural project, they chose to leave their salaried jobs, where they earned less than men. This was further confirmed when most married women interviewed indicated that the capital for starting their urban agricultural projects was initially provided and approved by their spouses. Obbo (1980) states that "urban women, in order to gain wealth, power and status, not only worked hard but capitalized on the traditional virtues of submission and services and their roles as wives or mothers" (p. 102). Earnings from urban agricultural projects were far greater than a woman would earn from a salaried job. For example, one person in a household engaged in a small business could net about ten times more than the average worker's monthly wage (Tripp, 1989). The Swahili term *Mama Miradi* (woman running a project) captures well the importance of having an informal, successful project in a city. In urban agriculture, successful projects for these women involve keeping dairy cattle and poultry for egg and broiler meat production. This has recently become such a dream for most urban women that at any point they may quit salaried jobs to start a project, frequently involving urban agriculture.

A few decades ago, agricultural activities were abhorred by urban women as occupations of the "uneducated beleaguered rural women." These activities today are considered to be urban economic saviors. This increased awareness of the importance of urban agriculture among women in Dar es Salaam has put greater educational demands on nonformal education provided by ALES. For the purpose of analysis, three types of nonformal education offered to three classes of urban women agriculturalists by ALES were identified. First are the senior elite urban women, who comprise about 10 percent of the urban women agriculturalists and who were more likely to have intensive contacts with the ALES agents. The senior elite women share all those characteristics described above in the discussion of the senior elite such as living in low-density areas and being more likely to keep dairy cattle. If they happen to be married, their spouses are more likely to be senior officers in the above-named offices, institutions, and companies, or running businesses.

Second are the middle-elite urban women, who comprise about 20 percent of the total women involved in urban agriculture. They are less likely to gain from nonformal education provided by ALES as compared to the senior elite women. Their urban agricultural projects are of medium size compared to those of the first group. Third are the underclass urban women, who constitute a majority, about 50 percent of the total women urban agriculturalists. They receive minimal nonformal education support from ALES. As described above under the characteristics of the underclass, they reside in high-density areas with poor roads, minimal or no running water, electricity, and sewerage, and their enterprises are small. Most normally grow crops under difficult conditions.

As the above indicates, the provision of nonformal education to urban agriculturalists in Dar es Salaam has favored members of the elite, both male and female. Given that it is plausible that there were other contributing factors that encouraged ALES agents to offer preferential treatment to members of the elite, what follows is a brief analysis of factors influencing nonformal education provision by ALES.

CONDITIONS RESULTING IN INEQUITABLE PROVISION OF NONFORMAL EDUCATION BY ALES

Prices and Scarcity of Animals

Prices and scarcity of animals provide the basis for confirmation of previously discussed theoretical perspectives posited by von Thuenen (cited in Kellerman, 1983), Shultz (1953), and Hayami and Ruttan (1985). Members of the elite bought most of the available dairy cows because of the intense demand created by the scarcity of milk in the city. Indeed, the scarcity of dairy cows and day-old chicks in Dar es Salaam had made both too expensive to be afforded by a majority of the underclass. For example, in August 1991, a cross-bred in-calf heifer in Dar es Salaam sold for between 120,000 to 150,000 Tanzanian shillings (T. shs.) (about $US 480 to 600), a 50 percent increase in price from that cited in a study by Mlozi, Lupanga, and Mvena (1989).[1] A purebred in-calf dairy heifer (a Friesian aged nine months), for example, was selling at T. shs. 300,000 (about $US 1,200) in 1991, and was difficult to find ("Urban Farming," 1991). Given that the average income of the underclass was T. shs. 5,000 to 7,000 (about $US 20 to 28) after the 1990 pay raise, owning a cow remained a dream for them. At the headquarters of MALCD, there was a long list of individual requests for dairy cows, and some people had been on the list for more than four years, yet were still unable to acquire cows through the ministry. Similar cases could be elaborated with the poultry enterprise.

When animals became available, they were allocated to the elite, who could afford the high prices. Members of the elite borrowed money from national banks with ease, since they had collateral and were acquainted with each other in the business and/or government system. Members of the underclass who aspired to borrow money from the banks faced many problems. These problems made the whole procedure a drudgery, and so cumbersome that eventually many of them lost their appetite for the loans. Banks discriminated against underclass borrowers who were considered to be "bad risks." Interventions by the state could aid in giving subsidies and loans to the underclass so that they could also purchase the animals and perhaps increase their access to government-provided nonformal education offered by ALES. A question to be considered is: How was the inequality between elites and the underclass, based on the acquisition of dairy cattle and day-old chicks, affected by their contacts with ALES agents? Agents were more likely to offer information to members of the elite, such as where to obtain the most productive milk-yielding heifers, how to construct a cow shed, how to brood day-old chicks and vaccinate them against notorious diseases, how to feed colostrum to a calf, where to obtain loans to start or expand a project, and so on. Part of the inequality, therefore, was due to the fact that nonformal education provided by ALES was more directed toward the elite who happened to keep dairy cows and chickens. This supports earlier-held views that change agents, be they ALES agents or otherwise, were more likely to offer skills and knowledge to well-off individuals in any given society (see Ban and Hawkins, 1988; Chambers, 1983; and Rogers, 1983).

Members of the underclass did not receive many visits from extension staff simply because they were considered to have less intensive agricultural and livestock activities, and often their activities were considered inferior by ALES agents. For example, ownership of dairy cows was more preferred by the elite, and they were more likely to receive nonformal education from ALES agents. Skills and knowledge imparted to the elite involved those regarding how to care for the newborn calf, how to mix a dairy meal, how to select and plant high-protein forages, how to diagnose mastitis and how to control and treat it, and so on. Milking one dairy cow for ten months, a member of the elite could earn ten times her/his usual income, when an annual income was assumed to be T. shs. 240,000 (about $US 960). For example, in August 1991, a liter of milk in Dar es Salaam city sold for T. shs. 120 to 150 (about $US .48 to .60). If an elite person kept three milking cows, an average in the 1989 urban survey (Mlozi, Lupanga, and Mvena, 1989), continuously milking for ten months (period of a lactation), he/she could earn T. shs. 2.2 to 2.7 million (about $US 8,800 to 10,800). The capital invested in buying a cow would therefore be recovered within one lactation period, after deducting a 20 percent expenditure from the earnings for animal drugs, labor, and feed. However, all those intensive activities require an authentic type of education on a continuous basis; here ALES agents became handy.

The Elite's Access to Transport

The social positions of members of the elites gave them access to government, institution, party, and company vehicles which they used to ferry ALES agents to attend to their projects. Some use was made of their own vehicles, though to a limited extent. This helped make it possible for members of the elite to gain skills and knowledge from the nonformal education provided by ALES agents. In contrast, members of the underclass were denied similar access to the skills and knowledge about urban agriculture offered by ALES, as most had no access to public transport and either used bicycles or walked. At the elite's homes, ALES agents not only imparted skills and knowledge concerning urban agriculture but also demonstrated how to perform certain activities. For example, they demonstrated how to inject a sick cow with antibiotics, how to regulate heat in a chick brooder, how to correctly sow forage seeds and cuttings, how to deworm cows, and so on. As ALES agents came to consider that being picked up was their right, those who did not conform to this expectation were seen as not in need of their services. In a country like Tanzania, which has an egalitarian modus operandi, those perceptions led to further domination and polarization of the underclass. Members of the underclass could certainly not "catch up with the Joneses."

Though provision of transport by elites to ALES agents was construed as a success by the "mother" ministry (MALCD), its social consequences were many. One possible explanation for the ministry's view is related to the failure of the government to provide ALES agents with a "tool kit" to ease their work, such as transportation. In a city like Dar es Salaam, plagued with unreliable public and government transport, being picked up by an elite person's car came to be considered a privilege by most change agents. Transport obviously had a significant impact on the agents' contacts with the elite and the underclass (see Table 6.1). Among the serious consequences of using public transport to pick up agents were the use of government, institution, party, or company funds for buying fuel; the wear and tear of vehicles; payments of drivers' salaries and overtime; and the lack of vehicles to perform other office duties. Urban agriculture practiced by the elite, viewed from that angle, was an implicit circumventor of two forms of equality. First,it utilized the meager foreign exchange (used in buying vehicles and fuel) painstakingly acquired by all Tanzanians, mostly the rural farmers. Second, access to transport came to be a factor fueling the inequitable provision of nonformal education by ALES agents favoring the elite urban agriculturalists.

Rewards to ALES Agents by Elite Members

One way the elite urban agriculturists secured continued nonformal education from ALES agents was by rewarding them, as shown below, whenever they turned up at the elite's projects. Kulaba (1989) reported that in 1989 about 72 percent of the urbanites in Dar es Salaam city earned supplementary incomes from a number of activities such as farming, dairy keeping, poultry keeping, piggeries, and so on. Similarly, that study found that about 56 percent of the respondents were in the upper-middle-income to high-income groups. These findings have been further documented by Mvena, Lupanga, and Mlozi (1991) in an urban agriculture study. For example, more frequent staff contacts were associated with high incomes, living in low-density areas, having projects meant for income generation, and being less susceptible to city bylaws presumed to control urban agriculture. These were characteristics inherent in the elite, who were more likely to give rewards to ALES agents, which in itself was construed as a way to ensure continued provision of inequitable nonformal education.

Rewards offered to ALES agents were of two types. First was the giving of tangible entities, which was common and included money; food in kind; part of the produce; a drink such as beer, coffee, or tea; and/or writing a recommendation for a promotion. Second were intangible rewards, which included goodwill, a verbal recommendation for promotion in the organization, compliments, and a show of appreciation by thanking. The reward system was an informal one, common with dairy cattle and poultry-keeping projects. Reward giving appeared to evolve from three main premises. First, there was a limited number of ALES staff, hence members of the elite were competing for services of the few. Second, the value of dairy cows and/or chickens was important, and their loss due to disease meant an economic catastrophe. Thus, it was important to have an agent provide the needed expertise, and this justified rewarding. Third, the final products obtained by the elite from these projects were far more valuable than the rewards given to the agents. From a psychological point of view, ALES staff were more inclined to provide nonformal education to the elite on the basis of the anticipated rewards than to the underclass, from whom they rarely, if ever, received such rewards. How then was reward giving to ALES agents construed as immoral, thus exacerbating the inequitable provision of nonformal education to the elite in the city?

Dickinson and Dawson (1989) indicate that motivational states operate through incentive processes and that such states appear to modulate performances of the individual. Boshier (1975) suggests that rewards are based on principles of behaviorism. When they are translated into observable reinforcements, rewards represent a powerful influence to change behaviors. Rewards in essence are "behavior modifiers;" this is linked to the Pavlovian tradition of association between cues and incentives in human psychology. Rewards to ALES agents were contingencies manipulated by the elite, that in essence modified the behaviors of the ALES agents. For example, there were times when ALES agents, without a formal request, went to the elite's homes to offer information pertaining to a new chicken or cattle drug for the control of a disease. Members of the elite were delighted with such resourcefulness and in return handsomely rewarded ALES agents in appreciation. Rewards received by agents increased their penchant to provide nonformal education, that is, skills and knowledge about urban agriculture, to the elite rather than to the underclass, thus perpetuating educational inequities in the city.

Pride in Working with the Elite

Pride in working with the elite was seen in the speed with which ALES agents responded to calls made by the elite. This study found that oftentimes there were far more home visits made by ALES agents to the elite's projects than to those of the underclass. Agents here offered skills and knowledge pertaining to a variety of themes in urban agriculture, including demonstrations of how to regulate heat in a brooder of day-old chicks, how to feed a newborn calf, how to seed spinach, how to vaccinate an ailing animal, how to judge a good milking heifer, and so on. Most of the information offered to the underclass was in the area of crop production, such as how to plant spinach, correct spacing, the best varieties to plant, and so on. ALES change agents indicated that they felt comfortable working with the elite because these people had meaningful urban agricultural enterprise projects on which they could work, while the underclass happened to have far less intensive projects. This was just the tip of the iceberg, as illustrated below. There were additional reasons to account for this, such as those concerning promotion and upward mobility.

Providing nonformal education to the elite was perceived by most of the ALES agents as a way to earn recognition and as a prerequisite for upward mobility in the MALCD organization. Members of the elite were perceived by many ALES agents as able to influence and talk to their bosses on issues concerning promotions, further training, increases in salary, and making positive recommendations. These abilities were considered to be lacking among the underclass, who occupied lower ranks in the social strata.

The pride the ALES agents attached to working with the elite cannot be overemphasized. Change agent contact among clients "is positively related to: higher social status, greater social participation, higher education and cosmopoliteness" (Rogers, 1983, p. 322). Rogers further maintains that more effective communication between change agents and their clients occurs when they are homophilous (that is, similar). This explains the reasons for more frequent contact between the ALES agents and the elite: Not only was the communication rewarding, but also the elite were much more similar to ALES agents.

The concept of self was paramount over that of community. The sense of recognition provided by the elite to individual ALES agents contributed to the agents' offer of fuller nonformal education to the elite, thus intensifying their urban agriculture projects. Yet Omi and Anyanwu (1981) maintain that the self and being are all in one in traditional African philosophy, while they are separate entities in Western philosophy. Rewarding and recognizing ALES agents was important for the elite to ensure a continuous flow of nonformal education for profit maximization from their urban agricultural projects, an attitude rooted in an individualistic ethos. This influencing of ALES agents was found lacking among the underclass, who in many cases depended on interpersonal, nonformal education channels, in which neighbors, friends, and family members featured prominently as sources of information.

DISCUSSION

The evolution of urban agriculture in most countries seems to have been shaped by economic considerations, the natural increase of the urban population, and rural-urban migration. Though the underclass may have differed slightly in levels of poverty from one country to another, they were a majority of the urban population.

The focus in this study has been how skills and knowledge about urban agriculture were provided to urban agriculturalists in Tanzania. This education has been referred to as nonformal education, and an analysis of the Tanzanian situation yields a number of questions which could also apply to other African countries. Studies indicate that, of the two prominent groups in towns and cities—the elite and the underclass—the latter were most likely to practice urban agriculture. In most African countries where urban agriculture was practiced by the underclass, the countries' policies, programs, and decisions concerning nonformal education were made by the elite and little or no effort was made to provide it to the underclass.

In Tanzania, for example, the elite benefited most from the nonformal education provided by ALES, thus profiting from agriculture projects. Projects also prospered owing to the presence of urban markets, access to government-owned vehicles, houses, infrastructure, and nonenforcement of bylaws. Here too, urban agriculture projects provided an essential source of food and income to the elite. The elite also were able to procure superior social and economic benefits and derive high social status and prestige from the projects. If urban agriculture is to continue in the urban milieu, "there is a pressing and evident need for innovative strategies at finding, mobilizing, and re-allocating educational and other resources so as to ensure a more equitable distribution of opportunities" (Rahnema, 1978, p. 71).

NOTES

The author wishes to thank Sokoine University of Agriculture (SUA) for permission to conduct the research, the International Development Research Centre of Canada (IDRC) for financial assistance, and Z. S. K. Mvena and I. J. Lupanga, colleagues in the Urban Agriculture Research Project. The comments by Nelly Stromquist are also appreciated. Views expressed herein are those of the author and in no way they reflect those of SUA or IDRC.

1. Two hundred and fifty Tanzanian shillings (T. shs. 250) were equivalent to one dollar ($US 1) as of 29 March 1992 (*Sunday News—Tanzania*, 1992, p. 5).

REFERENCES

Armstrong, A. M. (1987) Master Plans for Dar es Salaam, Tanzania: The Shaping of an African City, *Habitat International 11*(2): 133–145.

Ban, A. W. van den, and Hawkins, H. S. (1988) *Agricultural Extension*. New York: Longman Scientific and Technical.

Beatley, T. (1991) A Set of Ethical Principles to Guide Land Use Policy, *Land Use Policy 8*(1): 3–8.

Berry, D. (1978) The Effects of Urbanization on Agricultural Activities, *Growth Change 9*: 2–8.

Berry, L. (1990) Tanzania: Physical and Social Geography, in *Africa: South of the Sahara*, 20th ed. London, UK: Europa.

Boserup, E. (1970) *Women's Role in Development*. New York: St. Martin's Press.

Boshier, R. (1975) Behavior Modification and Contingency Management in a Graduate Adult Education Program, *Adult Education 26*(1): 16–31.

Brookfield, S. (1986) *Understanding and Facilitating Adult Learning.* San Francisco, CA: Jossey-Bass.

Bryceson, D. F., and Swantz, M. (1985) *Women in Development: A Creative Role Denied? The Case of Tanzania.* London, UK: Oxford.

Burgess, E. W. (1923) The Growth of the City, *Proceedings of the American Sociological Society 18:* 85–89.

Carroll, J. (1990) Tanzania, in *The African Review 1990,* 14th ed. (pp. 198–201). Edison, NJ: Hunter Publishing, World of Information.

Chambers, R. (1983) *Rural Development: Putting the Last First.* London, UK: Longman.

Christensen, C. A. (1986) *The American Garden City and the New Towns Movement.* Ann Arbor, MI: UMI Research Press.

Coombs, P. H. (1989) Formal and Nonformal Education: Future Strategies, in Titmus, C. (ed.), *Lifelong Education for Adults: An International Handbook.* Oxford: Pergamon Press.

Coombs P. H., and Ahmed, M. (1974) *Attacking Rural Poverty: How Nonformal Education Can Help* (pp. 57–60). Baltimore, MD: Johns Hopkins University Press.

Dickinson, A., and Dawson, G. R. (1989) Incentive Learning and the Motivational Control of Instrument Performance, *Quarterly Journal of Experimental Psychology 41*(1): 99–112.

Encyclopaedia Britannica. (1979) *Knowledge in Depth 7.* Chicago, IL: Encyclopaedia Britannica.

Ewert, G. D. (1991) Habermas and education: A comprehensive overview of the influence of Habermas in education literature, *Review of Education Research 61*(3): 345–378.

Freeman, D. B. (1991) *A City of Farmers: Informal Agriculture in Open Spaces of Nairobi, Kenya.* Kingston, Ontario: McGill-Queen's University Press.

Freire, P. (1985) *The Politics of Education: Culture, Power, and Liberation,* (Donaldo Malcedo, trans.). Westport, CT: Bergin and Garvey.

———. (1972) *Cultural Action for Freedom.* Harmondsworth: Penguin.

Gbadegesin, A. (1991) Farming in the Urban Environment of a Developing Nation—A Case from Ibadan Metropolis in Nigeria, *Environmentalist 11* (2): 105–111.

Habermas, J. (1974) *Theory and Practice.* Boston, MA: Beacon.

———. (1971) Knowledge and Human Interests (trans. J. J. Shapiro). Boston, MA: Beacon.

Hayami, Y., and Ruttan, V. (1985) *Agricultural Development.* Baltimore, MD: Johns Hopkins University Press.

Hyden, G. (1983) *No Shortcuts to Progress: African Management in Perspective.* Berkeley, CA: University of California Press.

Jeager, D. (1985) Lusaka, Garden City: The Agricultural Activities of City Residents, unpublished manuscript. The Netherlands: Tropical Institute.

Katz, S. (1980) *Marxism, Africa and Social Class: A Critical Review of Relevant Theories.* Montreal: McGill University, Center for Development-Area Studies.

Kellerman, A. (1983) Economic Spatial Aspects of von Thuenen's Factor Intensity Theory, *Environmental Planning 15:* 1521–1530.

Kleer, J. (1987) Small-scale Agricultural Production in Urban Areas in Poland, *Food and Nutrition Bulletin 9* (2): 24–28.

Kulaba, S. (1989) Local Government and the Management of Urban Services in Tanzania, in R. E. Stren and R. R. White (eds.), *African Cities in Crisis: Managing Rapid Urban Growth* (pp. 203–245). Boulder, CO: Westview Press.

La Belle, T. J. (1982) Formal, Nonformal and Informal Education: A Holistic Perspective on Lifelong Learning. *International Education Review 28:* 159–175.

Lado, C. (1990) Informal Urban Agriculture in Nairobi, Kenya: Problems or Resource in Development and Land Use Planning, *Land Use Policy 7* (3): 257–266.

Losch, A. (1954) *The Economics of Location* (W. H. Woglom and W. F. Stolper, trans.). New Haven, CT: Yale University Press.

Lubeck, P. M. (1987) The African Bourgeoisie: Debate, Methods, and Units of Analysis, in P. M. Lubeck (ed.), *The African Bourgeoisie: Capitalist Development in Nigeria, Kenya and the Ivory Coast* (pp. 3–66). Boulder, CO: Lynne Rienner.

Luzar, E. J. (1988) Strategies for Retaining Land in Agriculture: An Analysis of Virginia's Agricultural District Policy, *Landscape and Urban Planning 16* (4): 319–331.

Martin, J. (1991) Order of theoretical properties of holistic ethical theories, *Environmental Ethics 13* (3): 215–234.

Matson, F. W. (1973) *Within/Without: Behaviorism and Humanism*. Belmont, CA: Wadsworth.

Mazambani, D. (1982) Peri-urban Cultivation within Harare, quoted in Rakodi, C. (1988) Urban Agriculture: Research Questions and Zambian Evidence, *Journal of Modern African Studies 26* (3): 495–515.

Mitchel, J. C., and Epstein, A. L. (1959) Occupational Prestige and Social Status among Urban Africans in Northern Rhodesia, *Africa 29:* 22–39.

Mlozi, Malongo R. S., Lupanga, I. J., and Mvena, Z. S. K. (1989) Urban Agriculture: The Livestock Dimension and Its Implications, *Tanzanian Society of Animal Production Conference Proceedings,* no. 16. Morogoro, Tanzania: Sokoine University of Agriculture.

Mutlu, S. (1989) Urban Concentration and Primacy Revisited: An Analysis and Some Policy Conclusions, *Development and Cultural Change 34* (3): 611–639.

Mvena, Z. S. K., Lupanga, I. J., and Mlozi, M. R. S. (1991) A research report on the study of urban agriculture in four cities and two towns in Tanzania, unpublished manuscript. Morogoro, Tanzania: Sokoine University of Agriculture.

Nyerere, J. K. (1976) Declaration of Dar es Salaam: Liberated man—the purpose of development, *Convergence 9*(4): 9–17.

Obbo, C. (1980) *African Women: Their Struggle for Economic Independence*. London, UK: Zed Press.

Okpala, D. C. I. (1987) Received concepts and theories in African urbanization studies and urban management strategies: A critique, *Urban Studies 24* (2): 136–150.

Omi, E. A. R., and Anyanwu, K. C. (1981) *African Philosophy: An Introduction to the Main Philosophical Trends in Contemporary Africa*. Rome, Italy: Catholic Book Agency—Officium Libri Catolici.

Osborn, F. J. (ed.) (1965) *Garden Cities of To-morrow*. Cambridge, MA: MIT Press.

Peil, M., and Sada, P. O. (1984) *African Urban Society*. Chichester, UK: John Wiley and Sons.

Rahnema, M. (1978). Education and equality: A vision unfulfilled, in B. L. Hall and J. Robby Kidd (eds.), *Adult Learning: A Design for Action—A Comprehensive International Survey* (pp. 61–71). Oxford: Pergamon Press.

Rakodi, C. (1988) "Urban agriculture: Research questions and Zambian evidence," *Journal of Modern African Studies 26* (3): 495–515.

Rogers, E. M. (1983) *Diffusion of Innovations* (3rd ed.). New York: Free Press.

Sachs, I. (1985) Cultivating the cities, *Development Forum 2*: 5.

Sanyal, B. (1985) Urban Agriculture: Who Cultivates and Why? A Case Study of Lusaka, Zambia, *Food and Nutrition Bulletin 7* (3): 15–24.

Sawers, L. (1989) Urban Primacy in Tanzania, *Economic Development and Cultural Change* 37 (4): 841–859.

Schwerdtfeger, F. (1982) *Traditional Housing in African Societies*. Chichester, UK: John Wiley and Sons.

Shivji, I. G. (1976) *Class Struggle in Tanzania*. London, UK: Heinemann.

Shultz, T. (1953) *The Economic Organization of Agriculture*. New York: McGraw-Hill.

Skinner, E. P. (1974) *African Urban Life: The Transformation of Ouagadougou*. Princeton, NJ: Princeton University Press.

Streiffeler, F. (1987) Improving Urban Agriculture in Africa: A Social Perspective, *Food and Nutrition Bulletin 7*(3): 15–24.

Sunday News-Tanzania, 29 March 1992.

Tripp, A. M. (1989) Women and the Changing Urban Household Economy in Tanzania, *Journal of Modern African Studies 27*(4): 601–623.

Urban Farming in Line with Policy (May 1991), *Daily News—Tanzania,* p. 3.

Wade, I. (1980) Fertile Cities, *Development Forum,* September, p. 499.

Yeung, Y. M. (1988) Agricultural Land Use in Asian Cities, *Land Use Policy 5* (1): 79–82.

PART III

THE CITY AND EDUCATIONAL POLITICS

7

Education and Docility: The Dilemmas of Singapore and the Next Lap

Roger Boshier

Singapore is a small island republic in Southeast Asia that in the last thirty years has been transformed from a crumbling outpost of the British Empire to a modern city-state that surpasses even the wildest and most ambitious dreams of leaders that negotiated its independence. It is almost entirely an urban city-state. There are no wilderness or rural areas where the citizenry can gain respite from urban hubbub. As a result, shopping (in air-conditioned shopping centers) is a favorite weekend pastime. The closest approximation of ''country living'' is in Malaysia, but weekend queues at the border, coupled with other mutual irritations, mean that most Singaporeans construct their lives among the concrete towers that puncture the Singaporean skyline.

Singapore is about 42 kilometers long and 23 kilometers wide, and occupies a land mass of only 618 square kilometers. It is very close to the equator, has a population of about three million people and, if in China, would not rank among the ten largest cities of that country. Nearly 50 percent of the main island is built up and only 3 percent is deemed to be open space or to have recreational uses. Almost the entire infrastructure has been erected in the last thirty years, so that transportation, communication, health care, higher education, and most other systems are state-of-the-art.

In many respects, Singapore has become a model urban environment. It has a mixed-enterprise economy that has grown consistently, a strong currency, a low inflation rate, and a compulsory savings scheme that yields enormous revenues for government services. It has a reliable and busy port, flourishing shipbuilding and oil-refining industries, and considerable expertise in electronics and information-processing industries.

Singaporeans are fond of lauding their "success" (Drysdale, 1974). In a recent example Sandhu and Wheatley (1989) edited *Management of Success,* a 1,200-page celebration of Singapore's transformation from urban slum to modern city-state. During this process Singapore has been variously characterized as a fishing village, a political joke, a poisoned shrimp, a hedgehog, and global city. Part of Singapore's so-called success involved rebuilding the slum-ridden fabric of the old urban nucleus on the south side of the island which is now "a modern, efficiently serviced, tropical garden city" (Sandhu and Wheatley, 1989, p. vi). What is remarkable is that the government has managed to avoid much of the urban and environmental degradation so often associated with rapid economic or population growth. Thus the greening of Singapore has been hailed as a triumph of "holistic" planning" (Yeh, 1989).

About four-fifths of the population live in government-administered, predominantly high-rise flats, many of which are owned by the occupants. Most Singaporeans have a television, telephone, and other consumer goods found in the industrialized states of the West, with the exception of cars. Almost all homes are connected to sewers, life expectancy and infant mortality are comparable to or better than levels in the West, and there is a standard of living that will soon approximate that of neighboring countries like Australia or New Zealand and is second only to Japan among Asian countries. The utilities are modern, the new mass transit railway is clean and efficient, and Singapore International Airlines is consistently rated one of the best in the world. There are flourishing trees, well-kept parks, and public facilities mixed among new buildings. Singapore is an unusually attractive urban city-state.

Fresh water comes across the causeway from Malaysia. Electrical power is generated in oil-fired stations. Of the approximately three million people (Census, 1990) the largest group is Chinese, although considerable energy has been expended to disabuse visitors and neighbors of the notion that Singapore is a "third China." Singapore is a multilingual country, and the emphasis on English is more a recognition of geopolitical realities than a deference to former colonial masters.

Few institutions in Singapore have received as much sustained attention as education. It is seen as a crucial instrument in the pursuit of economic development, social stability, and national identity. The tightly knit urban-ness of Singapore has expedited the implementation of a human capital approach to education informed by a radical functionalist ideology with an emphasis on hierarchy, competition, measurement, and accountability. It is not significantly influenced by humanistic or social democratic assumptions that have shaped progressive or even less radical functionalist education systems in other countries. Because of the lack of natural resources the government long ago embarked on a functionalist program of human resource development in an attempt to become the Switzerland of Asia.

The transformation wrought in the last thirty years is undeniably impressive. But, for various reasons, the residents do not appear to be wildly excited about their "success." Indeed, many of the better-educated are emigrating to other countries and those who remain are extremely orderly and subdued. By 1991 the economic and political tasks set by the first generation of leaders had largely been accomplished and Singapore entered what the government has called the Next Lap. But in Singapore, as in other polities, it is now possible that, because of a better-educated citizenry, defeat could be snatched from the jaws of victory.

PURPOSE OF THIS CHAPTER

Within the context of the foregoing, the purpose of this chapter is to consider the extent to which Singapore's "urban-ness" intersects with and shapes the character of the assumptions that inform educational practice. In pursuing this purpose it will be necessary to describe the context for education and show how the twin pillars of Singaporean ideology (survival and pragmatism) threaten the capacity of citizens to develop cognitive processes and attitudes needed for the Next Lap. The survival of Singapore is threatened—not by Communists, communalism, Thai pirates, foreign workers, chewing gum in the mass transit system, Coca-Cola in schools, a lack of discipline in the work force, prying foreigners, long hair, *Time* magazine, the *Far Eastern Economic Review,* or Western individualism. Ironically, the chief threat to Singapore is psycho-educational and, strangely, stems from the fact nothing fails like success.

CONTEXT

Singapore was founded as a British colony in 1819 and, largely because of its strategic location on the Strait of Malacca, grew rapidly and attained considerable wealth and significance. By the turn of the century it was the fulcrum on which British interests in East Asia turned. It had a population with a well-developed work ethic, an efficient administration, and, even in the early days, a focus on human resource development and public education campaigns (the first was to exterminate rats). At first Singapore was a British residency (1819–30) and then part of the Straits Settlements (1830–1946) with a three-year hiatus during the Japanese occupation (1942–45). Later it was a crown colony (1946–58). In 1959 the colony made a transition to self-government when Lee Kuan Yew's People's Action Party (PAP) won forty-three of fifty-one seats in the newly created parliament. There was a brief merger with Malaysia from 1963 to 1965 but, since August 9, 1965, Singapore has been an independent republic.

If analysis is confined to economic matters, Singapore has been remarkably successful in generating growth and improving living standards. In 1957 the island had few manufacturing industries, a decaying urban infrastructure, rapid population growth of about 4.4 percent per year, widespread poverty, and an unemployment rate of 10–15 percent (Grice & Drakakis-Smith, 1985). By the mid-1980s the per capita GNP had reached $US 7,260—higher than Ireland or Italy, manufacturing industries were being developed, the physical and social infrastructure were of a high standard (the best in the region), and poverty had been dramatically reduced (Rigg, 1988).

Uniquely Urban Features

Architects, politicians, and planners given an opportunity to create urban environments like new capitals such as Canberra or Brasilia are very conscious of the fact that space is *structuring* as well as *structured by* individuals. The first generation of leaders in postcolonial Singapore inherited the decaying infrastructure of a British colony and were uninhibited in their enthusiasm for demolition and reconstruction. Each of the urban features in modern Singapore serves several purposes and is usually designed in a deliberate manner with overt and covert purposes in mind. For example, while the main road into the modern airport provides an impressive entrance for visitors, it can also double as an emergency runway in times of war. While the modern mass transit system efficiently moves the general population, it was also designed as part of the "total defense" system to quickly move armed forces reservists. The housing developments are an instrument of forced racial integration.

Singapore is a unique urban environment, comparable only to Hong Kong. There is no rural hinterland (except that in Malaysia or Indonesia), no influx of rural migrants, no barriers of space or distance that impede the participation of women in the work force, an almost complete absence of popular movements (they've been repressed, and even membership in Greenpeace could cause problems), low unemployment rates, and no longer any significant pools of unhealthy housing or shantytowns. Although much is made of Singapore's multicultural character, the dominant group is overwhelmingly Chinese. The citizens, although city-bound, frequently take a taxi to the airport, which provides ready access to various holiday destinations in Asia and beyond. In these and other respects Singapore does not manifest all the attributes of "urban-ness" described by Stromquist (Chapter 2, this volume). Most notably it is the absence of a hinterland, its small size, the public housing developments, the charisma of the "founding fathers," and its "Asian-ness" that distinguish Singapore.

In other respects, Singapore conforms to attributes of urban-ness described in Chapter 2 (this volume). For example, it is one of the leading exponents of a development model arising from a discourse of pragmatism and survival that emphasizes industrialization and free trade. Moreover, within the last thirty years Singaporeans have become adroit users of modern urban facilities, such as transportation. However, because of tight controls on electronic media (there is no private radio or television service), profound constraints on newspapers, and a history of skirmishing with foreign publishers of popular magazines (for example, *Time*) there is not the same kind of access to the diversity of opinions or perspectives found in comparable urban settings such as Hong Kong. In this respect, the citizens derive no advantage from living in a city. However, as a strategically important former outpost of the British Empire, Singapore incurs considerable advantage from its location on the Strait of Malacca. Entrepôt trade is still important and the process of bifurcation in the education system identified by Stromquist (Chapter 2, this volume) is exemplified in the creation of a "meritocracy" that, in accord with Confucian tradition, relentlessly separates the "leaders" from the "led."

Full employment, modern buildings and transportation systems, parking lots filled with modern cars, shopping malls jammed with fashionably dressed people, and teenagers crowded into McDonald's and Kentucky Fried Chicken all attest to the relative affluence of Singaporeans and their embrace of modernity and Western influences. However, in an exceedingly well textured account of "everyday life," Chua (1989) notes that icons of modernity and consumerism "float above a substratum of the mundane, uneventful reproduction of daily life which, for the overwhelming majority of the population, is enacted within the confines of the housing estates" (1989, p. 1013), where the day begins when food vendors set up stalls. Children wearing uniforms are hurrying to school by 7 A.M., low-income workers in jeans and T-shirts leave next, and white-collar workers are often collected by friends who need extra passengers in a car to save the levy made against those entering the central business district in rush hours. By 8 A.M. women are heading to the markets where food is purchased and social relations renewed. During the day older people socialize on the "void deck" (a common open area) in the housing development. When children return from school the ground-level playgrounds fill up and, in the evening, there is more socializing on the void deck and other spaces. If the rhythms of life in the housing developments seem unduly tied to "clock time," this is a consequence of Singapore's industrialization. "Industrial time-consciousness" is not confined to the workplace; it also pervades social relations (Chua, 1989).

Survival Discourse

When Singapore left the Malaysian confederation it weakened its access to a nearby and friendly market for industrial goods. This event enabled Lee's PAP government to attempt to unite what had previously been a splintered multiethnic population behind a common interest—the need for survival. Since 1965 the government has promoted an image of Singapore as a small and defenseless island without natural resources, surrounded by enemies—real and imagined—and filled with potential for fragmentation and internal turmoil.

The need for survival pervades every aspect of the sociopolitical and educational landscape. When Singapore was tossed out of Malaysia the survival of the nation became synonymous with survival of the individual. Finding the means to ensure survival became the only "practical" thing to do and thus "pragmatism" became the other leg in the "twin pillars" (Chua, 1991, p. 9) of the ideological system of the PAP.

After 1959 survival and pragmatism were translated into a pervasive economic developmentalist orientation which required a stable social and political climate. This led the PAP government to intervene in all aspects of personal, social, and political life. Radical unions were deregistered and replaced by PAP corporatist unions that worked with the government, population control measures were introduced, the mass media were restrained through annual licensing procedures.

Postcolonial governments often generate crisis narratives to periodically remind the citizenry of trauma associated with liberation. In Singapore the potency of these narratives is enhanced by the strategic location and urban-ness of the republic. By repeatedly focusing on the alleged fragility of the nation and its vulnerability to internal and external threats, the state's "originating agency is periodically reinvoked and ratified, its access to wide-ranging instruments of power in the service of national protection continually consolidated" (Heng and Devan, 1992, p. 343). Thus the administration of crisis revitalizes the leaders' claims to own the instruments of power. These involve overwhelmingly patriarchical narratives nested within the notion of a family ruled by a stern and uncompromising father. The metaphors deployed, the accusations leveled, and the explanations sought have invariably been aimed at population groups (such as graduate mothers) who do not reflect or give back the founding fathers' image of themselves.

There is frequent reference to the presence of potentially hostile neighbors, the possibilities for insurrection, the moral decadence of certain Western "values," and constant reminders concerning the lack of natural resources. It is hard to disentangle the contrived from the real threats. However, whether the "alleged Marxists" imprisoned without trial (see "Enemies of the State," *Far Eastern Economic Review*, 4 June 1987, p. 8) or Minchin's 1986 banned book constituted a real threat is only of passing interest in this context. Nor does it matter when banned books are suddenly permissible. What matters is that people have learned to fear state authorities and suppress unorthodox or lateral opinions, and this has immense implications for education.

Despite their fear of authorities, it appears that most people have largely accepted the government's definition of the situation and there has been a strong ideological consensus. This consensus has been considerably strengthened by the government's ability to improve the everyday life of most Singaporeans. Full employment, improved standards of living, and modern health, education, communications, and transportation systems do not come easy in a small urban country without natural resources. Hence the ability of the government to transform everyday life from a struggle for necessities to one in which there are choices has been applauded by most Singaporeans.

Twin Pillars

Prior to 1959, Singaporeans had been accustomed to a high degree of individual freedom but also to a lot of material privation. The PAP felt the citizenry had to become a disciplined industrial work force that would attract foreign capital. This provided a rationale for weaving a network of educational and other disciplining strategies.

A good example involved outcomes associated with public housing programs. By 1990 86 percent of resident households lived in Housing Development Board (HDB) flats (Census, 1990), compared to 69 percent in 1980. Although the HDB flats have provided reasonably decent—though boring—high-rise public housing for most Singaporeans, it has turned the working population into "clients of the state" (Chua, 1991, p. 10). The government has been able to contain the proportion of people from each ethnic group living in each housing block and thus diminish the possibility of political organization along racial lines.

Controversial decisions relating to family planning or allocation of public housing; the banning, censorship, or restriction in circulation of foreign publications; and the imprisonment without trial of social workers and community activists alleged to be Marxists (see *Far Eastern Economic Review*, 22 October 1987)—these are often defended on the grounds that the alternatives constitute a soft option. Thus, it is not surprising that perseverance, conformity, performance, and discipline are highly desirable values and that the education system is competitive and exam-oriented. Formal education is highly valued, and failure or the inability to secure one of the few places at the National University can incur a stigma. Parents who can afford it employ private tutors for their children.

In Singapore, policies rationalized on pragmatic grounds often turn out to be undemocratic in serious ways. All elements of life are harnessed to the pursuit of economic growth. Instrumental rationality, the operant arm of pragmatism, has been the dominant ideology. Vogel characterized Singaporeans as law-abiding, conscientious in their work, and orderly in their behavior. Most significantly, it was almost as if they had been "tamed by a very strict schoolmaster" (1989, p. 1049).

The government is intrusive and manifests an unparalleled sense of purposiveness and efficiency. According to Gopinathan (1987, p. 201), "The single-minded drive to achieve, to go one better, the passion with which the principle of cost effectiveness is pursued are abundantly clear both in national life and education." Hence the first generation of PAP leaders saw themselves as custodians of the future, and the personality of Lee Kuan Yew is a colossus that straddles the modern history of Singapore (George, 1984).

Because of its strategic location, dependence on tourists, and thriving port and airport, Singapore was thought to be vulnerable to undesirable Western influences and became famous in the 1960s for demanding haircuts for hirsute visitors. Today, Western and other pernicious influences are combated through relentless programs of mass education (delivered in formal, nonformal, and informal settings), national service, and school curricula designed to build a Singaporean identity.

SURVEILLANCE, KNOWLEDGE, AND POWER

Lee Kuan Yew, the founding father of all founding fathers, created and reinforced uncertainty to keep the children in line. In general, the children hold the father in a mixture of fear, respect, and admiration. During his administration he meted out strong punishment for "disobedience" and, despite outstanding achievements, often appeared unwilling to trust the children to abide by his wishes. For example, at one time he threatened to withdraw the "one person, one vote" principle after an electoral rebuke. The government's insistence on creating a disciplined labor force, coupled with his paternalism, created a fear and docility that operate in many spheres of social and political life. Although there is now a new prime minister, it is commonly assumed that Lee still makes important decisions and, as Singaporeans are prone to explain, when there is a huge banyan tree, it is difficult for other trees to grow under its shadow.

By the time Goh Chok Tong took over from Lee Kuan Yew on November 28, 1990, the economic developmentalist orientation of the previous thirty years, along with decades of largely corruption-free government, had led to improvements in the material well-being of the average Singaporean. Changi Airport, the mass transit system, and a thriving port, among many other things, were a testament to the Lee government. However, the remarkable achievements of the first generation of PAP leaders were achieved at considerable cost, and leading academics publicly expressed regret for the fact that "democracy has suffered" and that there has been "much use of legalized repression which sometimes violated the common understanding of democratic principles" (Chua, 1991, p. 10).

The Internal Security Act (ISA) is a conspicuous instrument of social discipline and has a pervasive and generalized effect on the political and educational culture. When linked to a state ideology wherein the "individual is lesser than the society" (Lee, cited in "Playing the Identity Card," *Far Eastern Economic Review,* February 9, 1989, p. 31) it serves to silence political opponents and narrow the range of options available for scrutiny in educational settings. Moreover, all citizens are aware that the government reserves the right to arrest and detain people without trial and, in such a small urban setting, surveillance can be achieved with ruthless efficiency.

The extent to which scholars or citizens can engage in the kind of scholarly inquiry or debate that is fairly routine in the West—and is of the open and critical kind needed for the Next Lap—is greatly constrained (see Gopinathan & Shive, 1987). These constraints are not "objective" but reside in the fear of ISA informants and suppression of "harmful thoughts" and avoidance of "sensitive issues." Chua (1991) argues that the Internal Security Act must be repealed. Repeal is "the sine qua non of establishing a democracy in Singapore" (1991, p. 29).

The situation in Singapore echoes Foucault's (1979) description of *le regard* (the gaze), a technique of linking and controlling power and knowledge by organizing visibility (Fraser, 1989) among various populations. This surveillance technique is of two kinds—synoptic and individualizing. The first, synoptic visibility, is based on the architectural design and organizations which made it possible to observe and control the population and various elements within it. Hence, prisons usually have cells arrayed around an observation tower. In Singapore it is manifested also in the design, administration, and organization of the public housing developments and the close government monitoring of voluntary organizations (such as the People's Association).

Individualizing visibility involves the exhaustive and detailed observation of individuals, their habits and histories. The individual becomes a "case," an object of inquiry and target of power (Foucault, 1979). Both kinds of gaze, synoptic and individualizing, involve practices which link knowledge to power. In Singapore, the government generally withholds information that would be needed by someone wanting to participate in a public or some other kind of debate or critique of government policy. The most pernicious aspect of surveillance concerns what Foucault called the "asymmetrical character of the gaze," which is unidirectional. Thus, in the prison, the warden can see the inmate but not vice versa. This unidirectionality of the visibility denies the inmates knowledge of when they are being watched. It makes them internalize the gaze and, in effect, surveil themselves (Foucault, 1979). Thus, Singaporeans automatically assume that Internal Security Department (ISD) officers or informants are present in their place of work, place of residence, voluntary organizations, and educational settings. Discourse is shaped accordingly. Whether ISA officers are present or absent does not matter. What counts is the introjection of the widely accepted assumptions concerning surveillance and, as shown later, this inhibits classroom discussions, enfeebles educational research, and causes scholars to "steer clear" of sensitive issues.

Electoral Dissatisfaction

Unfettered faith in Lee began to falter in 1980, along with the capacity of the survival/pragmatism ideology to command unswerving support. Although most Singaporeans were too fearful to voice opposition in public, in the privacy of the voting booth they had an opportunity to send the government a message. In most parts of the world the election of a few opposition candidates would be welcomed as an essential corollary of democratic functioning, but in Singapore such an event is treated as yet another crisis. The presence of a few opposition members brings no joy to the government.

By 1984 Singapore had experienced many years of social and economic stability, but the electorate had clearly become irritated with paternalism and authoritarianism. A better-educated electorate could create "electoral problems" for the government. In 1980 only 21 percent of the populace had a secondary school qualification, in contrast to the 39 percent who had high school qualifications in 1990. Moreover, only 2 percent of the population were university graduates in 1980, against 4 percent in 1990 (Census, 1990). Increasing education levels appeared to be associated with a decreasing willingness to accept orthodox government wisdom concerning what is good for the people. Moreover, better-educated people now had the skills to critically appraise the sometimes spurious and scientifically dubious reasoning that lay behind government announcements—such as those on eugenics and population policies and, for some, the "pragmatic" thing to do was pack up and leave. In the 1988 election the PAP won only 63 percent of the popular vote.

It was clear that many Singaporeans had expanded their aspirations and were tired of the relentless barrage of exhortations concerning pragmatism and survival. Goh Chok Tong now needed to distance himself from Lee's autocracy, and a handy way of doing it would be to claim to start a new era. He also had to deal with a strong lobby concerned by creeping Westernization and the need to reinforce "Asian values."

Singaporean government leaders believe that an ideology of individualism has led to the decline of Western economies (in relation to Japan). Although the Singaporean political culture applauds individual entrepreneurs, generalized individualism and Westernization is thought to contain the seeds of destruction. The president stated the problem in an address to parliament in January, 1989:

Singapore is wide open to external influences. Millions of foreign visitors pass through every year. Books, magazines, tapes, and television programmes pour into Singapore every day. Most are from the developed countries in the west. The overwhelming bulk is in English. Because of universal English education, a new generation of Singaporeans absorbs their contents immediately, without translation or filtering. . . . The speed and extent of the changes to Singapore society is worrying. We cannot tell what dangers lie ahead, as we grow rapidly more Westernized. (*Shared Values*, 1991, p. 1)

A white paper on shared values was released in January 1991 and identified the following:

• Nation before community and society above self
• Family as the basic unit of society
• Regard and community support for the individual
• Consensus instead of contention
• Racial and religious harmony

Of the five values, the one referring to support for the individual had been added to the four "core values" first identified by the government in December 1988.

It was hard to know why the need for a national ideology arose in the late 1980s, although some cynics claimed the problem resided in the fact that Singaporeans brought up on pragmatism "may seem to think that the logical conclusion of a 'pragmatic' way of life was to move on to another country, should it offer more opportunities than Singapore." The "brain drain" was a "ticking time bomb" according to one M.P. and, in government circles, was widely attributed to a lack of "emotional commitment." ("Pledge of Allegiance," *Far Eastern Economic Review*, February 9, 1989, p. 34). Perhaps it was hard to commit to a place that only has room for pragmatism.

Next Lap

When Goh Chok Tong was sworn in as prime minister on November 28, 1990, he said, "The torch has passed from one generation to the next. But the race continues. . . . I therefore call on my fellow citizens to join me, to run the Next Lap together" (Government of Singapore, 1991, p. 141). The notion of a Next Lap served to help distance the less autocratic Goh from the paternalism of Lee and the "handing of the torch" was soon followed by *Singapore: The Next Lap* (1991), a lavish government publication with color photographs on each page and an upbeat blueprint for the future of Singapore.

Subsequent discussion reinforced the fact that "Next Lap thinking" does not involve any erosion of government power in Singapore. As the minister of information noted, "The ship of state needs certain controls so that we can navigate and change directions quickly" ("Govt. Will Always Have to Balance Pressures," *Straits Times*, June 22, 1991, p. 1). Survival and pragmatism still provided the ideological buttressing for government policy, although the increasing dissatisfaction of the electorate had evoked a more sophisticated conceptualization of their meaning.

EDUCATION

The ideology of survival and pragmatism, coupled with economic developmentalism, have had an enormous impact and impose their own logic on educational practice. Investment in education is guided more by the need for social and economic efficiency than for any intrinsic worth or value. Three interrelated factors have molded thinking about education. All stem from the twin pillars (survival/pragmatism). First is the lack of natural resources and a limited land area. Secondly, there are structural factors—most notably the fact that this is a multiethnic, multicultural, multilingual, and multireligious city-state. The PAP believes that this heterogeneity should be preserved and is the key to political stability which is, in turn, the crucial element that attracts foreign investment. The third set of factors is situational. Government leaders still refer to the "crises" associated with the 1965 separation from Malaysia, the international oil crisis of the early 1970s and other "crises" of varying degrees of importance. The oil crisis and other factors associated with securing independence were experienced by other small nations but, in Singapore, they assumed "a potency and immediacy of critical proportions" (Tham, S. C., 1989, p. 492).

In a study of value premises that undergird the transformation of Singapore, Ho (1989, p. 685) identified the basis of education at the confluence of Tham's three interrelated factors. Education is "strictly practical and pragmatic, namely . . . job training through the inculcation of knowledge and expertise relevant to the kinds of professional skills required by the . . . economy." The education policy is "grounded on good, old fashioned virtues," since "the practical necessities of life must take precedence over matters of intellectual interest." This, he claimed, "goes down well" with most Singaporeans, despite the "occasional grumbles" about rote learning, cramming, the lack of creativity, and "the breeding of obedient bureaucrats and technocrats" (Ho, 1989, p. 687).

Ho identified the ideological underpinnings of education in clear terms but worried about the extent to which a narrow education nested within an economic developmentalist orientation can develop the "flexible intellect" and "inquiring attitudes" of the kind needed for the Next Lap. He further bemoaned the fact that liberal arts education has typically involved "little more than committing to memory" material needed for answering questions on exams. The true spirit of liberal education is not to turn people into "walking encyclopedias or microcomputers" but rather to develop the ability to think analytically and critically (Ho, 1989, p. 686).

Schooling

The school system is intensely competitive, exam-oriented, and hierarchical. It is designed to build a Singaporean identity and distinguish "leaders" from the "led." The process of streaming is under almost constant review, although its essence does not change. Young children are streamed into a "normal bilingual," "extended bilingual," or "monolingual" course. Exams are administered to these children and, although lateral transfers are supposed to be possible later in life, this initial streaming has a major and long-term impact on a person's career, with one stream heading to the university and another to vocational training. For assessment purposes the Ministry of Education maintains a bank of test items. At secondary school the top 10 percent of those who passed the primary school leaving exam are enrolled in a "special course" and will sit their "O"-level exams after four years. They are effectively bilingual and work in two languages.

The system is very competitive. In other sociocultural settings, educational authorities and citizens would not be comfortable with the loss of face (an important negative reinforcer) or erosion of self-esteem associated with it. Slow learners are "weeded out" at each level, and the psychological damage done by the system is less of a concern than the need to identify the most "meritorious," who will become the "next generation" of leaders.

The influential Goh report (1972) noted that out of every 1,000 pupils who enter primary school only 94 get into a tertiary institution. More recently Chua (1985) estimated that only 8 percent of each cohort survive the examinations and enter the university. The insistence on bilingualism in schools is controversial because, for about 85 percent of pupils, the two school languages are not those used at home. In an exam-oriented system that depends on language, educational "success" is greatly affected.

There is significant opposition to the kind of social Darwinism that streaming represents, but the government insistence on this can be understood when considered in the context of its obsession with genetics and sociobiology. Protests about streaming are seen as protests "in principle," which is antithetical to pragmatism. Streaming is alleged to work because it reflects "natural intelligence." Significantly, the study of social or political psychology was not encouraged in Singapore, and yet important population, educational, and other policies were based on it. For example, senior leaders appear to believe that most variance in intelligence is genetically determined and thus early streaming just reflects "nature." As Chua (1985) noted, instead of channeling resources to help the disadvantaged, resources are largely used to enrich those in relatively privileged positions. "Instead of attempting some distributive social justice, 'meritocratic' inequality is unapologetically accepted as a consequence of 'nature.' " This process is used to identify the no more than five percent that will lead the nation who, it is argued, will create benefits for all in some kind of trickle-down distribution of resources.

Continuing Education

Continuing education has become the umbrella term that encompasses a broad spectrum of training and adult education activities carried on under the rubric of *personal* or *community* development. Despite their benign appearance, almost all are shaped by economic developmentalism and, significantly, not much effort goes into educating older adults, handicapped people, or other "nonproductive" groups. There are few if any courses shaped around the so-called "sensitive issues."

A considerable amount of continuing education occurs in nonformal settings such as business and industry, professional associations, statutory boards, the armed forces, hospitals, community organizations, and the Extramural Department of the National University. The most notable agencies involved in formal education are the Singapore Polytechnic, largely involved with the training of technologists, the Ngee Ann Polytechnic, which offers diplomas in engineering, business, and computer studies, and the Nanyang Technological University, which offers practice-oriented engineering and related courses. The National University is very oriented toward professional development, and the annual intake is around 4,500. The total undergraduate enrollment for the 1989–90 academic year was 14,645. The total number of postgraduate students was 1,910, which comprised 11.5 percent of the total student population. By 1990 there were about 1,300 staff members *(Singapore, 1990)*. The National University Department of Extramural Studies offers a large range of noncredit courses to the public and has been at the center of attempts to train adult educators and foster the development of regional adult education organizations.

Agencies engaged in nonformal education offer "personal development" courses designed to provide "self-fulfillment." A wide range of courses are offered, many reflecting the new interests of a more affluent society. There are no entry requirements, and the prominent providers are the People's Association, which has strong ties to government, and the Armed Forces Reservists Association.

"Education for community development" is nested within an ideology of economic developmentalism and is concerned with improving the quality of life and broadening the range of options and activities available for individual Singaporeans. There have been a large number of "public education" programs designed to foster community development since 1959. These mass campaigns are used to educate, persuade, and cajole the populace about spitting, litter, pests, healthy lungs, family planning, drugs, road safety, speaking Mandarin, cancer, leprosy, smoking, courtesy, productivity, environmental awareness, cleanliness, parenting skills, the treatment of older people, and so on (Tham, K. W., 1986). Campaign goals are enforced, and various political and other father figures frequently lecture the populace about undesirable habits. These campaigns are one of the most prominent and interesting features of the educational landscape in Singapore and, at a time when other countries are attempting to educate the citizenry about AIDS and other important matters, there is little they can learn from the Singaporean experience. Data concerning the nature and execution of campaigns is not readily available.

Research

Pragmatic Bias. The pragmatic nature of education in Singapore constrains scholarship (see Gopinathan & Shive, 1987), and educational policy is not openly discussed. It is widely referred to as a "sensitive" matter. Because of the "sensitivity" surrounding education the Ministry of Education was sometimes slow to implement policies in the 1960s and 1970s.

In one of the few empirical studies on educational research in Singapore, Gopinathan and Gremli (1988) interviewed twenty researchers about the nature of their activity, the research process, and, most importantly in this context, their perceptions of the research environment. Most of the respondents were from the Institute of Education and the Regional English Language Centre;

others were from the Ministry of Education and the National University. The authors found that most educational research is initiated through a top-down approach. Most respondents were working on "assigned" projects. With regard to the climate for research there was some agreement concerning the need to steer away from research on "sensitive issues." Master's degree candidates were particularly wary of sensitive issues and tended to focus on "specific, pragmatic school-based problems." "Sensitivity" was also an issue reported by those evaluating curricula. Here there was considerable concern "not to be found too critical or negative" (Gopinathan and Gremli, 1988, p. 162). Some respondents said they had modified interim research reports so as to soften what might be perceived to be a criticism. Research on bilingualism, religious education, and streaming were among the "hot" issues. If the researcher is a foreigner, uncongenial results or interpretations are likely to be dismissed as the work of "colonialism" or as an insult to Singapore. In this climate simply allocating more resources to educational research will probably not significantly increase the quality or quantity of research.

Subjectivist Ontology. The safest research is atheoretical or descriptive, employs a quantitative methodology, and is cast within an objectivist ontology. Notably absent from educational research in Singapore are projects informed by subjectivist ontology.

Few studies use an action or participatory research methodology, or involve any kind of critique of existing theoretical frameworks or policies. Because of the hegemony of engineering and "hard sciences," there is little research on adult learners in Singapore. Learners are widely regarded as a constant. It is the content to be learned that attracts greatest attention.

The most outstanding piece of research nested within a subjectivist ontology was Heng and Devan's (1992) critique of "state fatherhood," which employed a postmodern/Foucaultian frame of reference. Another study located within subjectivist ontology was by Pratt (1992), a Canadian, who used phenomenography to study "conceptions of teaching" in Singapore. Conceptions are "representational models" composed of interrelated actions, beliefs, and intentions concerning teaching. After interviewing over 200 adult educators in Asia and North America he concluded that there are five deeply rooted conceptions, each of which can be categorized with a metaphor. The first, and most dominant in Singapore, is an *engineering* conception (Pratt, 1992a). Those who construe teaching as asking to "engineering," frame it as "content to be delivered." Teacher expertise is primarily associated with accomplished performances, efficient "coverage" of content, efficient time management, and development of instructional materials. Knowledge is assumed to be relatively stable and external to the learner. Learners are objectified. They are objects or a "target audience." Moreover, according to Pratt (1992, p. 210) teaching is understood to involve "finding efficient means to achieve a set of predetermined, nonproblematic ends." Learners are expected to passively absorb material "transmitted" through lectures or other "one-way" didactic processes.

DOCILITY AND LATERAL THINKING

The contemporary context for education largely stems from Singapore's unique demography, history, geopolitical position, and ideology. In many respects it does not manifest typical "urban attributes" such as those described by Stromquist (Chapter 2, this volume). The confluence of sociopolitical factors described above has created an obsession with human resource or professional development. Education is widely thought to be a process of transmitting information to learners who are largely passive and have little control over the content to be learned or the educational processes employed. Education is widely construed as rote learning and regurgitation of material found in textbooks or "modules."

Few citizens are able to secure information needed to challenge the assumed linkage between education and economic development, and learning acquired outside the framework of formal education is accorded little prestige or status. Unintended consequences might flow from the relentless pursuit of an economic developmentalist orientation. Thus, S. C. Tham noted that some educational commentators are of the opinion that

there is too much discipline and conformity to the detriment of self expression and individual freedom—a situation they believe could work against the government's plan to develop greater creativity or innovativeness as a desired behavioral quality. In the same vein, there is the view that, in exercising close supervision over manpower training to meet the needs of the economy, the government is abrogating a fundamental demand of education, namely that of meeting the need for self realization. (1989, p. 492)

The docility of the populace has created a formidable challenge for continuing education, because casualties of previous encounters with a system designed to "weed out" people are not enchanted by the notion of returning for a second or third dose. Nor do they want to sit through hour after hour of dreary lectures. There is doubt about whether they have the creativity and confidence deemed necessary for the Next Lap.

Sociobiology, telecommunications, computers, and related "high-tech" fields require imagination, diversity, playfulness, and the free exchange of ideas within a democratic context. Thus Lim (1983) wrote of the need for a "creative" society; a 1986 report on the economy said future strategies should encourage the development of more creative and flexible skills through broad-based education; and a plethora of consultants, including Edward De Bono, have been brought in to teach lateral thinking and creativity; but it is exceedingly difficult to "engineer" creativity among a docile populace, particularly when it flies in the face of an entrenched social history. It is not that small countries are incapable of technological innovation. The problem for the Next

Lap is rooted in decades of exaggerations about survival and pragmatism and autocratic education that may have all but eliminated the individual capacity for creativity, play, or imagining the future.

The government will be tempted to "source" lateral thinking programs, and quick-fix short courses or creativity "modules." But can creativity be "socially engineered"? (Wilson, 1978). It will be difficult to undo decades of social learning that has reinforced the suppression of unorthodox or lateral thought, and caused many people to lose face—an important consideration in Asian societies—or define themselves as failures. In addition there is a shortage of artists and others who might challenge "authority." None of this augurs well for the future.

It is ironic that Singapore should have reached this point, because PAP leaders used immense ingenuity to shuck off the British administration. But the intensely competitive education system retains its colonial structure and ethos. In many ways the Singaporean meritocracy contains strong echoes of the British class structure. Moreover, meritocracy is not just a procedure for selecting and promoting the best talent but creates an "aura of special awe for the top leaders" (Vogel, 1989, p. 1053) and provides them with a mechanism to discredit the "less meritocratic" opposition irrespective of the merit of their arguments. Compared to consensus-seeking Japanese bureaucrats who keep a low profile, Singaporean leaders "combine the articulate English debating style with the confidence of the Chinese mandarin and the raw energy and wit of the street-smart, local Chinese trader" (Vogel, 1989, p. 1053). This is one of the few countries in the world where an opposition politician can be discredited by publicizing his A- and O-level marks. Other leaders, such as Keith Holyoake, Norman Kirk, and Walter Nash, all former prime ministers of New Zealand, and John Major of Great Britain, turned their lack of formal schooling into an asset. This would not work in Singapore.

The education system is designed to lessen the effects of interethnic diversity and provide common experiences that will promote a Singaporean identity and build skills, knowledge, and values that contribute to national development. But education is symbiotically connected to the sociopolitical fabric, and the intense competitiveness, the traditional Confucian respect for the teacher (whose authority is rarely challenged), the fear of the ISA, and the pervasive impact of "pragmatism" do not create a receptive climate for the participatory (Botkin et al., 1979) or andragogical (Knowles, 1980) principles of education. It is the Chinese "stuffed duck" that best summarizes the situation. Many foreign-trained Singaporean teachers have learned to use participatory techniques and alternatives to "plowing through a textbook." But they are greatly constrained by what they think are the expectations of their employers and are wary of students who complain if there is any deviation from a teacher-centered process of "adult schooling."

CONCLUSION

Singapore stands as a remarkable testimony to the persistence and vision of the founding fathers. Because of the lack of a hinterland that could provide resources, breathing space, and a security buffer zone, the founders of modern Singapore early recognized that education was a critical instrument for nation building, economic development, and racial harmony. There is thus an extraordinary emphasis on formal education and an unrelenting commitment to highly integrated public education campaigns in nonformal and informal settings. As a result, Singapore sometimes resembles aspects of a "learning society" (Faure, 1972).

There is no rural hinterland, and few citizens can avoid official "gaze" or the educational messages hammered into them from billboards, television, radio, pamphlets, public events, and the exhortations of political leaders. But it is the radical commitment to human resource development in an intensely urban setting, coupled with a willingness to experiment, that distinguishes Singapore from other polities. Although this is still a tightly controlled society, scholars such as Heng and Devan (1992), who challenge patriarchy, loyal critics such as Chua (1991), who wants greater democratization, or Gopinathan and Gremli (1988), who want more imaginative and better research, and some Singaporean expatriates, have demonstrated that counter-hegemonic discourse is now possible.

The public housing developments are, without doubt, one of the outstanding urban features of Singapore and have been a potent instrument of racial integration and social control. But as Singapore moves into the Next Lap they represent new possibilities for community-based education. Moreover, if these buildings are appropriately wired almost every Singaporean could be hooked into computer networks that deliver educational and other services. There is probably no other urban area in the world that could be so easily transformed into a "wired city." Of course, this could lead to even more surveillance. But, since early 1991, the Goh Chok Tong government has created broader and more differentiated possibilities for education and dialogue than was previously the case and might permit the kind of uninhibited discussions that occur in other countries (see Boshier, 1990).

In Singapore, the reciprocal and dynamic links between space, architecture, politics, education, and psychosocial structures are probably more tightly woven than in any other comparable urban center. If the Singaporean authorities become less secretive, those in urban settings could learn much from the experience of this remarkable republic. In the meantime, Singapore's friends will watch with great interest as the very intriguing tapestry of this city-state rolls through the Next Lap and into the next century.

REFERENCES

Boshier, R. W. (1990). Socio-Psychological Factors in Electronic Networking. *International Journal of Lifelong Education, 9* (1): pp. 49–64.

Botkin, J., Elmandjra, M., and Malitza, M. (1979). *No Limits to Learning.* Oxford: Pergamon.

Census of Population 1990: Advanced Data Release (1991). Singapore: Department of Statistics.

Chua, B. H. (1985). Pragmatism of the People's Action Party Government in Singapore. *S.E. Asian Journal of Social Science, 13* (2): pp. 29–46.

Chua, B. H. (1989). The Business of Living in Singapore. In Kernial Singh Sandhu & Paul Wheatley (eds.), *Management of Success.* Singapore: Institute of Southeast Asian Studies, pp. 1003–1021.

Chua, B. H. (1991). Building a Democratic State in Singapore. Paper presented at the International Symposium, Institutions in Cultures: Theory and Practice. Singapore: National University of Singapore, 19–22 June.

Drysdale, J. (1974) *Struggle for Success.* Singapore: Times Books International.

Far Eastern Economic Review, 9 February 1989, pp. 32–37.

Far Eastern Economic Review, 4 June 1987.

Far Eastern Economic Review, 22 October 1987.

Faure, E. (1972). *Learning to Be.* Paris: UNESCO.

Foucault, M. (1979). *Discipline and Punish: The Birth of the Prison,* trans. Alan Sheridan. New York: Pantheon Books.

Fraser, N. (1989). *Unruly Practices: Power, Discourse and Gender in Contemporary Social Theory.* Minneapolis, MI: University of Minnesota Press.

George, T. J. S. (1984). *Lee Kuan Yew's Singapore.* Singapore: Eastern Universities Press.

Goh, K. S. (1972). *The Economics of Modernization.* Singapore: Asia Pacific Press.

Gopinathan, S. (1987). Education. In J. S. T. Quah, H. C. Chan, & C. M. Seah. (eds.), *Government and Politics of Singapore,* pp. 197–232. Oxford: Oxford University Press.

Gopinathan, S., & Shive, Glenn A. (1987). Scholarly Access: Opportunities and Problems in North-South Academic Relations. *Comparative Education Review 31* (4), pp. 490–508.

Gopinathan, S., & Gremli, M. S. (1988). The Educational Research Environment in Singapore. In S. Gopinathan & H. Dean Nielsen (eds.) *Educational Research Environments in Southeast Asia,* pp. 137–183. Singapore: Chopmen in Association with S. E. Asia Research Review and IDRC (Canada).

Government of Singapore. (1991). *The Next Lap.* Singapore: The Government of Singapore.

Grice, K., & Drakakis-Smith, D. (1985). The Role of the State in Shaping Development: Two Decades of Growth in Singapore. *Transactions, 10* (3): p. 351.

Heng, G., & Devan, Janadas (1992). State Fatherhood: The Politics of Nationalism, Sexuality, and Race in Singapore. In A. Parker, M. Russo, D. Sommer, & P. Yaeger (eds.), *Nationalisms and Sexualities,* pp. 343–364. New York: Routledge.

Ho, W. M. (1989). Value Premises Underlying the Transformation of Singapore. In

Kernial Singh Sandhu & Paul Wheatley (eds.), *Management of Success*, pp. 671–691. Singapore: Institute of Southeast Asian Studies.

Knowles, M. S. (1980). *The Modern Practice of Adult Education*. Chicago, IL: Follett.

Lee, K. Y. (1978). Preface to the *Report on the Ministry of Education 1978*. Singapore: Government Printers.

Lim, W. S. W. (1983). Towards a Creative Society. In S. W. Saw, & R. S. Bhathal, *Singapore: Towards the Year 2000*. Singapore, pp. 156–162. Singapore Association for the Advancement of Science.

Minchin, J. (1986). *No Man Is an Island*. Sydney, Australia: Allen and Unwin.

Ministry of Education. (1986). *Education in Singapore*. Singapore: Public Relations Unit, Ministry of Education.

Pratt, D. (1992). Five Conceptions of Teaching. *Adult Education Quarterly 42* (4): pp. 203–220.

Pratt, D. (1992a). Singaporeans' Preferred Conception of Teaching. Personal communication with the author, December 1, 1992.

Rigg, J. (1988). Singapore and the Recession of 1985. *Asian Survey 28* (3): pp. 340–352.

Sandhu, K. S., & Wheatley, P. (eds.) *Management of Success*. Singapore: Institute of Southeast Asian Studies, 1989.

Shared Values (1991). White Paper presented to Parliament by the president, Republic of Singapore.

Singapore, 1990. (1990). Singapore: Psychological Defence and Publicity Division, Ministry of Communications and Information.

Singapore: The Next Lap. Singapore: Government of Singapore, 1991.

Straits Times (June 22, 1991). Govt. Will Always Have to Balance Pressures.

Tham, K. W. (1986). National campaigns. In *Singapore: Taking Stock: Readings for the General Paper*, pp. 41–57. Singapore: Federal Publications.

Tham, S. C. (1989). The Perception and Practice of Education. In Kernial Singh Sandhu & Paul Wheatley (eds.), *Management of Success*, pp. 477–502. Singapore: Institute of Southeast Asian Studies.

Vogel, E. (1989). A Little Dragon Tamed. In Kernial Singh Sandhu and Paul Wheatley (eds.), *Management of Success*, pp. 1049–1066. Singpore: Institute of Southeast Asian Studies.

Wilson, H. E. (1978). *Social Engineering in Singapore*. Singapore: Singapore University Press.

Yeh, S. H. K. (1989). The Idea of the Garden City. In Kernial Singh Sandhu & Paul Wheatley (eds.), *Management of Success*. Singapore, pp. 813–832. Singapore: Institute of Southeast Asian Studies.

8

Neighborhood Associations and the Fight for Public Schooling in Rio de Janeiro State

Nelly Moulin and Isabel Pereira

Public schools in Brazil were created by the slaveholding society to satisfy the educational needs of an incipient middle class and never managed to fully meet the needs of the population. The first Brazilian constitution (of 1824) stated that every citizen had the right to receive free elementary education. In fact the whole class of slave workers, an absolute majority of the population, was excluded from this universe. On the other hand the elite, composed of the big landowners, from the beginning sent their children to the private (mainly religious) schools in Brazil or abroad.

In a country with an essentially agricultural economy, the dispersed rural habitat contributed to the isolation of the rural population, making it difficult to provide education to the poorer rural class. This situation remained the same for many decades, up into Brazil's republican period. Public schools began to appear and slowly spread throughout the country aiming to meet the needs of the urban middle class, which represented a small part of the population. They were supplemented by private schools, first of a confessional nature, and later secular.

It is necessary to recall that in a slaveholding society "work" was always perceived as "physical work" and was relegated to the slaves. Therefore the school aimed to prepare the bourgeoisie to perform intellectual and artistic activities, concentrating on general culture. Women usually spent a few years at the religious schools and then were excluded from formal education. At home they dedicated themselves to music, embroidery, knitting, and to activities other than those of the slaves (Sodre, 1972).

The antidemocratic imperial school seemed to satisfy the demands of the public which it was oriented to. Commenting on the social and historical context, Fernandes says: "During the slaveholding and *senhorial* regime, Brazil had an aristocratic teaching system, extremely refined and efficient for its social and cultural purposes" (Fernandes, 1966, p. 4).

The aristocratic teaching system that provided general culture to a small part of the population continued to be considered a teaching model, spreading throughout the country even after Brazil's imperial period. Because this teaching system was inadequate to satisfy the needs of the popular classes and because of structural difficulties caused by the socioeconomic and demographic conditions referred to above, Brazilian society in the second half of the twentieth century was composed of a small and very well educated elite and a huge mass of illiterate people (more than 50 percent). Lambert (1959), in an excellent analysis of "the two Brazils," states: "According to the 1950 census which, like all other censuses is very optimistic about the subject, almost half of the Brazilian population, i.e., 49.5 percent, knew how to read and write" (p. 207).

THE STRUGGLE FOR MODERNIZATION

Since 1930 Brazil had been trying to develop its industrial sector rapidly. The process of industrialization generated important social, economic, political, and cultural changes. However, the lack of a literate population—one of the requirements for economic modernization—was an obstacle to this objective.

In the cities that grew around the new industries, the rising industrial elite was taking from the rural aristocracy the exclusive control of the country. Little by little, some of the rural inhabitants moved to the cities, where they expected to find work and better living conditions. Another demographic flow was formed by migrants leaving the more densely populated northeast region and moving toward the southeast and south, where the industries were flourishing. Most of these migrants formed the urban proletariat, and faced a very low standard of living.

To give an idea of the evolution of the urbanization process, Table 8.1 presents the Brazilian population distribution by rural and urban areas during the last five decades.

As Table 8.1 shows, in 1940 only a little more than 30 percent of the total population was urban, while 70 percent was rural. The predominance of the urban population appears only by the 1970 census, when its percentage had risen to more than 55 percent. In the 1980 census the situation became more dramatic. Although there were high overall population growth rates in the 1960s (2.89 percent per year) and in the 1970s (2.48 percent per year), the number of inhabitants in the rural areas in 1980 is lower than in the 1960s.

Table 8.1
Brazilian Population Distribution by Area, 1940–80

Years	Rural Areas Population	%	Urban Areas Population	%	Total
1940	28,356,165	68.76	12,880,182	31.24	41,236,315
1950	33.161,506	63.84	18,782,891	36.16	51,944,397
1960	38,987,526	54.91	32,004,817	45.09	70,992,343
1970	41,603,810	44.02	52,904,744	55.98	94,508,554
1980	38,566,297	32.41	80,436,409	67.59	119,002,706

Source: IBGE Foundation, 1989.

The urbanization process was very disorganized, and the increase in the services and assistance required by the population growth was not satisfactory. The housing problem led to the occupation of hills, swamps, and the peripheries of the cities, where slums were built without any planning or sanitary facilities.

It was necessary to increase the number of public schools, to multiply the number of teachers, and to make teaching a more democratic activity, extending it to the popular classes and eliminating its aristocratic character. The school system did expand, but teaching maintained its traditional nature and old model. The profound changes required by the new social classes and by the technological and economic development did not happen.

EMPHASIS ON TECHNICAL EDUCATION

In 1964, when there was a military coup, only 45 percent of the Brazilian population lived in urban areas. The urbanization process was accelerated by a new economic order in the following decades. The dictatorial regime, supported by multinational capital, adopted an economic model focusing on industrial development. Modern technology and know-how were introduced in order to guarantee quality and large-scale export-oriented production. These products, designed to satisfy the consumption needs of the bourgeoisie and the technocratic groups (who earned high wages), were essential to sustain the economic model (Furtado, 1972).

The wages of the working class were "frozen" so that large profits could be shared by the national bourgeoisie and multinational capital. The agricultural sector was neglected and this led to smaller crops, high rates of rural unemployment, and the subsequent exodus to the large cities of those rural workers who sought work and social assistance. As mentioned earlier, the urbanization system did not adjust to the accelerated population increase. The existing urban housing and sanitary infrastructures, as well as transport and health care services, could no longer meet the needs of the whole population.

Government expenditures dedicated to social services, and specifically to the educational reform, were insufficient to provide the population with basic needs. Technical and vocational education received some government attention, as they were the source of skilled workers for the industry. Secondary technical education was the only school level taken into account in the state budget. The other educational levels, from preschool to college and university, were neglected by the government and were left for the private sector.

WHERE EDUCATIONAL PROBLEMS STAND TODAY

In spite of some government initiatives to reduce illiteracy, the absolute number of illiterate people older than fifteen years continued to grow (Table 8.2). This trend is unlikely to be reversed if the high levels of failure during the first school years and of school dropouts of still-illiterate students are not overcome.

At present there are approximately 20 million illiterate people in Brazil (IBGE, 1989) out of a total population of 146 million. These figures are more surprising when compared with statistics that show some Brazilian companies to be among the richest in the capitalist world. The contrast between such a rich elite on the one hand and the 50 percent of the population who live in poverty and the 20 million people who are illiterate on the other is both worrisome and shameful.

Changes toward a more democratic educational structure would involve offering to every citizen, equally, the possibility of getting instruction and of participating more in the country's society, production, and economic wealth.

Table 8.2
Evolution of Illiteracy in Brazil, 1940–80

Years	Population above 15 years (millions)	Illiterate People above 15 years (millions)	Illiteracy Rate %
1940	23.6	13.2	56.17
1950	30.2	15.2	50.48
1960	40.1	15.8	39.35
1970	54.3	17.9	33.01
1980	74.5	19.5	26.00

Source: IBGE Foundation, 1989.

Needless to say, investments in education should be the starting point of any economic development program, since the better instructed and more capable the population of a country is, the more productive it will be. If there is enough wealth being created, why is there such a lack of political will to promote social changes, including those in education?

One of the positive aspects of the urbanization process is that the organization of the population into groups, associations, and parties is favored by the urban agglomerate and by the concentration of workers in the factories. Such organizations allow workers to have their needs and claims for significant social change in Brazil represented and defended by their leaders.

Assuming that education and training for productive activities are basic instruments for any improvement in the standards of living of the marginal population—who do not yet benefit from the country's wealth—we may ask: What has Brazilian civil society been doing through its organized groups, particularly its neighborhood associations, to fight for wider access to a basic, adequate, universal, and free education? This is the general point that this paper intends to discuss, starting from the analysis of the struggle for public schools in the city of Rio de Janeiro.

THE POLITICAL EDUCATION OF THE POPULAR CLASSES

Political participation is still an incipient practice among the Brazilian popular classes. Up to the 1930s Brazil was essentially an agricultural country whose social and economic context did not favor the process of political awareness. It can be said that the political consciousness of the Brazilian citizen began very late, influenced by the atmosphere of industrialization and urbanization during the modernization of the country. However, this democratic process was interrupted many times, being replaced by long dictatorial periods when free demonstrations and participation in the political life were not allowed. We believe that it is necessary to follow the process of political consciousness of the popular classes in Brazil in order to understand what is unusual about the urban social movements and to identify their strategies for struggle.

Patronato and Clientelismo

Up to the 1930s the large landowners constituted the hegemonic political class. Under their influence and protection there was a dependent group of relatives, friends, and workers—the *clientela*. The landowners or patrons maintained with their *clientela* a relationship known as *patronato* (patronage), which included political loyalty to the patron. The diffuse pattern of settlement, the isolation, and the high illiteracy level in the rural areas are the factors that contributed to the low interest of the rural worker in politics. Nevertheless, the participation of these workers in elections was relatively high, even though they had to travel long distances to vote. As there was no solid political awareness, the masters—the large landowners—manipulated (and still manipulate) their employees, telling them for whom they should vote. The masters instructed their workers on how to vote, supplying even the transportation to take them to the polling places. Sometimes the vote was paid for as if it were a service. Gifts were also exchanged for votes. Thus voting was not recognized as a citizen's right; on the contrary, it was seen as an obligation to the master. In fact, the prestige of the master or political leader was measured by the size of their *clientela*.

As the industrialization process started, a new class of urban entrepreneurs emerged to challenge the political power of the landowners. The agrarian economy, which was vital for the country until then, was surpassed by the industrial economy. The decay of the landowners' economic prestige was followed by a reduction of their political prestige. The *patronato* system became vulnerable as employees started to question their master's power. As progress reached the countryside, new ideologies spread, which further contributed to weaken the *patronato* system. In the cities the different migrant groups lost their political references, left behind in the archaic rural society. They cut the ties of loyalty that used to attach them to their former masters, yet sought no political training nor showed interest in getting involved with political parties.

This undefined political situation both in the countryside and in the cities was considered by a few politicians an immense source of votes to be exploited. They were the so-called "demagogues" that took advantage of this moment of social disorder to establish a new relationship with their *clientela*, based on exchanging favors: Votes were exchanged for protection and public services as if these services were governmental gifts. This type of relation has been termed by the political scientists *populismo*. This phenomenon happened not only in Brazil but also in the rest of Latin America.

Ianni (1989) considers *populismo* as well as the mass movements "to be a political phenomenon generated inside the broad modernization process of Latin American society" (p. 4). In Brazil *populismo* was one of the characteristics of the dictatorial government of President Getulio Vargas (1930–45). This government recognized the workers' rights, but at the same time the state was identified directly with the people and was supposed to harmonize the interests of the society. Therefore the existence of political parties and the participation of the people in the exercise of power were considered unnecessary. We find this passage in Ianni (1989): "The state is proposed to and imposed upon the society as if it were its best and unique interpreter, without the intermediation of the parties. [Getulio] Vargas would have said that 'voting doesn't feed anyone' " (p. 90).

Vargas left the government in 1945 and then there was a return to the democratic regime, with the reopening of congress and the organization of political parties. Nevertheless, *populismo* never disappeared. In its democratic form *populismo* emphasized the labor unions, but they were kept under the control of the government, which determined their functioning and structure.

During the détente period that followed the Vargas dictatorship, the working class had the necessary conditions to build its political consciousness, to participate more in the social movements, and to improve its class demands. At the same time, the strength of *populismo* as well as the power of mobilization demonstrated by the labor unions and by the mass of workers at the beginning of the 1960s engendered its own end. In 1964 President Goulart was overthrown, accused of turning Brazil into a "republic of unions." The increasing political participation that had been a conquest by the people was then interrupted.

Military Dictatorship

From 1964 to 1983 Brazil was under a military regime and democratic practices were banished from the country. For about twenty years the Brazilian population was kept away from political participation. Any individual or group demonstration, especially coming from schools or factories, was seen as "subverting the order" and was repressed by the police. During that time it was not possible to learn political practices nor to develop a new popular leadership that could fight for social rights.

At first the economic model adopted by the authoritarian regime led to a decrease in inflation rates and to some economic growth. However, in the early 1970s several factors, notably the world oil crisis in 1973, demonstrated how fragile the model was. This model was based on capital and income concentration, recessionary policies, and increased dependence on foreign capital and technology; it was also responsible for the rise in the foreign debt. The social crisis became worse when wages were "frozen," which caused a fall in the purchasing power and standard of living of the working class. In addition to the rising inflation and unemployment rates in the big cities, violence began to threaten citizens' personal security.

Given this situation, the authoritarian regime's legitimacy began to be questioned. The failure of the adopted economic model undermined the prestige of the political forces in power. In this context, and accompanied by increasing poverty and very low standards of living, popular demand movements began to appear, mainly in the poorer areas. These groups started to demand state initiatives in order to solve their basic housing, sanitary, transport, health, and educational problems. These social movements marked the return of the working class to the political scene and the opening of new channels for expression. Among these grass-roots initiatives, the neighborhood associations stand as one of the most important.

THE NEIGHBORHOOD ASSOCIATION MOVEMENT IN RIO DE JANEIRO

Rio de Janeiro City was the country's capital from 1763 to 1960, when Brasilia became the seat of the federal government. Even after this, Rio remained an important city, maintaining strong commercial and industrial activity, surpassed only by the city of Sao Paulo. The present population of Rio is around ten million people, the second highest in the country, again surpassed only by the city of Sao Paulo, with approximately twelve million.

The political and economic position of Rio attracted migrants from other states. Near the midpoint of this century, Lambert (1959) pointed that 42 percent of Rio's population of 2.3 million people were migrants. The city grew in a very disorganized and uneven way. The infrastructure created favored the neighborhoods of the upper class, neglecting the urban periphery and the suburbs. Slums, disorderly groups of poor houses with no proper water, light, transport, or sanitary conditions, were built on the city hills. It is especially in these neighborhoods, where the infrastructure is precarious, that residents' associations became stronger in the 1970s.

Origin and Nature of the Neighborhood Associations

Although these popular movements had been created many decades before, they were excluded from the Brazilian political scene after 1964. The emerging social mobilization of the neighborhood associations in the 1970s is a striking phenomenon, given the circumstances prevailing at that time. Even in the absence of an atmosphere of free political expression, these movements demonstrated a huge capacity for mobilization and became an effective channel for mediation with the state.

The Catholic church, with its *pastorais operarias* groups, and the left-wing militants are said to have helped to create these movements in the majority of neighborhoods. Jacobi points out that "in many neighborhoods, societies of neighborhood friends are organized and articulated by militants connected with the Church, with left wing militants from different political origins and with industrial workers living in these areas" (Jacobi, 1990, p. 230).

The support received from political militants could have represented a political articulation able to broaden the local claims. However, as Jacobi mentions in his study, "The leadership tried to expand the struggle's scope, but it basically concentrated on neighborhood-specific problems" (p. 230).

There is solid evidence that the drive of the neighborhood associations is concentrated on their immediate interests and on the problems that affect their daily lives. Thus, their movement has a focus on better living conditions. They do not contest nor get involved with the socioeconomic and political questions that generated their local problems.

The Rise of the Neighborhood Associations

Step by step, the number of neighborhood and slum associations increased, and associations were also created in Rio's middle-class neighborhoods. In the 1980s this process became more intense. In 1983, there were 249 known neigh-

Table 8.3
Neighborhood Associations in Rio de Janeiro by Date of Creation

Year	Neighborhood Associations Created	Percentage of Total to Date
Up to 1980	129	16.5
1981	82	10.5
1982	83	10.5
1983	143	18.0
1984	89	11.5
1985	87	11.0
1986	92	12.0
1987	49	6.0
1988	3	1.0
No information	23	3.0
Total	780	100.0

Source: IBASE, 1990.

borhood associations; there were 700 by 1987. This process is shown in Table 8.3, which depicts the annual creation of associations.

The increase in the number was not even, as an unusual growth rate occurred in 1983. A study by the Brazilian Institute of Social and Economic Analysis (IBASE, 1990) indicates that the majority of neighborhood associations in 1983 appeared in the southern zone of the city, where the middle class lives. The study attributes this strong mobilization to media support and to the publicity concerning successful campaigns. It should also be noted that in late 1982 both a governor and a mayor from the Democratic Labor Party (PDT), with a socialist political platform, were elected to assume their office on 15 March 1983, for a four-year period. During this period (1983–87) a very impressive number of associations were created (see Table 8.3). However, after 1987 the rhythm of increase was not the same, though the number of existing associations was maintained.

In 1978 the Federation of Neighborhood Associations of Rio de Janeiro (FAMERJ) was founded in order to consolidate community demands and to reinforce their pressure on the state. Another federation of neighborhood associations was created to assist and represent the organized slum movement, the Federation of Favela Associations of Rio de Janeiro (FAFERJ). FAMERJ en-

Table 8.4
Members of Boards of Directors of Neighborhood Associations in Rio de Janeiro by Age

Age	Percentage
Below 20 years of age	2.0
From 21 to 30 years old	19.5
From 31 to 40 years old	31.0
From 41 to 50 years old	22.5
51 years old or more	21.0
No information	4.0
Total	100.0

Source: IBASE, 1990.

compasses the urban area associations, from both middle-class and poor neighborhoods; FAFERJ includes only the slum associations. As a consequence, their demands differ in focus, since the slums still have to give priority to infrastructural needs that in middle-class neighborhoods have already been satisfied. Both of these federations must have contributed to strengthening the neighborhood movement and expanding the scope of its action.

Reasons for Creating the Associations

The main reasons for the numerous neighborhood associations that appeared in Rio de Janeiro may be explained by the data published by IBASE in 1990. Focusing on a universe of 780 neighborhood associations comprising the FAMERJ, IBASE found that the main causes for the emergence of these movements in the city of Rio were the fight for housing or landownership (62 percent), followed by the fight for infrastructural services: basic sanitary provisions, electricity, and garbage collection.

The struggle for education was not among the first popular claims, except in the peripheral metropolitan area of Rio. In this area, Baixada Fluminense, education was the basic concern in 50 percent of the movements.

Who Joins These Movements?

We assume that urban social movements are spontaneous, heterogeneous, and that they group different social classes. In these cases homogeneity is obtained through fighting together for the same objectives, not because of similar

Table 8.5
Members of Boards of Directors of Neighborhood Associations in Rio de Janeiro by Level of Schooling

Schooling Degree	%
Never went to school	0.5
Elementary school	23.0
Complete elementary school	22.0
High school	27.0
University	15.0
No information	12.5
Total	100.0

Source: IBASE, 1990.

characteristics of the participants. According to IBASE (1990) the FAMERJ and FAFERJ congresses usually "gather men and women from different religions, races, ages; sometimes whole families" (p. 12).

About 85 percent of the neighborhood associations started with the support of the church. It is very difficult to know the precise number of their affiliates owing to the lack of updated files and to the multiple affiliation criteria. Some neighborhood associations consider all residents affiliated. Therefore the figures that follow (see Table 8.4) depict only the associations' leaders and cover a total of 7,417 members of the boards of directors in the 780 neighborhood associations of Rio.

Regarding sex composition, the IBASE findings indicate that women occupied only 36 percent of the administrative positions in the neighborhood associations. Women can be found directing only such areas as education and child care. This greater male participation in leading positions does not happen only in Rio de Janeiro State. In Recife, capital of Pernambuco, more women than men participate in neighborhood associations, and the women's share is more than 50 percent in 75 percent of the associations. Nevertheless, women are presidents of only 22 percent of these entities (pp. 29–30). Regarding the age distribution in the associations' directories, we notice a remarkably even participation among people of all ages (except for those under twenty-one) (p. 13). This fact was corroborated in the interviews.

The neighborhood associations that are members of FAMERJ represent communities from very different realities, with contrasting social and economic profiles. The amount of education of the directors of the associations also varies according to the type of community (see Table 8.5). In the poorest communities, the level of schooling is lower than in associations representing middle-class neighborhoods. Considering that the illiteracy index of Rio's population was 11 percent in 1988 (IBGE, 1989), the schooling level of the directory members is higher than that of the population they represent (IBASE, 1990).

THE STRUGGLE FOR PUBLIC SCHOOLS

The movements' leaders adopt different practices to fight for public schooling, depending on who their main supporting groups are—the church, political militants, or professionals. Each of these agents has its own platforms and presents alternative forms of action in order to preserve its relationship with the communities. The church created grass-roots communities *(comunidades de base)* to recover its prestige among the people. The left-wing political militants tried new ways of articulating and integrating with the working class.

To guarantee their own survival these agents combine their interests with those of the neighborhood residents. At one time the neighborhood associations seemed to be "the only possible 'forum' for political resistance and survival" (Jacobi, 1990, p. 232). In a way, the political experience and training of the militants provide the necessary stimulus to sustain the mobilization, which also guarantees the adoption of more progressive fighting strategies.

Referring to the ideological nature of the militants' activity, Jacobi observes: "It was important to persist in working on the basis of a closer daily relationship with the population . . . to try to break the traditional practices, considered by them as paternalistic and apolitical" (p. 232).

Jacobi reiterates the importance of these agents when he points out that "even though the political context favored a demanding and politicizing atmosphere, the very low political level of the majority of residents was an obstacle to their more active participation" (p. 223).

In fact *clientelismo* was never completely excluded from the strategies adopted by the neighborhood associations in their fight for public schools. Oliveira (1985) distinguishes two types of relationships between the surveyed communities and the state and its representatives. One is a *clientelista* relation; the other is independent, outside the formal political system.

An example of the first procedure was found by Oliveira in the Parque Uniao Association, a slum association active during the 1960s and 1970s. The *clientelista* practice was used when votes for certain deputies were exchanged for the construction of two public schools. But in 1980 this association's leadership rejected this practice, thus showing an increasing political consciousness as a movement.

It should be emphasized, to avoid being too idealistic, that even with this political progress, sometimes a return occurs and *clientelista* practices appear in the associations. Even though the directorates of some movements do not adopt these practices, they cannot prevent other politicians from maintaining this type of relationship with members of their communities.

It is worth mentioning the experience of the Association of Vila Vidigal. This association also had the support of a mothers' group, which was organized to pressure the city's secretary of education. Jacobi (1987) believes that the free access to the secretary "helped the people to form a demystified opinion about the authorities' role" and contributed as well to the opening of "a wider interaction space" (p. 18), as the layers of bureaucracy were bypassed and demands became clearer.

After fighting from 1981 to 1985, supported by the group of mothers, Vila Vidigal's neighborhood association managed to enlarge the sole public school in the neighborhood at that time. Paulo Roberto Muniz, the association's director, reported that after the enlargement of this school, the community decided to present claims for the construction of another school:

The groups of mothers were organized to reform the school. . . . These groups had meetings, visited the Secretary to try to enlarge the school. We struggled a lot (from 1981 to 1985) and then we obtained it in 1985. . . . When the reform was over we realized it no longer satisfied the community's needs. . . . Then we started fighting for another school. It was a harder dispute. (Muniz, 1989)

We observed that the strategies adopted by the neighborhood associations varied according to the way the state responds to their demands, and according to the government's level of commitment to the community. Sometimes the government itself was the agent that stimulated the society to participate in the fight for education in Rio de Janeiro.

In 1982 the first direct election for state governor took place, and a socialist candidate (from PDT) was elected in Rio de Janeiro. The leaders of the communities were then invited to discuss general teaching problems, including the creation of a parent-teacher association in each school. The participation of the community in the decision-making process was emphasized, and they could intervene in the election of the school's principal. Francisco Alencar, FAM-ERJ's president from 1983 to 1985, declared in an interview:

I believe that 1983, when Brizola's government began, is an unquestionable watershed. . . . The Democratic Labor Party (PDT) group composed of Professors Darcy Ribeiro and Maria Yedda Linhares managed to openly discuss the school's problems and the need for education, and to elaborate a teaching project with the population. After that we realized that a few neighborhood associations began to consider teaching a service as important as basic sanitation, health and housing. (Alencar, 1989)

After the late 1970s, and especially during the 1980s, there was a change in the political panorama that allowed a political evolution of the neighborhood associations. Generally speaking, the associations presented a more mature performance after that, maintaining their autonomy while relating to the state and to the politicians. Afterward, many communities realized that social services need not be "paid" with votes. On the contrary, they asserted that the provision and maintenance of these services were a state duty.

THE NATURE OF CLAIMS

In order to identify the nature of the neighborhood associations' demands in their fight for public schooling, we analyzed the annals of the three first FAMERJ congresses.

In 1983, seventy neighborhood associations participated in the first congress. At that time Jo Resende was elected president of the association. (Later he became the city's vice-mayor.) During the debates two objectives were defined: to refurbish the schools and to make them more democratic. On the basis of these goals, the final report outlined strategies to obtain:

1. Free and public schools.
2. Better school facilities.
3. The creation of nurseries in the neighborhood.
4. Concrete results from the government's commitment to make education a priority. (FAMERJ, 1983, p. 25)

In addition, the different neighborhood associations that participated in this congress committed themselves to surveying their neighborhoods' educational situation, and to identifying the positive and negative aspects of the school-community integration. However, the four main actions were too broadly defined and were never really implemented.

During the second FAMERJ congress the debates on education were already better oriented and the definitions were much more precise. This indicated that the discussion was grounded on a more critical ideology and that it aimed at a social transformation. At this congress, which took place in June 1985, 316 representatives of neighborhood associations participated and were given the right to vote for the federation's president. Professor Francisco Alencar was elected. The debate included strategy proposals for education. The way FAMERJ understood schooling at that time can be shown in its educational report, which was produced by the Educational Committee during the second congress:

We consider that the educational process should aim to construct a free and fair society where education is not an instrument of domination used for private interests, designed to attend to a minor part of the population, and oriented to the elite. [We believe] that in this society the school may play its role in forming politically conscious and critical citizens. It is necessary to emphasize how important it is that the community participate in the debate on teaching democratization, on free access to education, and on curricula development. (FAMERJ, 1985, p. 2)

Several proposals with this progressive approach to schooling were debated and approved by vote during this second congress, including:

1. Fighting against the reproduction of the values of the dominant ideology in the sphere of teaching, with the support of students' groups, teachers, and all other segments of society.

2. Fighting for improving the quality of teaching, for in-service training of the teachers, and for adapting the curricula and the programs at the elementary and high school levels to the students' reality. This should be done with the participation of parents, students, teachers, and neighborhood associations. Subjects such as agrarian reform, unemployment, and income concentration should be included in the schools' curriculum.

3. Fighting for refurbishing of school buildings.

4. Fighting for direct elections with the participation of teachers, parents, employees, and community associations.

5. Fighting for increasing the number of high schools. (FAMERJ, 1985, p. 20)

During FAMERJ's third congress, in May 1987, 700 neighborhood associations participated and elected Almir Lima as the new president of the federation. It is important to observe the increase in the number of participating associations, from the first congress in 1983 (70) to the third in 1987 (700). This is an indication that FAMERJ is becoming stronger and that the neighborhood associations are fighting with increasing unity. However, 1987 was also the year of the end of Brizola's government. The new governor did not consider education an issue of high priority. The associations' claims concentrated on protecting the benefits introduced by Brizola's government, such as the longer school period, changed from four to eight hours a day.

In the third FAMERJ congress the main topics discussed and issues defined were the following:

1. Public and free education at all levels, including the university.

2. Immediate opening of the full-time schools that were already built and the guarantee that others would be built.

3. Election of school principals by parents, teachers, students, and employees.

4. Creation of public nurseries and kindergartens in the neighborhoods and in work-places. (FAMERJ, 1987)

As can be noted, there is not exactly an evolution in the purpose of the claims. There is an attempt to guarantee what had been won before, such as the election of principals and the full-time school. The associations also tried to amplify the struggle's scope when they made a claim for public and free higher education.

By and large we observe that the associations' main concern is still the fight for schooling, for increasing the number of enrolled children, teachers, and

school buildings, and the amount of school equipment. The neighborhood associations have not reached the stage of fighting for an educational system that
includes better teaching quality, well-trained teachers, and more adequate curricula and instruction. Nor are they fighting for equal educational opportunities.

The interviews with the federations' presidents and with the associations'
directors support this conclusion. Irineu Guimarães, president of FAFERJ, is
aware of the fact that there is still a long way to go until they reach the stage
of higher level demands: "We are growing up but there are still many children
out of school, and we have to fight for more schools. We are waiting for the
right time to fight for a democratic and better education" (personal communication, 1989). The statement of Alencar, former FAMERJ president (1985–87),
presents the same opinion: "There's a very slow evolution from 'wanting to
build or reform schools,' to 'wanting good quality teaching.' From presenting
claims for concrete buildings to discussing deeper educational questions" (interview, 1989). These communities still spend most of their time discussing
how to build and improve the infrastructure of the schools. This makes it difficult to develop discussion on other important matters such as teaching quality
and school democratization.

SCOPE AND LIMITATIONS OF THE NEIGHBORHOOD
ASSOCIATIONS IN RIO DE JANEIRO CITY

The analysis of urban social movements in Brazil, especially those that
emerged during the military dictatorship in the 1970s and 1980s, shows several
features present also in the Spanish urban movements, the ones most studied
to date. Castells (1983) considers that social movements emerge as a spontaneous popular initiative, free from the influence or control of the power elite and
the political parties. Some authors, such as Telles (1983), believe that the Brazilian movements had the capacity to establish "a practice that seemed to break
the tradition of subordination and *clientelismo* that mark the *populismo* years"
(p. 3). Rosa and Raichelis (1985), adopting the same line, emphasize how
important it is that the neighborhood associations "affirm their autonomy"
when defining the forms and the direction of their fight (p. 78).

We believe that the neighborhood associations in Rio are not totally independent of the parties nor of the elite. We found evidence of a *clientelista* relationship when some demagogic individuals influenced the movements. This is not
surprising if we remember that *populismo* lasted until not too long ago, and
that it strongly marked the behavior of the Brazilian politicians and people.

Another point stressed in the literature is the antistate character of the social
movements. The state is viewed as the enemy against whom the associations
must be mobilized. However, from 1983 to 1987 education was considered a
priority by the Rio de Janeiro State government. An official educational plan
was designed to be implemented during this period, including the construction

of 500 new school buildings. In-service training of teachers, curricular reform, and a school day expanded from four to eight hours were among the other measures. In this particular case, it seems that the state emphasis on education was a major trigger inducing new popular demands. So the movement of the associations represented an answer to state stimulation and included education among the social benefits to be fought for.

There is no single answer or method to measure how successful the movement for public school has been in Rio de Janeiro. First of all, the nature of the demands has been very timid, very few, and limited to quantitative features. In addition, after 1987 the movement was not able to maintain some of the benefits already obtained, such as the eight-hour school day. However, it is important to recognize that in Rio de Janeiro, the neighborhood associations have an intrinsic value, independent of how successful they might be in implementing their initiatives. Considering the authoritarian context in which the movement was brought forth, the role it fulfills in developing the notion of citizenship and awareness for civil rights is unquestionable.

The existence of the movement itself has been part of the process of learning citizenship practices. It contributed to informing the workers about social problems, and helped them to form a critical consciousness. We concur with Meksenas (1989), who believes that the process of organizing and fighting for the democratization of the school is an educative process, since it also introduces learning how to participate. Gohn (1982) observes the "formation of a collective self-consciousness" as the result of the movement's daily practice.

The Federation of Neighborhood Associations of Rio de Janeiro represented the first step in the career of some politicians. They started by being candidates for FAMERJ's presidency. There they gained enough experience and exposure to be elected to public posts later. Jo Resende was elected vice-mayor of the city. Others, such as the current member of the City Council Francisco Alencar, were elected for positions of popular representation.

The actions of the neighborhood associations of Rio are criticized for restricting the fight's focus to regional matters. This could bring the risk of weakening the movement once their claims are satisfied. Expanding on this point, Alencar (1990) declares: "The main virtue of the neighborhood associations, that of touching questions of daily life politically, may also be its major limitation as they do not refer to the whole society, nor observe the city and its contradictions" (p. 158).

Another limiting factor in the neighborhood associations' struggle for public education is their excessive emphasis on the expansion of school facilities and enrollment. It is necessary to enlarge the scope of the claims to include the discussion of such issues as the quality of teaching, the equality of educational opportunities, the prejudice against slum children, and the high level of school failure in the popular classes. Finally it is necessary to alter the present type of relationship with students, where the school and the teacher play the role of mediators in the interests of the ruling class, imposing their linguistic code and inadequate curricula, controlling the information, and thus reproducing mechanisms of social stratification.

REFERENCES

Alencar, F. R. (1989) Personal interview.

Alencar, F. R. (1990) *Movimento Associativo de Moradores do Rio: uma nova política está na rua.* Rio de Janeiro: M. A. thesis, Fundação Getulio Vargas.

Castells, M. (1983) *The grassroots and the city.* Berkeley, CA: University of California Press.

FAMERJ. (1983) *Relatório do I Congresso.* Rio de Janeiro: FAMERJ.

FAMERJ. (1985) *Relatório do II Congresso.* Rio de Janeiro: FAMERJ.

FAMERJ. (1987) *Relatório do III Congresso.* Rio de Janeiro: FAMERJ.

Fernandes, F. (1966) *Educação e sociedade no Brasil.* São Paulo: Dominus.

Furtado, C. (1972) *Análise do modelo brasileiro.* Rio de Janeiro: Civilização Brasileira.

Gohn, M. G. (1982) *Reivindicações populares urbanas.* São Paulo: Cortez.

Guimarães, I. (1989) Personal interview.

Ianni, O. (September–October 1989) A questão social, *Revista da USP.*

IBASE. (1990) *Rio de Janeiro: Radiografia das lutas de bairro no estado—1988/1989. Mapeamento das organizações comunitárias filiadas a FAMERJ.* Rio de Janeiro: IBASE.

IBGE Foundation. (1989) *Brasil. Séries estatísticas retrospectivas.* Rio de Janeiro: IBGE.

Jacobi, P. R. (1987) Movimentos sociais urbanos numa época de transição: límites e potencialidades. In Emir Sader (ed.), *Movimentos sociais na transição democrática.* São Paulo: Cortez.

Jacobi, P. R. (1990) Movimentos reivindicatórios urbanos, estado e cultura política: reflexão em torno da ação coletiva e dos seus efeitos político-constitucionais no Brasil. In S. Larangeira (ed.), *Classes e movimentos sociais na América Latina.* São Paulo: Hucitec.

Lambert, J. (1959) *Os dois Brasíls.* Rio de Janeiro: INEP-CBPE.

Meksenas, P. (1989) *Sociologia da educação: introdução ao estudo da escola.* Rio de Janeiro: Paz e Terra.

Muniz, P. R. (July 1989) Personal communication.

Oliveira, S. (1985) *Associação de moradores, formato diferenciado de participação e representações de interesses.* Rio de Janeiro: M.A. thesis, State University of Rio de Janeiro.

Ribeiro, D. (1986) *O Livro dos CIEP.* Rio de Janeiro: Bloch Editores.

Rosa, C. M., and Raichelis, R. O. (December 1985) O serviço social e os movimentos sociais. *Serviço Social e Sociedade 6,* pp. 74–97.

Sodre, N. W. (1972) *Síntese da história da cultura brasileira.* Rio de Janeiro: Civilizacão Brasileira.

Telles, V. S. (January 1983) *Autonomia e subordinação na prática dos movimentos sociais.* São Paulo: ASESP.

9

The Growth Machine and the Politics of Urban Educational Reform: The Case of Charlotte, North Carolina

*Roslyn Mickelson, Carol Ray,
and Stephen Smith*

At least since the appearance of *A Nation at Risk* (National Commission on Educational Excellence, 1983), the allegedly weak condition of the American educational system has been a topic of discussion among parents and political leaders. *A Nation at Risk* legitimized claims of critics who contended that America's schools were a threat to this country's economic, social, and political well-being. Even today, hardly a month goes by without a high-level conference, task force, foundation report, or governmental study reinforcing the 1983 report's claims that the horrible state of America's schools makes it impossible for the United States to compete effectively in the international economy. Clearly, educational reform is an important item on the agenda of people throughout the country. The rhetoric of school reform today is, to a large degree, grounded in this particular formulation of the educational crisis facing the nation. It is not surprising, then, that business leaders at both the local and national levels have become increasingly involved in the politics and process of school reform.

This chapter examines how political battles over educational reform have recently developed in one urban school district, Charlotte-Mecklenburg, North Carolina, from 1987 to 1992. The theoretical perspective used to interpret this case study is the growth machine model of urban politics, which analyzes cities as political entities in which the ethic of growth pervades virtually all aspects of urban life (Logan and Molotch, 1987, p. 13). The growth machine is a powerful configuration of interlocking businesses, associations, and governmental units. The growth elite is composed of activists who are owners and top officers of local newspapers, ultilities, supermarkets and department stores, property investment and real estate development firms, and banks and other financial institutions (Logan and Molotch, 1987, pp. 70–74). Top executives of regional firms headquartered in a city, directors of museums and other cultural institutions, and leaders of universities and community colleges are also supporters of urban growth. Members of the growth elite rely on an urban place for income from sales and rents. Their ability to move their income-producing activities to a new locale is limited. Because the markets for their enterprises may become saturated if growth is slow, growth elite activists compete with other cities to attract new businesses and, thus, new residents who will consume the land, retail services, and products of local growth elites' products or services.

Individual growth elite activists act on behalf of community growth by virtue of their organizational position, rather than their personal goals. As capitalists of place, united by a doctrine of value-free development, members share a set of class interests. Aggregate growth, from their perspective, is a public good which benefits the whole community. Growth brings jobs, expands the tax base, and pays for the urban infrastructure (Logan and Molotch, 1987, pp. 32–33). There is, however, a tension between generating the taxes needed to provide the necessary infrastructure for business and establishing a "good business climate" to attract growth.

By creating a "good business climate" through sympathetic local government, all manner of favorable incentives for companies who relocate can be provided. Important among these incentives are low taxes. Moreover, a key growth machine actor, the local Chamber of Commerce, may promote its city as offering harmonious and progressive race relations and fine public schools. These qualities imply a literate and disciplined work force available to relocating firms, as well as good schools for the employees who relocate with their families. Any public policy or political agenda of any group that may hinder growth and development is opposed by the growth elite (Logan and Molotch, 1987, p. 32). Similarly, growth activists try to hamper any activities that may generate public controversy or social unrest, for these may discourage prospective newcomers.

Charlotte, North Carolina, a rapidly growing city of 400,000 in a metropolitan area of over one million people, serves as a good illustration of the growth machine model. Its Chamber of Commerce and other growth activists actively campaign to attract firms to Charlotte and are, by all accounts, highly successful. The low costs of living, land, labor, and taxes are quite appealing to prospective firms, and the city's growth activists have generally been able to promote the community's race relations as harmonious and, until recently, the Charlotte-Mecklenburg schools as excellent.

Three key issues make this urban district especially worthy of study. First, a great deal of the tension involved in urban school reform derives from the fact that the growth elite has been highly successful in persuading firms to relocate in this county. Charlotte's attractiveness to corporate leaders was recognized by *Fortune* magazine, which, in the fall of 1991, ranked the city as having the seventh best business climate in the nation (*Fortune*, 1991). Yet, what makes this place attractive to business—low taxes and cheap labor—has negative consequences for the local infrastructure. Schools (as well as roads, sewers, and other basic elements of the infrastructure) are seriously underfunded and have become the target of much criticism, especially by new residents in the area. In 1987, vocal relocated executives confronted the growth elite and were successful in bringing the question of the quality of the local schools into public debate. Their efforts culminated in a 1987 Chamber of Commerce Task Force on Education and Jobs. The creation of this task force and the recommendations of its final report herald the intersection of the local reform movement, the Reagan/Bush administrations' school reform plans, and questions of educational equity.

Second, *Swann v. Charlotte-Mecklenburg*, the 1971 landmark Supreme Court case allowing within-district busing as a remedy for dismantling segregation, originated in this district. By most accounts, the district's busing plan has been one of the most successful, if not *the* most successful metropolitan desegregation plan in the country (Hochschild, 1984; Gaillard, 1988; Monfort and Orfield, 1988). Consequently, attempts to reform Charlotte's educational system inevitably raise especially vivid questions about the relation among the proposed reforms, school desegregation, and educational equity in urban settings.

Finally, the relationship between local reform efforts and the agendas of national education, business, and political leaders is singularly apparent in Charlotte. The Charlotte-Mecklenburg district's superintendent, his administration's current and past association with the federal Department of Education, and the district's selection by the Reagan administration as a site for the examination of parental school choice suggest the importance of Charlotte as a case study of the politics and process of urban educational reform.

HISTORY OF DESEGREGATION IN CHARLOTTE

Any discussion of recent educational reform efforts in Charlotte must be placed in the context of the history of this countywide district's efforts to desegregate its schools. African-Americans—schoolchildren, parents, educators, as well as attorneys, who were sometimes the targets of both actual and threatened violence and whose steadfastness was the *sine qua non* of whatever progress was made—first challenged the segregated schools in the 1960s (Gaillard, 1988). Following the Supreme Court's decision to uphold federal district court judge James McMillan's judgment in *Swann*, a wide multiracial coalition of the district's residents made a determined effort to overcome segregation's poisonous legacy and to help bring about the implementation of what became widely understood as "the law of the land." Critical to these efforts was the role of many white business, religious, and civic leaders and the growth elite, whose involvement in mitigating potential racial conflict dates back to efforts to desegregate public accommodations in the mid-1960s.

Legend has it—and there is substantial evidence to support it (Gaillard, 1988; Piedmont Airlines, 1985)—that during the early 1960s Charlotte's growth elite activists cast their eyes northward to Greensboro, North Carolina, saw the social unrest surrounding the lunch counter sit-ins, and concluded that desegregation of public accommodations was inevitable. These leaders reasoned that it would be in the community's best long-term interests if they could control the process and thereby avoid negative headlines and possible violence. Shortly thereafter, Charlotte desegregated its public accommodations. Accounts of this period report that a group of prominent white businessmen invited a group of prominent black businessmen to a very visible luncheon at a downtown restaurant.

Almost a decade after the desegregation of public accommodations, Charlotte faced a similar challenge. In 1971 the Supreme Court upheld the decision of Judge McMillan, who had ruled in *Swann v. Charlotte-Mecklenburg* that busing was an appropriate remedy for school segregation. Once again far-sighted business leaders concerned about Charlotte's business climate joined with religious and civic leaders to forge a consensus among the warring factions. They helped craft a solution which desegregated the schools in ways that ultimately led to continued racial and social peace as well as rapid growth and economic prosperity for the city. In doing this, Charlotte's reputation as a good place to live, work, and relocate one's business remained untainted. Economic growth and development flourished throughout the following two decades.

The growth machine model of urban politics articulates nicely with what several observers (Gaillard, 1988; Orfield, 1981) describe as the particular social and political conditions which enabled Charlotte to desegregate in the 1970s. The growth elite is perhaps best exemplified by the activities of W. T. Harris, who, because of the regional supermarket chain bearing his name and his service as chair of the Board of County Commissioners, was one of the city's most prominent businessmen and civic leaders. At a crucial point in the desegregation consensus-building process in the 1970s, he played a pivotal role by lobbying opponents to accept mandatory busing for school desegregation (Gaillard, 1988, pp. 143–50).[1]

The peaceful and successful desegregation of Charlotte-Mecklenburg schools in the mid-1970s must be understood within the context of that specific historical period. No matter what the level of personal commitment or opposition to equality of educational opportunity through desegregated schooling among members, as a coalition the growth elite was unified in its support for and activities on behalf of desegregation. For example, one growth elite activist, Charlotte developer and then school board member C. D. Spangler (currently the president of the University of North Carolina), not only supported the policy as a board member, but sent his children to newly desegregated schools in the heart of the black community.

Arguably, the best indication of continued support by the growth elite and the larger community for Charlotte's busing plan occurred in 1984 when President Reagan visited Charlotte as part of his campaign for reelection. Departing from his standard campaign speech, he criticized busing as a "social experiment that nobody wants" (Gaillard, 1988, p. 152). Unlike virtually all his other remarks, these comments about busing "were greeted with silence: uncomfortable, embarrassed, almost stony." As the *Charlotte Observer* subsequently said in an editorial entitled "You Were Wrong, Mr. President," the city's "proudest achievement of the past 20 years is not the city's impressive new skyline or its strong growing economy. Its proudest achievement is its fully integrated school system" (Gaillard, 1988, p. 153).

By the late 1980s, however, the consensus about Charlotte's schools that civil rights activists, the growth elite, and a wide range of other citizens had worked so hard to build was in danger of unraveling. In part, this was due to the very success of the growth elite in persuading businesses to relocate to Charlotte. Relocated firms typically bring top-level managers, professionals, and technical personnel and their families to their new site. Unlike many longtime Charlotteans of various races and classes who are familiar with the city's desegregated schools and often proud of their history, many relocated middle-class whites from the North and Midwest find little in the school system of which to be proud. Moreover, the desegregation plan crafted in the 1970s had been regularly altered, but never overhauled to address completely the changing demographics of the county. Consequently, certain students faced extremely long bus rides and others in naturally integrated neighborhoods were bused to outlying schools. Unhappy corporate families complained to the top management of their firms about the local schools.

The economic prosperity of relocated firms, unlike the prosperity of the growth elite, whose business success is intimately tied to local and regional economic development, is more heavily dependent on national if not international markets. These firms' relocated employees have little interest in or knowledge of the history of current local agreements and alliances (Logan and Molotch, 1987, p. 84). Nor do they share the pride in or understand the fragility of the consensus around many school issues. To this difference can be added other forces which have dramatically shaped recent battles about educational reform—the demands not only of national corporate officers but also of local businesspeople that the schools do a better job of preparing and training the non-college-bound work force. These demands are linked to the escalating nationwide concern about the allegedly deplorable state of the country's schools, and various doubts about the district's pioneering busing plan. Moreover, the federal government's role in school desegregation has changed dramatically during the past twelve years. While the federal courts and the executive branch have at times played different roles in school desegregation, today the administration and the courts are actively pursuing the dismantling of existing school desegregation plans across the nation (Carr and Ziegler, 1990). Finally, the policy of school choice, central to President Bush's "America 2000" program (U.S. Department of Education, 1991), may also jeopardize desegregation and educational equity (Blank, 1991; Cookson, 1992; Clune and Witte, 1991; Gewirtz, 1986; Merl, 1991; Metz, 1991; Moore, 1991; Nakao, 1989; Orfield, 1991; Thernstrom, 1990).

These factors set the stage for a turning point in Charlotte's educational history: On 31 March 1992 the Charlotte-Mecklenburg school board unanimously approved a plan to end districtwide busing for desegregation. The policy adopted in its stead is a voluntary integration plan which utilizes parental choice of magnet schools, the creation of midpoint schools (between black and white neighborhoods), and the location of new schools only in areas with at least 10 percent black residents. The adopted plan contains several amendments designed to address the concerns of those who feared the end of busing for desegregation would result in the resegregation of the district. Before voting to end busing and begin parental choice of magnet schools, the school board reaffirmed its commitment to its proclaimed mission to "become the premier urban integrated system in the nation. . . ." (*Charlotte Observer*, 1992a).

The remainder of this chapter will examine closely three recent phases of school reform. First, the Charlotte Chamber of Commerce's Task Force on Education and Jobs; second, the elections for the Charlotte-Mecklenburg Board of Education; and finally, the developing role of the Charlotte-Mecklenburg district as an archetype or test case for the Bush administration's program for educational reform, and the influence of the increasingly close links between national and state actors involved in defining the reform agenda on the school reform decisions made in Charlotte.

THE CHAMBER OF COMMERCE TASK FORCE

Perhaps the best indication of the extent to which the consensus around Charlotte's schools was in danger of unraveling is illustrated by the issues raised by the Task Force on Education and Jobs formed by the Charlotte Chamber of Commerce in late 1987. The impetus for this task force came from several top executives of large firms that had recently relocated to Charlotte. In early 1987 these men approached the Chamber of Commerce with complaints about the schools. Bolstered by national discussions about inferior schools, critics charged that the schools were inadequate and, therefore, the labor pool from which they hired entry-level workers was defective. Non-college-educated new workers not only lacked many literacy skills but, most importantly, they lacked the work ethic. These corporate leaders expressed dissatisfaction with the "products" of the schools who had troublesome traits like "immaturity," "failure to show up on time," and a sense that businesses "owe them something." Most worrisome was the absence among young workers of "social discipline that respects and understands authority." One employer observed, "It's just like they have their own unions 'cause they can leave one job and just go down the street to find another." Another business leader complained, "They need to learn to do what people tell them." The relocated corporate officers demanded that the Chamber of Commerce "do something about the schools" because it was the Chamber that lured their firms to Charlotte in the first place.

In response to this pressure, the Chamber of Commerce initiated the Task Force on Education and Jobs in November 1987. Its membership included representatives from relocated firms, local businesses, elected officialdom, the school board, the school district administration, and local civil rights organizations. The Task Force's formal mission was to identify the work force needs of local business, assess the degree to which schools were meeting these needs, and propose reforms. What is needed, the Chamber's director said in his opening address at the first meeting of the Task Force, are "higher education skills and capabilities" to "match employers' needs" so that the United States can successfully "compete with other countries," and so that Charlotte can "compete with other cities."

The field research for this study began with the first meeting of the Task Force.[2] Prior to the first meeting the researchers approached the chair of the Task Force, the chancellor emeritus of the university where they taught, and requested permission to observe the deliberations of the Task Force. On the first day of the Task Force, he introduced the researchers and asked if any of the participants objected to their presence. Although the Task Force meetings were not open to the public, no one objected. From November 1987 to August 1988 the researchers observed at all the meetings of the Task Force, at its business subcommittee meetings, at final report-writing sessions, and at other public events concerning education. They took field notes and kept interpretive journals. After the Task Force completed its work in August 1988, they conducted semistructured in-depth interviews with key members of the Task Force, the school district's administrative staff, civic leaders, and major business leaders who represented both the growth elite and relocated firms.

The second phase of the research entailed examining business-led school reform efforts at the national level. During 1990 the authors conducted lengthy interviews with policy analysts in public and private research institutions and in government bureaucracies. During the present phase, field observations have continued with the Charlotte-Mecklenburg Educational Foundation and the World Class Schools panel, as well as interviews with local and state figures active in school reform, including educational officials, and also members of the judiciary, the general public, and the business community.

While the quality of the work force was the formal topic of the Task Force, informally, a number of relocated executives turned their sights toward another target—the class- and race-desegregated schools their relocated employees' children attended. Top executives of many firms which had recently moved to

Charlotte were besieged by complaints about the schools from their upper- and mid-level managerial and professional staffs.[3] Prior to moving to Charlotte, these families typically lived in homogeneously white, upper-middle-class suburbs where the schools' population reflected the demographics of the suburbs. Charlotte's race- and class-integrated schools were very different from the public schools previously experienced by the relocated families. The relocated executives wanted the Chamber to play a role in beginning to dismantle the desegregated school system.

Among the controversies that growth elite activists believe hinder urban economic development are those concerning race and school busing (Logan and Molotch, 1987, p. 60). Charlotte's growth elite, including the officers of the Chamber of Commerce, made a decision prior to the formation of the Task Force that desegregation and busing would not be part of the official agenda. Informants told the investigators that even before the Task Force was announced publicly, its leaders had decided that any discussion of busing would open a Pandora's box that growth activists wished to leave closed. When an antibusing activist requested permission to address the Task Force, for instance, the executive director of the Chamber of Commerce refused the request.

At the first meeting of the Task Force, its chair appointed a business subcommittee to identify the needs of local business and to make recommendations to the entire Task Force.[4] Relocated executives dominated (and one chaired) the subcommittee. Representatives of the growth elite attended but did not participate actively in discussions. A Chamber of Commerce representative was an exception. He played the role of keeping the subcommittee on task; that is, whenever relocated executives brought up the topics of desegregation or busing, he steered the discussion back to the formally mandated reason for the Task Force. At the subcommittee meetings, nonetheless, the researchers learned of the depth of the antipathy toward local desegregated schools shared by relocated executives. These sentiments surfaced both in formal discussions and informal conversations before and after the subcommittee meetings (for greater detail see Ray and Mickelson, 1989 and 1990).

The subcommittee's deliberations led to two policy recommendations which, if implemented in the schools, relocated members argued, would improve them and ultimately produce better workers. First, they advocated more extensive tracking and second, with greater force and conviction, they called for the consolidation of vocational education in one centralized high school rather than the current plan, which disperses the programs throughout the eleven comprehensive high schools in the district. The relocated executives suggested that the vocational-technical magnet high school should be located in the central city near businesses which could donate resources and expertise. Charlotte's African-American community is also concentrated in the central city (see Figure 9.1).

Historically, vocational education has been aimed disproportionately at working-class and minority youth (Lazerson and Grubb, 1974; Shor, 1986;

Figure 9.1
Black Population Distribution in Mecklenburg County, 1990

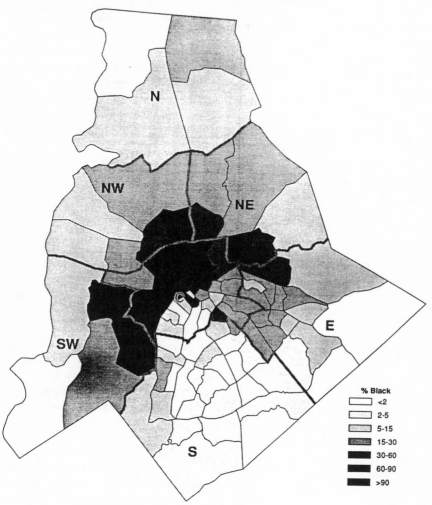

Wrigley, 1982). If the subcommittee's recommendations were implemented, the centralized vocational high school would likely siphon off from the other ten suburban schools a large proportion of the working-class and minority student population which vocal critics among relocated business leaders argued "doesn't want to learn and ruins the schools for the serious students who do."

Following the subcommittee's presentation of its recommendations, the educators responded. They literally salvaged these two proposals by presenting overwhelming counterevidence that greater tracking and centralized vocational education would not provide better workers for a variety of pedagogic, curricular, and developmental reasons. They even invited expert witnesses, including a former governor active in educational reform, to testify to that effect. Moreover, educators argued that in addition to the stigma attached to vocational education as the curriculum of the "losers," it also fails to prepare students for the contemporary workplace because the narrow vocational skills taught are vulnerable to obsolescence due to rapid technological change. Finally, a major outcome of centralized vocational education of which the educators were certain was that it would seriously undermine desegregated education in Charlotte because vocational education students were (and still are) traditionally from working-class and minority families. Educators were unanimous in declaring desegregated education a nonnegotiable aspect of district policy. Importantly, they argued that maintaining desegregated education was crucial for any attempts to offer equality of educational opportunity.

But having pulled the rug out from under the relocated business executives' analysis of the problem and having denigrated their key reform proposals for improving the future work force, the educators were forced to offer their own analysis. It is crucial to recall that the educators perceive desegregated education as a central element in their efforts to provide equality of opportunity for "at-risk youth." Their argument against tracking and centralized vocational education was part of a larger strategy to maintain this policy. Nevertheless, educators then had to explain the apparent deficiencies found among entry-level workers. They claimed that the source of the problem was not the schools in general or the current vocational education programs in particular. The problem was the nature of the student who traditionally enrolls in these courses and then becomes the entry-level worker that business must hire, namely low-income and minority youth. And the reason that these youth were marginal students who later become disappointing employees was that their parents had failed to motivate them, monitor them, and provide them with "good role models."

The definition of the problem facing businesses proffered by educators concentrated on the "children at risk" and their parents. The solution educators recommended, flowing from this assessment of the problem, was an expansion of early childhood education. Consequently, even though educators believed desegregated education was crucial to attempts to offer equality of educational opportunity for minority students, in order to preserve desegregated schooling Charlotte's educators ultimately indicted the poor and their children as the source of the problems in the schools and later in the workplace.

In the end, the perspective of the educators prevailed in no small part because it was supported by the growth elite. The final report of the Task Force stressed that poverty and the poor were here to stay. The major recommendations of the Task Force followed the analysis of the problem offered by educators and called for an expansion of early childhood education. The relocated business executives failed to convince the larger Task Force that greater tracking and centralized vocational education were appropriate solutions; in the report the recommendation for highly centralized vocational education appeared as one of many peripheral suggestions. Educators and growth elite representatives on the Task Force joined together and controlled the debate in ways that maintained (at least for a time) the legitimacy of claims that Charlotte is a good place to live, work, and relocate one's business.

The indirect challenge to desegregation failed. But relocated executives won a subtle victory. Recall that they were deeply concerned with "the disgusting things which go on at the end of the bus ride," presumably caused by ill-behaved and poorly motivated black and working-class students. The final report of the Task Force highlighted precisely these students, the so-called children-at-risk. In other words, the final report upheld indirectly the relocated executives' analysis of what is wrong with the schools. Most importantly, the criticism and reform of the Charlotte-Mecklenburg schools became legitimate political discourse following the release of the final report of the Task Force.

SCHOOL BOARD ELECTIONS

School board elections were the second arena in which the political battles over school reform were fought. Throughout the two decades since the *Swann* decision, the community's leaders have embraced Charlotte's desegregated schools as its "proudest achievement." Although, as indicated above, the late 1970s and early 1980s were characterized by broad community support for Charlotte's school system and its desegregation plan, this support was not unanimous. For example, as early as 1978, just three years after the federal court had announced its satisfaction with the school board's busing plan and when much of Charlotte's political community was committed to making desegregation work, an education writer for the *Charlotte Observer* noted that "transplanted Northerners" were especially angry at busing. He quoted one recently arrived Charlottean who said, "When we moved down here from Albany, [New York], we bought a house out here in Providence Plantation [an affluent outlying neighborhood] so we could get our kids out of inner-city schools. But dammit, you got us anyway." This woman illustrated the core theme in Charlotte's antibusing movement of that decade: "The most vocal and highly organized opposition comes from suburbs filled with transplanted Northerners transferred to Charlotte by large corporations shifting their operations to the Sunbelt. The parents are disappointed with what they consider an inferior Southern school system, and their irritation is compounded by the forced busing many had expected to leave behind in Northern cities" (Nadler, 1979, p. 315).[5]

Unlike the current dissatisfaction described in the previous section, the sentiments described by Nadler failed to mobilize enough votes to win a school board election from the mid-1970s through the mid-1980s. This was due, in large part, to the consensus among the growth elite that antibusing sentiments were not "good" for the city and its future growth and development (Logan and Molotch, 1987). The image of Charlotte conveyed by civic, business, and religious leaders was one of the "New South," a place where all people of goodwill can live and work in ecumenical and racial harmony. Not until 1986 did a conservative fundamentalist Christian, campaigning on a school prayer and neighborhood school platform, get elected to the school board. She was the first outspokenly antibusing candidate to win election to the school board since the desegregation battles a decade earlier.

Between the 1986 and 1988 elections (board elections are held every two years), several developments internal to the school district administration allowed antibusing forces to mobilize. Jay Robinson, the widely respected school superintendent, resigned to take a position with the University of North Carolina system. A native North Carolinian who strongly supported busing, Robinson had charisma and an intimate knowledge of the region's politics, both of which provided a bulwark against earlier incipient challenges to Charlotte's desegregation plan.

Chosen to replace Robinson in 1987 was a Northern educator with little experience in the South, Peter Relic. He made it clear that he was committed professionally and ethically to desegregation. A strong believer in participatory democracy and openness, he attempted to guide the school district according to these principles. During his first year in office Relic decided to sponsor a series of five community forums to permit the public to react to the proposed biennial adjustments in the pupil reassignment plan and to legitimate any changes which would occur.

These forums took place in early 1988 before the school board elections and included many vitriolic denouncements of busing largely from people who were not native Southerners.[6] Knowledgeable observers believe this series of forums provided a platform for critics, many of whom were newcomers to the community, who were waiting for "a window of opportunity" to challenge the desegregation plan. Both supporters and opponents of busing attribute these community forums with providing the newcomers not only the opportunity to speak out against busing and desegregation, but with the opportunity to organize their forces as well.

Their efforts were largely successful. In the 1988 election, four pro-busing/ integration incumbents (with twenty-eight years of collective school board experience) were defeated. The four new members included a woman who campaigned on a specific anti-busing platform and three men who agreed that bus rides ought to be shortened and that magnet schools should be explored as viable alternatives to busing for integration. An analysis of voting by precincts indicates that the 1988 election brought to the polls large numbers of residents of southeast Charlotte, an area with a disproportionately large number of transplanted Northerners. At the same time, voter turnout in the other areas of the city was minimal. The makeup of the school board at this time included two outspoken opponents of busing, four proponents of it, and three people whose position was somewhere between the others.

After the 1988 election, there was widespread speculation offered both in the media and by several informants that the days of busing for desegregation were numbered.[7] Given the changing demographics of the city and the results of the 1988 election, many supporters of desegregated education dreaded the 1990 school board election, especially because three of the four pro-desegregation members were up for reelection.

Approximately a dozen candidates sought election for the four places on the school board that were on the ballot. None of the three pro-busing incumbents sought reelection; however, the anti-busing incumbent (first elected in 1986) did. The field of candidates included several people whose campaign literature and yard signs called for an end to forced busing, the expansion of neighborhood schools, and school choice. Ignoring many of the complexities of the policy, opponents of busing made parental choice one of their rallying cries— along with a return to neighborhood schools. The joint advocacy of parental choice of schools, a return to neighborhood schools, and an end to busing for desegregation suggests the population of citizens to whom the policy of choice was targeted: disenchanted, affluent white suburbanites active in the efforts which resulted in the Chamber's 1987 Task Force.

The 1990 election results disappointed the anti-busing constituency. With the exception of the anti-busing incumbent first elected in 1986, none of the anti-busing candidates was elected. In fact, the three seats vacated by supporters of busing were filled by white newcomers to the board, all of whom fundamentally supported busing as a tool for desegregation.

As in most elections, the candidate selection process played an important role in explaining results. The growth elite was actively involved in the campaigns of two of the successful white candidates who supported desegregated schooling. One of the successful candidates, a highly respected child advocate who had never before sought elective office, had initially hoped to manage the campaign of the second successful candidate, a banker personally connected to the growth elite. Instead, members of the growth elite encouraged the child advocate to run and offered to make generous campaign contributions. Members of the growth elite said they did not want any "fringe candidates" winning a seat on the board. When asked what "fringe candidate" meant, the child advocate replied, "You know, supporters of school choice." Recall that in the 1990 Charlotte school board elections opponents of busing linked this policy position to school choice. The growth elite feared that public rancor surrounding any debate over an end to busing in Charlotte would jeopardize the city's efforts to attract a National Football League franchise as well as tarnish the city's image in a more general public relations sense. According to informants, this is why the growth elite actively supported and financially backed the two white pro-desegregation candidates for the school board. The third pro-desegregation candidate was an incumbent and a black minister popular throughout the city. He, the child advocate, and the conservative Christian incumbent won seats on the board in the general election. The fourth seat would be filled by the winner of a runoff election between the pro-desegregation banker supported by the growth elite and the anti-busing/parental choice "fringe candidate."

The school board runoff election was held simultaneously with the Democratic Party's senatorial candidate runoff election. One of the two runoff candidates was former Charlotte mayor, Harvey Gantt, an African-American whose candidacy galvanized both liberal white Democrats and large segments of the African-American community to turn out at the polls. Independents and Republicans were less likely to vote in this runoff election. Analysis of voting returns by precinct indicates that the residents of affluent, conservative, white southeast Charlotte voted to support the anti-busing/parental choice candidate but turned out in too few numbers to offset the large turnout in other areas of the city, particularly in the black community (*Charlotte Observer*, 1990).

Shortly after the new school board was seated in 1990, Superintendent Relic resigned. The new board, now composed of two conservative anti-busing members, two moderates, and five individuals committed to desegregated schooling, faced its first major task: the hiring of a new superintendent. Their choice of John Murphy in the spring of 1991 positioned the district to be at the center of national educational reform efforts.

CHOICE AND FEDERAL SCHOOL REFORM EFFORTS

While proclaiming that public education is a local and state responsibility, both the Bush and Reagan administrations took unprecedented steps to shape and channel school reform. Market-oriented policies and practices, like parental choice, were central to these efforts. Choice was supported by both the Reagan and Bush administrations, the latter's support in part indicated by the selection of Lamar Alexander as secretary of education and David Kearns, former CEO of Xerox, as deputy secretary. Both men were ardent advocates of parental choice of schools. President Bush's "America 2000" program proposed to Congress called for the expansion of parental choice in the public schools and, in some cases, private schools as well (Heritage Foundation, 1991). The connection between this policy initiative and Charlotte was both direct and indirect. The direct link was Charlotte's selection in 1989 by the Bush administration as one of five districts nationwide whose efforts at implementing school choice would presumably serve as a model for the rest of the country, although at the time of its selection choice in the Charlotte system consisted of five "optional" schools. The second connection involved Superintendent John Murphy and his efforts to restructure education and create a "world-class educational system" in Charlotte. This policy initiative involved direct and indirect connections with the federal education bureaucracy as well as with state and nonstate actors active in market-oriented educational reforms.

A little over a year after the 1987–88 Chamber of Commerce Task Force on Education and Jobs filed its final report, members of the Reagan administration invited Charlotte to participate as one of five pilot districts in an experimental federal policy/program of parental choice of schools. In November 1989 a Department of Education conference called "Choosing Better Schools" took place in Charlotte. The conference opened with a video address by President Bush, who proclaimed, "Choice works!" and included as speakers then U.S. secretary of education Lauro Cavazos and David Kearns, then CEO of Xerox and subsequently the deputy secretary of education.

Because of concerns about the federal government's pilot choice program and its track record on school desegregation, many parents and educators voiced their fears about a districtwide choice plan for Charlotte. They made clear their concern that such a plan would be a Trojan horse, threatening and eventually destroying desegregation and equitable educational experiences for all children. That meeting ostensibly in support of choice turned into a forum dominated by citizens leery of such plans (see Ray and Mickelson, 1989, 1990 for more detailed accounts of these events). In 1989 few if any changes resulted from the conference or from Charlotte's initial designation as a pilot district for school choice. The decision to adopt parental choice was to come three years later.

THE NEW SUPERINTENDENT

With the arrival in the summer of 1991 of a new superintendent, Charlotte's centrality to the federal government's efforts to reform education intensified and parental choice once again became a topic of public debate. John Murphy, whose reform efforts as superintendent of schools of Prince George's County, Maryland, attracted national attention, had a reputation as one of the nation's best superintendents. Former secretary of education William Bennett described him as "one of the three best superintendents in the country and I can't recall the names of the other two" (*Charlotte Observer*, 1991). During his tenure in Maryland, Murphy developed a close working relationship with researchers in the U.S. Department of Education's Office of Educational Research and Investigation (OERI) which, with the approval of then secretary William Bennett, used the district as a pilot site to test the utility and validity of recent educational research. As one associate of Murphy's tells it, Murphy

kind of popped into the U.S. Education Department . . . and he being as research driven as he is said, "Look, I want to call your bluff, if you say there's research out there that can make a difference, I'll open up Prince George's County System to you. Set up any kind of operation you want to try to take that research and force us to make those changes, and let's see if it works. And besides we'll do it in a way that you [informant] still work for the U.S. Department of Education so when we learn what we learn here you can take it back there [OERI]. . . .''

Bill Bennett was the secretary then. We met with him and he agreed. So for about a two-and-a-half or three-year period I [informant] was still an employee of OERI but stationed, if you will, in Prince George's County trying to see if we couldn't establish a prototype there that would be in formal touch with the R&D network around the country and try to make the changes that would be necessary. What was really interesting about that experience . . . is that there was a convergence of two things. One, is that there was my sense that we either knew or could tap into what R&D was generating around the country and what was effective. And then there was the superintendent's sense of what kind of system you had to create in which to embed that, those new practices, to increase the chances that they would succeed.

WORLD CLASS SCHOOLS

When Murphy came to Charlotte in the fall of 1991 he brought with him several of his Prince George's County team members, including the former OERI employee previously on loan to the Maryland district. Murphy also brought with him access to an extensive network of federal education officials and researchers, as well as national figures in educational research and school reform. Nothing better illustrates this than Murphy's ability to assemble a team of national education experts to redesign the Charlotte schools and create a prototype of a world-class school system. The funding for this project came from two private sources associated with the conservative political agenda. Soon after he arrived, Murphy announced that in December of 1991 a panel of national educational experts had agreed to participate in a World Class Schools Panel which would sketch the broad contours of the reforms needed in the district to make Charlotte graduates competitive nationally and internationally. The national education leaders participating in the effort included William Bennett, former education secretary; Ernest Boyer, president of the Carnegie Foundation for the Advancement of Teaching; Denis P. Doyle, author and senior fellow at the Hudson Institute; Chester E. Finn, Jr., Vanderbilt University professor; Patricia A. Graham, Harvard University professor and president of the Spencer Foundation; John Slaughter, president of Occidental College; Donald Stewart, president of the College Board; and Matina Horner, vice president of TIAA-CREF. James A. Kelly, president of the National Board for Professional Teaching Standards, served as the moderator.

Both the composition of the World Class Schools Panel and the words Murphy used to define its purpose suggest that he shared many of the Bush administration's assumptions regarding the centrality of market principles to school restructuring. In his letter inviting the experts to participate in the World Class Schools Panel, Superintendent Murphy said,

Recently we have seen the publication and wide acceptance of a number of books extolling the virtues of redefining and completely overhauling the schools. The works of

Chester Finn, David Kearns, Denis Doyle, and the America 2000 initiative recently announced by President Bush and the Secretary of Education, reflect this orientation and have begun to "set the stage" for meaningful change to occur. These authors and others have begun to lay out the parameters of a "world-class school system" which would re-establish our nation's pre-eminent position in economic, technical, and cultural matters. We now have a clear sense from a philosophical point of view [how] to make a difference and only need the will and opportunity to translate their philosophical points into a detailed specific plan for restructuring an entire school system. (Murphy, 1991)

The first meeting of the panel experts, which took place in Charlotte on 18 December 1991, was closed to the public but was videotaped. Both the comments of several informants and an analysis of the videotape and the minutes of the first meeting indicate that the panel's primary discussions addressed "the student competencies desired" in a world-class school system. The meeting revolved around issues of standards, curricula, expectations, assessment, and the possibility that 30 percent of students who are "at-risk" might need special schools. Doyle, Finn, and Bennett cautioned against permitting the poor or *"the pathologically impaired"* [authors' italics] students to drive the whole educational program. Parental choice was mentioned as a necessary reform by three members but only in passing. According to a school board member, this was because Murphy had warned the group not to push school choice or vouchers lest such discussions alienate the school board (which at that time had not yet decided to accept the recommendation to replace mandatory busing with a choice plan which was to come forth in several months).

The focus of the second meeting, held on 17 March 1992, was the redesign of the educational delivery system. This meeting was open to the public, and the first author was present. Several members who attended the first meeting were not present and two panel members attended for the first time. Moments before the panel began its work, one of the panelists who missed the first meeting exclaimed to Denis Doyle, "I don't have a clue what we're doing here." Doyle assured the panelist that all that was necessary was to sit around and chat about the educational issues on the agenda. The issues which were bantered about in the next six hours of free-ranging conversation included (in the order in which they were raised) mastery learning, tracking, organization of schools by grades and classrooms, report cards, IEPs (individualized educational plans), early childhood education, technology, cooperative learning, children at risk, coordinating services for children at school sites, discipline, and finally, parental choice. Chester Finn raised parental choice as a discipline strategy: "People behave better if they've chosen a place to go to school." Donald Stewart responded, "Choice is a most difficult issue . . ." Finn jokingly interrupted, "I thought I just handled it." Everyone laughed. Arguing that "choice will not solve the discipline problem," Stewart cautioned that race and class issues complicate choice plans. Graham noted that "the details make or break a choice plan." Kelly reminded the group that school structure is not a powerful explanatory variable and that school choice drew its strength from its ability to connect parents back to schools. Just before the group adjourned for lunch, Kelly summed up the choice debate, "There is nominal agreement that more choice is desirable."

The final meeting of the World Class Schools Panel, held on 29 April 1992, was almost an anticlimax. This is because during the period between the second and third sessions, a far-reaching reform had been adopted when, on 31 March 1992, the school board voted unanimously to institute a system of parental choice among magnet schools as an alternative to busing for desegregation (see below). The meeting's official agenda covered obstacles to reform such as "lack of student readiness to learn, teacher competencies, and regulatory restrictions on local schools" (*Charlotte Observer*, 1992b). When the final session drew to a close, the panelists praised Murphy's vision and requested feedback about reform efforts in one year.

The actual utility of the World Class Schools Panel's deliberations for school reform in Charlotte remains unclear. The Panel's stated goal was to establish general concepts and principles, while the actual reforms were to come from the community of Charlotte itself. In interviews shortly after the third meeting several growth activists and two school board members stated that they believed the discussions of the panel were so far-ranging and general, that the informal value of the enterprise was to legitimize any reforms Murphy might propose. Subsequent interviews with members of the World Class Panel confirmed their analysis. Several World Class Panel members expressed incredulity that anyone would seriously think three day-long meetings and one community "summit" where the Panel's recommendations were presented to citizens could be anything other than symbolic politics. This view is consistent with the lack of prior knowledge about the World Class School Panel's endeavor expressed by one member before the second meeting, and the absence of communication with members about important reforms adopted by the district during the time period the panel was deliberating. Given the centrality of parental choice to the national school reform agenda, for example, it is striking that panel members were not systematically informed about the district's decision, made between the second and third meetings, to substitute parental choice and magnets for busing for desegregation. Upon learning of the new plan during a luncheon conversation, Finn turned to Murphy and requested details: "None of the panelists have been informed about the magnet plan. Can you tell me about it?"

CHOICE IN CHARLOTTE

When the definitive history of school desegregation is written, the date of 31 March 1992 will be noted for two reasons. The first is that the Supreme Court ruled in *Freeman v. Pitts* that the De Kalb County (Georgia) schools were not required to bus children to achieve racial balance when racial imbalances persisted because of population shifts beyond the control of the school district (*Freeman v. Pitts;* Walsh, 1992). The second is that on this date the Charlotte-Mecklenburg school board decided to open a series of magnet schools to replace crosstown busing for desegregation. Soon after assuming office in July 1991 Murphy hired a consultant to redesign the pupil assignment plan in the district. After several drafts and a great deal of pressure from various white and black community groups, the final plan was adopted unanimously by the school board in a public meeting. Although a number of amendments aimed at preventing resegregation were attached to the magnet plan, the standing-room-only audience of citizens, roughly divided between blacks and whites, reacted in quite different ways: Whites applauded enthusiastically; blacks sat motionless and silent.

Within the African-American community, however, there was a great diversity of opinion concerning magnets and choice. While certain leaders argued that the magnets would jeopardize the hard-won educational gains wrought by desegregation, others supported the choice plan. Emblematic of this diversity is Dorothy Counts-Scoggins, who was a teen in the late 1950s and one of the first blacks to desegregate Charlotte's schools. A photo of her surrounded by angry, hostile whites was beamed across the world and contributed to Mr. and Mrs. Swann's decision to file suit against segregated schools (Gaillard, 1988). Today Mrs. Counts-Scoggins supports school choice and her cousin Stephanie Counts is the school district's director of magnet programs and served on President Bush's National Commission on School Choice.

This support notwithstanding, when originally proposed, the magnet plan galvanized the relatively quiescent black community into action concerning school reform in Charlotte. Community meetings were held over a period of several weeks. In response to the original magnet plan enormous pressure to redesign it was placed upon school board members by activists, including attorneys whose firm originally argued the *Swann* case. The original plan was widely perceived to be unfair to blacks, who would shoulder disproportionately the burden of busing. The plan was modified slightly by the superintendent, his staff, the consultant, and board members so that the onus of busing would be less on black children, and more on whites. However, following the magnet plan's adoption, representatives from the Atlanta, Georgia regional headquarters of the NAACP flew to Charlotte. An NAACP representative lamented that the black community had not done more to prevent this from happening. The representative of the Charlotte NAACP responded that the organization had been trying to prevent the dismantling of the desegregation plan but "the deal had already been cut." The leader of the Black Political Caucus, a retired principal, added, "Our children have been maligned for years, our teachers and administrators have been transferred and demoted. We have been told that 'it's a done deal.' The president of the Chamber of Commerce told me, 'Fred, we hired this man [Murphy] to do a job.' " Activists summarized the reaction of the black community as "too little, too late." In fact, the day after the school board's decision, a highly placed individual in city government observed, "The real end to the busing plan did not occur the other night at the school board meeting. It occurred increasingly over the past couple of years as the power structure lost confidence in [the school system] and hired Murphy, a recognized change agent" (*Charlotte Observer*, 1992b, p. 12A).

In a striking reversal of their position of two years before, members of the growth elite supported the adoption of the magnet plan. For example, an editorial by the *Charlotte Observer* claimed,

Charlotte-Mecklenburg must have a school system that is a source of unity and pride, not division and rancor. Bitter fights over the schools, in court or in the polls, would be expensive and destructive. . . . But the prospects are exciting. To paraphrase the superintendent, this is not a moment to be so concerned about failure that we sacrifice success. Tuesday's unanimous vote and the new plan it endorses ought to bring a welcome optimism and fresh energy to our schools and our community. (*Charlotte Observer*, 1992a, p. 8A)

A member of the editorial board of the local newspaper, explaining the marked reversal of its position on both issues during the last year or so, summarized the coalescence of local forces that shaped the decision to replace busing with parental choice:

Politically, practically, philosophically, the system of busing, it seemed to me, had just about used up its public mandate. I think there is widespread, justified dissatisfaction with the results of public education for most children here. Combine this with the physical difficulty and the political difficulty of maintaining the system of integration as the white population bulges to the south, and as the roads become more and more crowded with rush hour traffic. It's becoming politically more difficult as more and more people move into the county who haven't a clue to why we're doing this [busing for desegregation]. In fact, they have moved from an all-white suburb to an all-white suburb, the difference being that where they came from, they also had a virtually all-white school system and here they find themselves part of a county school system. So the politics of it are becoming difficult. The third is the philosophical difference. Upper-middle-class white people and upper-middle-class black people have not been affected greatly by school busing because they choose where to live in ways as to not make it a problem. And so the people who are really trapped in situations [busing assignments] they don't like, lack the economic resources to get out of busing, and it seemed to me there is a widespread feeling, which I share, that the mandate for busing has pretty much run its course.

DISCUSSION

Since *A Nation at Risk* legitimized renewed criticism of the public schools, educational excellence has been pitted against educational equity in much of the public debate over educational reform (Mickelson and Ray, 1990). Conservative critics of public education have long contended that a central problem of the schools is the absence of quality. The events described indicate that discourse about school reform in Charlotte was framed in precisely these terms. In the words of Chester Finn, "The sad fact is that for close to two decades now we have neglected educational quality in the name of equality" (quoted in Aronowitz and Giroux, 1985, p. 32). The extent to which the Charlotte-Mecklenburg system will become a world-class system (that is, excellent) is uncertain. But several points can be made on the basis of the past five years' political battles over school reform in Charlotte. The national rhetoric on restructuring and changes in educational programs invariably emphasize excellence, not greater educational equity. Although the official policy goal of the district adheres to the principles of equity, the structural reforms enacted, particularly the substitution of magnets and choice for desegregation by busing, represent the potential for quite opposite outcomes. There is a growing body of evidence that seriously questions whether school choice enhances school achievement or promotes desegregation, two critical elements of educational equity (Blank, 1991; Cookson, 1990; Clune and Witte, 1991; Gewirtz, 1986; Merl, 1991; Metz, 1991; Moore, 1991; Nakao, 1989; Orfield, 1991; Thernstrom, 1990; Witte, 1991).

Much of the current discourse about education is phrased in terms of a concern that equity jeopardizes excellence. Why? Perhaps it is because as the economy shrinks, so do people's hearts and their largeness of mind. In the Charlotte context, this theme expressed itself in increasing opposition to desegregated schooling. This opposition, as is argued at length elsewhere (Mickelson and Ray, under review) derives from black and white middle-class perceptions that their children's economic opportunities in a downsized and recession-prone economy depend more than ever on a high-quality education. Middle-class families are more sharply aware that they cannot simply pass their social and economic standing on to their children; the latter must earn their own position in the middle class (Ehrenreich, 1989; Mickelson and Ray, under review). To earn this position, a "good" education is necessary (though perhaps not sufficient). While it has always been difficult for parents to assess accurately the extent to which desegregated schools might influence their children's chances of admission into a "good" college and of obtaining a "good" job (Braddock and McPartland, 1988), today, given the shifting and tenuous economy, the risks of desegregated education are perceived as too great.

Fear of downward mobility for the next generation suggests that the core of the opposition to busing increasingly assumes more of a class (rather than racial) character. This is the case in Charlotte. For example, much of the opposition to busing and desegregated schooling centers around the presence of working- and underclass black youngsters in the outlying suburban schools. These children's alleged lack of motivation and discipline is perceived to affect the classroom atmosphere adversely. Both black and white middle-class parents have expressed concern about discipline and lack of homework in terms which link these to the presence of working- and lower-class children bused into suburban schools. A middle-class white father criticized the schools for placing his children "who are ready and able to learn" in the same class with poor minority youth who are not: "Do we back everything up to operate at that speed? Which is what we've been doing for many years." A middle-class black mother complained, "If I wanted my children to go to school with children from the projects, I'd have bought my house next to them."

CONCLUSION

The history of the events between 1990 and 1992 indicates that the growth elite changed its position regarding school choice. Its change of heart was instrumental in the process which led the Charlotte-Mecklenburg school district to abandon busing for desegregation and embrace parental choice and magnets as the core policy for achieving integrated education. Why? The perceived quality of Charlotte schools remains a crucial issue for the growth elite. For example, at a 1992 board meeting of the Charlotte-Mecklenburg Educational Foundation the county commissioner who directs the county's efforts to attract business to the area complained about the problems he faces recruiting firms to relocate in Charlotte: "Public schools are *the* thing looming over companies' relocation decisions. The perceptions of outsiders is that our schools are terrible, that they'd be throwing their children into a wasteland. Companies even factor private school tuition [for upper level management] into their relocation costs. We need to tell the right story for economic development."[8] At the same board meeting where these sentiments were expressed, a vice president of one of the region's largest utilities added: "During conversations I've had [with executives of firms considering relocation to Charlotte], I'm always asked, 'What private school do your kids attend?' They are incredulous when I tell them that I consciously send my kids to public schools."

The necessity of altering these perceptions, for example, led the Chamber of Commerce to fly Superintendent Murphy to Los Angeles in early 1992 so that he could assuage fears about the schools held by employees of Occidental Life Insurance Company, which was contemplating a relocation to Charlotte (O'Brien, 1992). It is not surprising, then, that in the summer following the decision to replace mandatory busing with choice, but before the actual implementation of the changes, a group of anonymous business leaders approached the school board with a request for permission to reward Superintendent Murphy with a $25,000 bonus for the spectacular accomplishments of his first year in office. Since districtwide achievement tests scores had not improved, the primary accomplishment of his first year was symbolic—the end of mandatory busing for desegregation. Because teachers had received no raises that year, the board declined the business leaders' offer but instead, in a highly controversial move, gave Murphy a $10,000 bonus.

The growth machine model is a persuasive framework for understanding urban politics at the heart of the school reform efforts in Charlotte over the past five years. Schools are but one institution in the urban landscape of concern to growth activists. "In the end, the appropriate level of social service [that is, schools] often depends, not on an abstract model of efficiency or public demand, but on whether the cost of that service fits the local growth strategy—past and present" (Logan and Molotch, 1987, p. 65).

Local pressures on the school system to improve are likely to intensify. Such pressures led the growth elite to play a different role in the early 1990s from the one they played on the Chamber of Commerce Task Force and the 1990 school board elections. In both instances, the growth elite took positions somewhat at odds with those of relocated corporate leaders and transplanted Northern executives. The growth elite played a safe, conservative role; it did not want to rock the boat. It was leery of the social and racial upheaval that might result from the reorganization of secondary education (for example, the creation of a centralized vocational high school), or the abolition or alteration of the busing plan, or support for board candidates who advocate school choice. Such upheavals were perceived as jeopardizing Charlotte's reputation as a good place to do business.

But as Charlotte entered the 1990s, the urban political landscape shifted. Growth activists came to believe that the potential gains from school choice were worth the risk. A prominent growth activist claims that the old desegregation plan had become politically untenable given the newcomers to Charlotte, practically unmanageable given the suburban sprawl in the county, and philosophically questionable in the current political climate. That is to say, the prestigious imprimatur of the national movement to reform education was firmly stamped on Charlotte's own efforts. The confluence of local and national factors placed Charlotte growth elite activists in the middle of the murky waters of school reform where they had either to swim against the current defined and shaped by national reform leaders, or go along with the flow. They chose the latter.

This case study of school reform in Charlotte illustrates a number of themes common to the politics of education in the urban context at this point in the late twentieth century. First is the growth of the black middle-class at the same time the ranks of the underclass swell. The divisions among middle-class blacks around issues of schooling and self versus community interest demonstrate that, contrary to popular stereotypes and media images, African-Americans are far from a monolithic social group, an observation we share with many other analysts (cf. Wilson, 1987, 1980). Because African-Americans in Charlotte did not speak in one voice on the issue of school reform, it was very difficult for whites who supported desegregated education to ally themselves with blacks who wished to fight the replacement of busing with a magnet/choice plan.

Second, the explicit terms of the school reform discourse cast equity as a threat to excellence. Twenty years ago this was not true, in part because the contradictions in the political economy were not as intense. But today, the racial and class polarization of major urban centers in the United States and abroad are increasingly reflected in the schools and in the politics of educational reform. Because the goals of equity and excellence are currently so sharply counterposed in the discourse of school restructuring, a political and ideological basis exists for the most privileged members of the society to utilize their superior political power, resources, and cultural capital to reclaim public schools for their children in order to restructure them at the expense of the children of the least privileged. The growing tears in the social fabric are apparent in the politics of urban school reform in Charlotte and across the nation.

NOTES

1. Several years later (1978), Harris chaired a business advisory group at the request of the Board of Education. Desegregation was no longer the broadly divisive issue it had been earlier in the decade. The group's task was merely to review the district's organizational structure, and make recommendations for improvement. Harris's views on the school system and how desegregation affected Charlotte are exemplified in his 1984 comments to a National Education Association commemoration of *Brown:*

I have looked at a lot of school systems across the country. We have got absolutely the best school system in these United States. I will say to you that any school system that isn't doing what ought to be done ought to get about it because they can make progress. We elected a Black mayor, and we are proud of him. . . . I would say to you that prior to school integration, we couldn't have done that, regardless of how good he was. We have grown tremendously. (*Charlotte Observer,* 1984)

2. The field research for this project was conducted jointly by Roslyn Mickelson and Carol Ray from December 1987 through July 1990. In September 1989 the two were awarded a National Science Foundation Grant (SES 8910865) to support the study. From the summer of 1990 to the present, the field research for this project has been conducted by Mickelson with the assistance of Stephen Smith.

3. High-ranking executives frequently enroll their children in private schools. However, the top three secular private schools are located in southeast Charlotte and have stiff academic standards for entrance. In addition, their tuition fees can be up to $8,000 per year per child. Despite these factors, the schools usually have long wait lists (*Charlotte Observer,* 1989).

4. The close links between the growth machine and the Task Force are illustrated by the choice of the latter's chair, the chancellor emeritus of the University of North Carolina at Charlotte, Dean Colvard. Before taking the position of chancellor of UNC Charlotte, Colvard had been instrumental in conceiving and bringing to fruition the Triangle Research Park in the Raleigh-Durham–Chapel Hill area of the state. In recent years he has worked successfully to bring a similar university research partnership to Charlotte.

5. We are grateful to Robin Wages for calling Nadler's chapter to our attention.

6. This was obvious from the prefatory remarks made by speakers ("I just moved here from upstate New York . . .") or their decidedly non-Southern accents.

7. Judge James B. MacMillan, who still sits on the federal bench, claimed that even

when he retires, it will take a long time to reopen the *Swann* case, present arguments, and get a ruling which may overturn the busing order (MacMillan, 1991). This was before the De Kalb decision and the numerous reforms instituted by Dr. Murphy during the 1991–92 school year.

8. In the spring of 1991 the president of a local utility (the same one who advocated choice as the single most important reform the school district can undertake) chaired a task force, the outcome of which was the establishment of a private foundation designed to support education in Charlotte. The Charlotte-Mecklenburg Educational Foundation (CMEF) began its work in the summer of 1991. At that time the first author (Mickelson) initiated field observations during its board meetings and meetings of various subcommittees. The twelve active members of the board are all members of the growth elite and the first executive director was the Chamber of Commerce vice president for education. The mission of the CMEF has three parts: (1) make education the highest priority for all stakeholders in the success of Charlotte-Mecklenburg, (2) develop and broker the community resources available to the schools, and (3) improve the community perception of the quality of public education.

REFERENCES

Aronowitz, S., and H. Giroux. (1985) *Education under Siege*. South Hadley, MA: Bergin & Garvey.

Blank, R. (1991) Educational Effects of Magnet Schools, pp. 77–110 in W. Clune and J. Witte (eds.), *Choice and Control in American Education, Volume 2: The Practice of Choice, Decentralization, and School Restructuring*. Philadelphia: Falmer Press.

Braddock II, J. H., and J. M. McPartland. (1988) The Social Consequences of Desegregation. *Equity and Choice*. (February): 5–11 passim.

Carr, L. G., and D. F. Ziegler. (1990) White Flight and White Return in Norfolk: A Test of Predictions. *Sociology of Education 63*: 272–282.

Charlotte Observer. (1984) Eloquent Words about Schools. May 28: A10.

Charlotte Observer. (1989) Charlotte's Rich and Influential Often Choose Private Schools. August 20: A1 passim.

Charlotte Observer. (1990) Tate Buoyed by Black Vote. June 6: A1.

Charlotte Observer. (1991) School Experts Launch Search for Radical Change. December 19: A1 passim.

Charlotte Observer. (1992a) As Era of Busing Ends, Another Chance Now to Lead. April 5: A12.

Charlotte Observer. (1992b) Experts End Debate on Schools' Future. April 30: C5.

Clune, W., and J. Witte. (1991) *Choice and Control in American Education, Volume 2: The Practice of Choice, Decentralization, and School Restructuring*. Philadelphia, PA: Falmer Press.

Cookson, Peter W. (1992) Introduction to the Choice Controversy: Current Debates and Research. *Educational Policy 6*(2): 99–104.

Ehrenreich, B. (1989) *Fear of Falling: The Inner Life of the Middle Class*. New York: Pantheon.

Fortune. (1991) Best Cities for Business Editors. (November 4) *124*(11): 52.

Freeman v. Pitts, 89–1290.

Gaillard, F. (1988) *The Dream Long Deferred.* Chapel Hill, NC: University of North Carolina Press.

Gewirtz, P. (1986) Choice in Transition: School Desegregation and the Corrective Ideal. *Columbia Law Review.* (May), pp. 729–799.

Glenn, C. (1989) Parental Choice and American Values, in Joe Nathan (ed.), *Public Schools by Choice: Expanding Opportunities for Parents, Students, and Teachers,* pp. 41–54. St. Paul, MN: Institute for Learning and Teaching.

Heritage Foundation. (1991) Assessing the Bush Education Proposal. *Issue Bulletin* no. 166.

Hochschild, J. L. (1984) *The New American Dilemma.* New Haven, CT: Yale University Press.

Lazerson, M., and N. Grubb. (1974) *American Education and Vocationalism: A Documentary History 1870–1970.* New York: Teachers College Press.

Logan, J. R., and H. L. Molotch. (1987) *Urban Fortunes: The Political Economy of Place.* Berkeley: University of California Press.

MacMillan, J. B. (1991) Personal interview. Charlotte, NC: December.

Meier, D. (1991) Choice CAN Save Public Education. *Nation.* March 4: 1 passim.

Merl, J. (1991) Failed "System for Choice" Serves as Lesson to Schools. *Los Angeles Times.* March 12. A1 passim.

Metz, M. H. (1991) Potentialities and Problems of Choice in Desegregation Plans, in W. Clune and J. Witte, (eds.), *Choice and Control in American Education. Volume 2: The Practice of Choice, Decentralization, and School Restructuring,* pp. 111–118. Philadelphia: Falmer Press.

Mickelson, R. A., and C. A. Ray. (1990) Markets, Values, and the Business Vision for School Reform: A Retreat from Educational Equity. *Humanity and Society* 14: 345–372.

Mickelson, R. A., and C. A. Ray (under review) Fear of Falling from Grace: Downward Mobility, the Middle Class, and School Desegregation.

Monfort, F., and G. Orfield. (1988) Change in the Racial Composition and Segregation of Large School Districts, 1967–86. National School Board Association (June).

Moore, D. (1991) Voice and Choice in Chicago, in W. Clune and J. Witte, (eds.), *Choice and Control in American Education. Volume 2: The Practice of Choice, Decentralization, and School Restructuring,* pp. 153–198. Philadelphia: Falmer Press.

Murphy, J. (1991) Letter to World Class Schools Panel Members (August 13).

Nadler, M. (1979) Charlotte-Mecklenburg, in N. Mills (ed.), *Busing U.S.A.* pp. 310–320. New York: Teachers College Press.

Nakao, R. (1989) Desegregation and Informed Choice in San Jose, CA. Paper presented at the Annual Meetings of the American Educational Research Association. San Francisco, CA.

National Commission on Excellence in Education. (1983). *A Nation at Risk: The Imperative for School Reform.* Washington, DC: U.S. Government Printing Office.

O'Brien, K. (1992) Education on Minds of Executives. *Charlotte Observer.* Jan. 6: C10.

Orfield, G. (1981) Why It Worked in Dixie: Southern School Desegregation and Its Implications for the North, in A. Yarmolinsky, L. Liebman, and C. S. Scheiling (eds.), *Race and Schooling in the City.* pp. 24–43. Cambridge, MA: Harvard University Press.

Orfield, G. (1991) Do We Know Anything Worth Knowing about the Educational Effects of Magnet Schools? in W. Clune and J. Witte, (eds.), *Choice and Control in American Education. Volume 2: The Practice of Choice, Decentralization, and School Restructuring,* pp. 119–125. Philadelphia, PA: Falmer Press.

Piedmont Airlines [U.S. Air]. (1985) The Charlotte Area Report. *Pace Magazine,* April. Winston-Salem, NC.

Ray, C. A., and R. A. Mickelson. (1989) Business Leaders and the Politics of School Reform. *Journal of Education Policy 4:* 119–137.

Ray, C. A., and R. A. Mickelson. (1990) Corporate Leaders, Resistant Youth, and the Politics of School Reform in Sunbelt City: The Political Economy of Education. *Social Problems 37:* 101–113.

Shor, I. (1986) *Culture Wars: Schools and Society and the Conservative Restoration, 1969–1984.* Boston, MA: Routledge and Kegan Paul.

Swann v. Charlotte-Mecklenburg Board of Education, 402 U.W. 1 (1971).

Thernstrom, A. (1990) Thinking about Choice. Paper presented at the Annual Meeting of the American Political Science Association. August 30. San Francisco, CA.

U.S. Department of Education. (1991) *America 2000. An Educational Strategy.* Washington, DC: U.S. Department of Education.

Walsh, M. (1992) High Court Eases Federal Guidelines for Desegregation. *Education Week.* April 8. p. 1 passim.

Wilson, W. J. (1980) *The Declining Significance of Race.* Chicago, IL: University of Chicago Press.

Wilson, W. J. (1987) *The Truly Disadvantaged.* Chicago, IL: University of Chicago Press.

Witte, J. F. (1991) First Year Report. Milwaukee Parental Choice Program. November. The Robert LaFollette Institute of Public Affairs, University of Wisconsin-Madison.

Wrigley, J. (1982) *Class Politics and the Public Schools.* New Brunswick, NJ: Rutgers University Press.

PART IV

THE EDUCATIONAL EXPERIENCE OF WOMEN AND MARGINAL STUDENTS

10

Rural Students in Urban Settings in Africa: The Experience of Female Students in Secondary Schools

N'Dri Assie-Lumumba

Rural and urban categories, within the framework of an analysis of the impact of the global economic system on Africa, cannot be separated from each other, as advocated by some modernization theoreticians in the West. They must be approached as phenomena that are dynamically linked with each other. However, from a policy analysis perspective, one must take into account the fact that each category has its own peculiarities due to historical development and thus they must be explained both globally and locally when dealing with different social systems, including education.

Rural and urban classifications include cultural, economic, political, and demographic phenomena. *Rural sector* is defined as a social categorization in which the economy is characterized by low and/or small-scale production at all levels. In the case of Africa, the rural social, economic, and political systems and institutions are shaped by strong relationships based on the extended family system. This categorization is not synonymous with backwardness or poverty.

Urban sector is defined as a classification in which the social, economic, and political institutions are more complex and the interactions among them are established on the basis of bureaucratic and impersonal relationships. Demographically, in Côte d'Ivoire and in many other African countries, according to censuses and other official documents, an urban area has a population of at least five thousand people. The urban infrastructures are more complex and provide services associated with heterogeneous populations with diversified demands. However, the urban categorization is not synonymous with development.

Although the urban and rural definitions are simple and therefore do not reflect the complexity of these two phenomena, they provide an idea of the basis of their internal dynamics and their relation to educational distribution in Africa, particularly in terms of gender representation in the African educational systems.

During the two decades that followed the attainment of political independence in most African countries in the early 1960s, constant growth in all levels of educational systems led educational planners and policymakers to believe that by the 1980s African countries would have achieved at least one of the major targets identified in the first regional meeting of 1961 in Addis Ababa: universal primary enrollment. Indeed, in the 1960s, and to a certain extent in the 1970s, African countries realized unprecedented educational expansion as measured by the growth in enrollment rates and the proportion of public expenditure allocated to education. At that time they spent between 20 and 30 percent of their state revenues on education. However, with regard to gender, the overall situation of access to and continuance in education is still characterized by profound imbalance. The combined effects of a complex set of past and present economic, political, cultural, and institutional factors which work at the local and international levels contribute to this continued unequal representation of girls and women in African educational systems. The bases for unequal enrollment include region, size of the community (for example, urban versus rural areas), social class, and gender.

It has been argued by many that the issue of gender inequality in educational opportunity in Africa must not focus exclusively on the simple question of access, as the quality and relevance of education are crucial aspects that must be addressed. (See also Assie-Lumumba, 1992a and 1992b). But, as the majority of African countries have not reached even universal primary enrollment, an analysis of some of the conditions that explain attendance is also relevant.

The thrust of this paper is to analyze the experiences of female students of rural origin who attend secondary schools in urban centers. The extent to which the urban settings enhance or hinder the chances of these students of pursuing their educational career is analyzed. The first section of the paper deals with the sociogeographic factor in the distribution of education. The second part addresses the question of the representation of female students in the educational system. The third section is an analysis of the experiences of female secondary school students in the urban milieu. The analysis will be generalized and examples are drawn from various African countries. However, the focus is the Ivorian case.

SOCIOGEOGRAPHIC BACKGROUND IN THE DISTRIBUTION OF EDUCATION

Occupation and organization of space is not neutral (Assie et al., 1978). The distribution, appropriation, and organization of space reflect the social structure of society and interaction of various groups and classes in society. For example, the location of institutions mirrors the power structure in a given social and historical context. Thus, in colonial Africa the classical location of Europeans was the highlands. The administrative posts were often located on the slopes or on the tops of hills, if there were any. Sometimes, the highlands represented several types of power.[1] In Kenya, for example, the British colonists took the highlands which were more fertile, leaving to the Africans the less fertile portions of the lowlands.[2]

In many colonial African cities, the *Plateau* neighborhoods were the residential areas of the colonists and/or the administrative/business centers, church, police, and military forces on which the administration relied for its security and continued control over the actual and potential challengers of colonial domination. This tradition, which was inherited by the African political leaders following independence, has since been reinforced. The distribution of services related to the power structure follows this tradition. For example, in Abidjan the police academy and headquarters, the *gendarmerie* camp, and other military facilities are located in or near Cocody, the residential area of the political elite. The military camp of Akouédo is well known to many students and opposition members who, upon their arrest for activities considered subversive by the government, are transferred there for "political resocialization" and other forms of punishment. Although the specific area is not hilly enough to allow the location of this camp on a high location, it is near the wealthiest neighborhood and the university campus.

The colonial towns and cities in Africa were deliberately used to reinforce the Western values received by African youths in the colonial schools. In French colonies, for example, formal education was established on an elitist foundation, from the village school to the federal institutions and, later on, to the metropolitan French schools. As Bouche comments, French education was geared to producing the needed civil servants, which "often easily reduced exclusively the role of village school to the first stage in the process of selecting the future elites, and it was useless for those who stopped their studies at that level." (Bouche, 1975). The same process of screening went on to the highest grades.

In the case of French West Africa, on the basis of an order of 1903 and its Ivorian application of 1911, the hierarchical structure of education and its orientation from the village to the towns can be summarized as follows:

Village schools, which provided four years of preparatory and elementary courses in reading, writing, and speaking, served as a means to sort out the most capable pupils to feed the regional schools. Regional schools comprised the complete elementary school and the *cours moyen*, for which some pupils were selected from the village schools. Not all pupils finished their education at the *cours moyen*. Among those who graduated, earning the *certificat de fin d'études* with either the "agriculture" or "manual work" options, the highest achievers were selected for further education.

Urban schools had the complete primary grades. Beyond the primary-elementary level, two types of schools existed: *école primaire supérieure* and vocational schools.[3] Federal schools were established for all students from French West Africa, with the centralized administrative headquarters located in Dakar.[4]

The African students were taught technical skills and the values targeted by the administration. As expressed by some French administrators *(chefs de poste)*, it was important to make African pupils see and imitate the way of life in the administrative centers which were actual or potential towns and cities, with features unknown in the villages from which the pupils came. An important aspect of socialization of African children consisted of making them understand, appreciate, and accept the relationship between schooling and urban life. It should be noted that in the early years of colonization, the problem of urban employment did not exist. Despite the crude colonial rules embedded in separate laws for the Africans and the Europeans, the Africans who received formal education and/or lived in urban areas with jobs in the Westernized sector of the economy were promoted to a status which, in the Westernizing context, was higher than that of the ordinary Africans with no schooling.[5] Colonial education was an effort of the governing classes both in the metropolis and in smaller urban centers in the colonies to create infrastructures which would support their social, economic, and philosophical systems (Lumumba-Kasongo, 1990). Thus, formal education, Westernization, better-paid jobs, more comfortable working conditions for the formally educated Africans, and so on were associated with the town or city. The colonial town/city became a dynamic place both in terms of internal contradictions and through its emancipatory/liberating potential. Although the phenomenon of large human clusters forming towns/cities was not alien to African societies, the new type of urban center and the perceived or actual opportunity for further education and socioeconomic attainment reached an unprecedented magnitude. These new types of urban centers became the basis for international exchanges, commerce, ideals, ideas, values, and industrialization.

In African countries, including Côte d'Ivoire, external sociohistorical and sociogeographic factors that played important roles in the beginning of colonization were reinforced as new social forces evolved. Since European education was introduced by the Europeans themselves, through either the colonial administration or the missionaries, it was in areas where the Europeans settled that formal education started and spread. The legacy still persists.

The urban areas have more school facilities and higher enrollment rates. The classic case in West Africa, for example, in former French as well as British colonies, is the striking imbalance between the north/hinterland with limited school facilities and the south/coastal areas with more facilities. Other areas selected by the Europeans on the basis of their economic, military/strategic, or religious importance in the hinterland later became urban centers.

In Côte d'Ivoire, the southern region—and particularly the southeast, which includes Abidjan—is characterized by a higher degree of urbanization, that is to say the establishment of the modern infrastructure and services that can promote and support the activities of the peripheral capitalist economy and the maintenance of the state apparatus. The current types of Ivorian schools (primary, secondary, and postsecondary) operating in the urban centers are excellent indicators of the social status of the towns/cities or of the specific neighborhoods within the urban areas. One of the most striking features of the educational system in Côte d'Ivoire, as in many other African countries (especially former French colonies), is that all secondary schools are located in urban areas. In addition to the rural-versus-urban imbalance, within the large urban areas there is also a sociogeographic division that affects, in clear patterns, the distribution of schools, in both number and type.

In Côte d'Ivoire, public funds are unequally distributed to the various secondary school institutions. Even in the public academic schools, the students receive unequal treatment. The *clientèle* of those schools is clustered around social-class lines. For example, students who come from the most privileged class (as measured by area of residence, and the level of parental education and occupation) are more likely to attend the *lycée,* which represents the secondary school par excellence and leads to institutions of higher education than the youth of socially disadvantaged parents and from rural communities. These less privileged students are more likely to attend the short-stream CEG *(Collège d'Enseignement Général).* According to the legal and administrative rules, students are assigned to these schools by a national commission. Although specific criteria of selection such as age and achievement score on the secondary school entrance examination are set, in reality other factors such as the power and influence of parents easily override the seemingly meritocratic criteria. Furthermore, a variable such as age in an African school setting is in reality a proxy for social class (Assie, 1982; Assie-Lumumba, 1983; Assie-Lumumba and Lumumba-Kasongo, 1991). Children from poor rural communities where subsistence needs are great and where there are few schools enter school late and are likely to repeat, thus finishing primary school at an older age than their middle-class counterparts.

The geographic distribution of schools mirrors the location of different social classes in the social structure. The geographic site of schools in Abidjan is a striking example of unequal distribution of educational facilities in relation to social class. Abidjan is composed of several neighborhoods/districts of differing statuses. Le Plateau, which in the colonial period was the center of the administration and was separated from the African neighborhoods either by the lagoon or by military and police headquarters, is today downtown Abidjan with its skyscrapers and services. Cocody has become the residential zone for the Ivorian "old" elite/Westernized families,[6] the diplomats, the Western technical assistants, and university students, to cite only a few. Among others, Treichville and Adjamé, which were the "neighborhoods for the natives" in the colonial era, and also Marcory, are today popular neighborhoods for the medium- and some low-income Africans. Port-Bouet, Koumassi, Abobo, and the popular section of Yopougon draw their dwellers from the low-income, semiskilled, and unskilled populations, and new unemployed rural immigrants. These districts are the most popular places for the masses and the lumpenproletarians. They form more than half of the Abidjan's population. In modern political and economic terms, they constitute the periphery. The type of public academic secondary schools that are located in those neighborhoods is an eloquent illustration of the social significance of geographic location. All the institutions in Le Plateau and Cocody are *lycées* and *collèges modernes,* while there are no *lycées* in the popular districts. Some *collèges modernes* are located in those areas, but the low-status secondary schools in Abidjan are in Treichville, Adjamé, Port-Bouet and Yopougon. The university and other institutions of higher education, near the police, *gendarmerie,* and military camps as mentioned earlier, are also located in Cocody, although students' residences are scattered throughout the city.

It is important to note that the private nonreligious schools at the secondary level are also urban-oriented. The main and overt goal of the owners of those institutions is to maximize monetary returns. While the demand for education is expressed all over the country, ability to afford the high private cost is not spread equally among social groups in terms of occupation or area of residence. Monetary funds are more available to urban dwellers who are wage earners or merchants than to rural populations. Also, the number of the actual and potential clientele is greater in large urban centers: youths who have failed and/or have not been allowed to take the secondary school entrance examination, public secondary school students who have been dismissed, and those who want or need a temporary place while looking for an opportunity in the public institutions. The cost and the distribution of private institutions contribute substantially to deepening the gap between the urbanized southern region and the less urbanized region of the north.

On the whole, even at the primary level of education, public as well as the private schools are more available in urban areas. All secondary and postsecondary institutions are located in urban areas. For the overall school-age population, access to postprimary education requires urban residence.

In the next section, the overall representation of females in the school system is analyzed. In the subsequent section the focus will be narrowed to the experience of the rural students who attend secondary schools in urban centers.

FEMALE REPRESENTATION IN THE EDUCATIONAL SYSTEM IN CÔTE D'IVOIRE

The issue of gender imbalance in access to education did not have and still does not have any relevance in the indigenous African social context. As was the case in African communities in the pre-European experience, in rural areas today—especially when there are not enough school facilities—every child in society has an education and he/she is expected to contribute to the various social activities from childhood to adulthood. Scarcity of facilities became an issue with the introduction of schooling and its requirement for access and success.

According to the UNESCO statistical review (UNESCO, 1991) prepared for the Sixth Regional Conference held in Dakar (Senegal) in July 1991, the proportion of females among the student population in Ivorian primary schools grew from 41 percent in 1975 to 44 percent in 1988. The corresponding figures for the secondary level are 33 percent and 40 percent, and 25 percent and 31 percent for the tertiary level. In 1990, the illiteracy rates for the adult population were 40 percent for males and 63 percent for females. Only a few African countries which have reached universal primary enrollment and three countries in southern Africa (Botswana, Lesotho, and Swaziland for some cultural and economic reasons) have equal or higher representation of the female population in schools. Even in these cases, the general trend of female underrepresentation tends to be reestablished toward the end of secondary and in higher education levels. A variety of factors, some general and others more specific to certain social groups or regions, explain the persistence of gender imbalance in education.

Colonial administration, based on its structures of power and its political economy, brought to the colonies the values of the metropolis, where females' education was not considered as important as that of the males for a long time. In restructuring African societies, this administration developed or reinforced patriarchy in them. Even missions in practice favored male domination, though officially they claimed to promote equality. While ''schools for chiefs' sons'' were created by various colonial administrations to train future male leaders, the administrations and missionaries designed home economics curricula to train African girls as wives and mothers tied to their homes with limited access to occupations in the public sectors. The male population received an education which, although also geared to preparing the African men to work for the benefit of the Europeans and their respective countries, was set according to the world vision of the European dominant class that only men can exercise an activity in the public sphere and earn a living to support their families. As a result, African girls' education was nearly reduced to sewing and embroidery. Yet, as active participants in agriculture, trade, and craft production, they also needed relevant training in these fields to increase their productivity.

Some of the factors explaining differential education among males and fe-

Table 10.1
Percentage of Repeaters at the General Secondary Education Level

	1980	1985	1988
Males	10.5	18.3	17.7
Females	15.2	21.7	20.5

Source: UNESCO (1991, p. 38).

males can be found in African culture itself. Men as well as women were submitted to the difficult colonial rules for forced labor, for example. But when there was room for a little choice, Africans tried harder to protect the women from external influences. For in many societies, women are considered the foundation for values, and are responsible for the perpetuation and preservation of those values. In addition, the conditions in the schools were especially hard. So, parents themselves were particularly opposed to enrolling their daughters and nieces.

These major factors, among others, explain the low proportion of females enrolled in schools, even at the primary level, in the specific case of Côte d'Ivoire. Despite the constant increase in the absolute and relative number of females, the problem of unequal enrollment still exists at all levels of the educational system. As will be shown, the problem is not only the initial unequal opportunity for enrollment but also unequal chances to continue once in the system.

The primary school gross enrollment ratios were 89.0 and 82.5 percent for males and only 59.4 and 58.4 percent for females in 1980 and 1985, respectively. The corresponding figures for secondary school are 25.6 and 26.6 percent for males and 10.9 and 11.3 percent for females. The figures for the postsecondary level are 4.7 and 3.8 percent for males and 1.0 and 1.0 percent for females (UNESCO, 1991). As a result of unequal initial distribution of education along gender lines, the illiteracy rates continue to be higher among females than among males.

The figures in Table 10.1 above indicate that Côte d'Ivoire's school system, as in many other African countries, has an overall low internal efficiency. As can be seen in the table, repetition rates are high among both male and female students, but they are even higher among females. These figures are consistent with previous trends. The problem of low internal efficiency worsened during the 1980s. The increase in the number of students who do not perform well enough to be promoted to the next grade can be an indication of the difficult conditions in which many students must study.

In Table 10.2 there appears a striking difference based on sex in the first cycle or lower secondary level, where the proportion of female students promoted to the next grade is lower than that of males. The smallest difference is 2.1 percent in the fourth grade, and the maximum is in the first grade at 13.4

Table 10.2
Rates of Promotion, Repetition, and Dropout between 1976–77 and 1977–78

Grade* and Sex		Promotion	Repetition	Dropout
6e	M	89.8	3.8	6.4
	F	76.4	8.8	14.8
	Total	85.9	5.2	8.9
5e	M	85.4	5.5	9.1
	F	75.2	10.9	13.9
	Total	82.8	6.8	10.4
4e	M	77.9	11.2	10.9
	F	71.0	15.7	13.3
	Total	76.2	12.3	11.5
3e	M	31.2	14.2	54.5
	F	29.1	18.2	52.7
	Total	30.8	15.1	54.1
2e	M	76.0	12.3	11.7
	F	73.5	12.6	13.9
	Total	75.5	12.3	12.2
1ere	M	82.0	10.6	7.4
	F	84.1	10.7	5.2
	Total	82.4	10.6	7.0
Terminale				
	M	–	25.6	–
	F	–	24.0	–
	Total			

Source: Assie, 1982, citing Ministry of National Education, *Statistiques: Année Scolaire 1977–78,* p. 68.

*6e to Terminale grades correspond to first to seventh (or final) grades of secondary school. The first four grades correspond to the first cycle, while the last three grades represent the second cycle.

percent. In the cases of repetition and dropout or dismissal, the proportion of female students is higher in both categories, although the percentage of males in the category of students dismissed is also high and even higher in the fourth grade.

In the second cycle the advantage of males decreases and the situation is reversed, as in the sixth grade of secondary school, where 82.0 percent of males are promoted, as compared to 84.1 percent of females. Thus, in the upper grades there are fewer females than males leaving school, while they have fewer chances than males to perform well in lower levels of the system.

The phenomenon of female higher academic performance has been found in other Third World countries as well as in industrial ones. Such findings have been reported in a study concerning eleven countries.[7] More specifically, in the first cycle of secondary school, the success rate of female students is higher than that of males in seven out of ten countries. In the second cycle, the proportion is ten out of eleven countries.

Although female students tend to have higher success rates than males in the upper grades of secondary school the point is not that females are more talented than males. Rather, "the fact that they had to overcome more difficulties to reach the level of the examination becomes an advantage" (UNESCO, 1970, p. 10). Students from the least advantaged social origins (with parents who are illiterate farmers or urban workers) face adverse conditions which can prevent them from actualizing their academic potential. Female students from these origins are more likely to face even greater obstacles against academic success.

In the majority of African societies, agriculture continues to be one of the most important socioeconomic activities, providing food and cash. In agriculture and petty trade, for example, female labor is highly prized. Within the structures of the sexual division of labor in the village communities, even when agricultural activities are performed by both females and males, men's daily activities take place in the fields while women both work in the fields and are in charge of domestic work as well (for example, cleaning the house and courtyard, taking care of the children, fetching water, cooking). Analyzed next are some of the experiences of students who have moved from those rural origins to urban settings and the implications this migration has for the education of females in the urban secondary schools.

FEMALE STUDENTS FROM RURAL MILIEUS IN URBAN ENVIRONMENTS

There are at least three categories of students of both sexes from rural origins in urban school settings. One group is the offspring of recent migrants from rural areas. Such students are among those who have moved to urban areas with their parents or other relatives who are themselves rural dwellers who have migrated from the rural communities. The second group is composed of students whose own parents still live in rural areas, but who have joined more stable relatives in urban areas. The third category of students is composed of those who have passed the secondary school entrance examination and are assigned to specific secondary schools located in urban areas.

As Little explains, one among the various reasons that African youths move "townwards" is that

few secondary schools and facilities for technical training exist outside the main towns and government offices and business establishments are also there. Not only does this make urban residence virtually essential for the educated classes in general, but it brings in nearly everyone who is looking for advancement, especially in "white collar" forms of employment. (Little, 1974, p. 11)

A large proportion of the urban dwellers are not integrated into the so-called modern sector and for a living rely on various activities classified as informal. The first difficulty of the general population of migrants from rural areas who live in the urban peripheries, particularly the unemployed and those who perform jobs classified as informal and unskilled, is the lack of access to urban services and facilities, including schools. The types of secondary schools in those districts are often of low quality, with overcrowded classes staffed with less qualified teachers. They include public academic schools and professional and technical schools. In the public schools in Abidjan, for example, as was indicated earlier, the *lycées,* which receive the highest share of government revenues, are the most costly, especially those with boarding facilities located in wealthy districts, while the nonelite schools are in the peripheral neighborhoods such as Abobo, Adjamé, Koumassi, Treichville, and Yopougon.

Regarding the second of the three categories of students specified above, Little is correct in stating that "people in the villages sometimes send their sons and daughters to urban relatives to be taught a trade or 'minded' while at school. . . ." (Little, 1974, p. 11). The rural students who live with Westernized urban relatives usually experience a new material security and comfort, and they have the opportunity to attend schools with higher quality. Their chances for academic success are enhanced. However, they go through a phase of profound acculturation and adaptation. They must adapt to a new social environment. The homes they live in do not necessarily provide a real continuity from the village. Although Westernized individuals speak African languages in many homes, European languages are more commonly used, at least as compared to the village community. Even in countries where there is a major lingua franca, many ethnic groups have their own languages. Thus language, style of living, food, social relations, and so on may be different from those in villages. Communication, even with relatives, may take time. It is well-known that peers influence each other. In the situation of rural and urban youth in contact in the urban context, the general tendency is for the rural child to be assimilated or at least acquire new ways of doing things in the culture of the urban life that are consistent with those of the urban/Westernized relatives. Thus, the pressure for adaptation and adjustment, especially on girls, can be difficult. The lives of these girls can be full of hope, high aspirations, and expectations. Yet, as they cannot share all their social experience of the rural context even with these relatives, they are likely to go through phases of loneliness.

The third category of female students of rural origins is composed of those whose only official purpose for moving to the urban areas is to attend secondary schools upon their success in the secondary school entrance examination and their assignment to a specific school in a town/city. As indicated earlier, in most African countries, including Côte d'Ivoire, there are no secondary schools in rural communities. Given the concentration of secondary schools in urban areas, rural students who move into those urban settings must cope with a new, complex, and often cosmopolitan urban environment. Although the material living conditions are the key factors in these students' lives, the cultural component of socioeconomic status and area of residence should not be dismissed. In their educational journey from the village primary school to the city secondary schools, African students in general encounter several cultural shocks or at least face some important needs for adaptation. For the students of rural origins, the cultural shock in the urban settings is one stage among several others. The first important shock they experience occurs when they start attending school and come into daily and intense contact with new requirements of behavior, a new language, timetables, and a set of values inherent in the European type of education. Although there are no statistics on the specific distribution of these three groups, it is fair to assert that the third category comprises the largest number.

Unlike the two other groups of students, who live with relatives, although in different socioeconomic environments, this third group encounters different realities for living. Those who attend boarding schools or have access to the boarding facilities are in a better environment to focus on their work. For most female students in this category, who do not have access to any boarding facilities, the conditions can be truly miserable.

It must be noted that one of the major generalized African cultural traits is hospitality (the basis for African humanism). In this broad context, the government, which designs and implements the policy of assigning students to regions other than their own, may certainly count on this African tradition which dictates that guests be treated with special attention. The host must provide to the "stranger"[8] the best meal that she/he can afford (even sometimes beyond her/his means), offer a comfortable place to sleep, be courteous, and so on. Certainly, as Pellow explains in the case of the Ashanti,

the values implicit in the term *Akwaba* (welcome) carry over in a more genuine way in the daily lifestyle of the urban Ghanaian's room, compound, and immediate neighborhood. Just as the compound is the home base of the extended family in the traditional milieu, there is always room in its urban equivalent for one more. If there is a shortage of beds, mats can be found for sleeping. (Pellow, 1977, p. 42)

In the context of migrant students however, it is a totally different social reality. It occurs on a large scale and is a national problem. Those who cannot find a "guardian" or *tuteur/tutrice*[9] from their region of origin must be thankful to any person who is willing to accept them. In some cases parents travel to the towns where the secondary schools are located in order to find a place for their children. However, most of the time students must find a host themselves. Then it becomes a matter of pure chance to find a host family with goodwill and material resources to make the living and study conditions comfortable. Indeed, although a few students may be fortunate to find new homes which provide support and comfort, the majority of them are less fortunate.

They must accommodate to different food[10] or at least a different way it is prepared. One of the major problems arises when there are too many people living in the same home. This situation occurs often in small towns where there are no boarding facilities. In such cases, the capacity of the local population to welcome the students is quickly exhausted. This leaves students in precarious conditions where the environment is not conducive to academic success, even when the hosts are generous and full of goodwill. Female students who are fully involved in domestic work can indeed become overwhelmed with responsibilities and housework.

Boarding facilities offer the best study conditions for students of low socio-economic status who otherwise would use study time for housework. But in Côte d'Ivoire boarding facilities have been scarce even in large or prestigious secondary schools such as *lycées*. Furthermore, there are none in low-status schools such as CEG *(Collège d'Enseignement Général)*, where the majority of students are from low socioeconomic backgrounds, mostly of rural origins. Most of CEG students from poor social origins must cope with daily social obstacles. In addition to the negative effects of housework, the problem of adolescent fertility is exacerbated by the lack of sex education and of sexual control or discipline for these young students away from home.

Although there are no hard facts showing the sociological causes of secondary school student pregnancy, it is fair to state that most of these cases stem from simple ignorance and/or inability to use means of protection besides abstinence. Rural students in urban areas, as young as twelve years, find themselves in charge of their lives away from parental authority and presence, even if the *tuteurs/tutrices* become surrogate parents and sometimes take this responsibility seriously. In other cases, the *tuteurs* themselves and other adult or adolescent males in the household may sexually abuse these teenage girls, for whom they are supposed to have become surrogate relatives. Other students, particularly those from modest origins, decide, for lack of alternatives, to have sexual intercourse with men in or outside the household who can provide financial resources to secure the necessary material means for survival. Lack of funds to acquire certain basic needs such as sanitary napkins, toothpaste, school supplies, and so on may be a source of serious constraints. Even food, which is produced by the families themselves in the rural/farming communities, requires money in the urban context. Transportation to and from school can put additional pressure on the needy students. All these constraints may lead poor/rural students to enter into relations, which in turn may lead to unplanned and unwanted pregnancy. Some have talked about this as a form of prostitution among such students. Today, with the decline in the economic power of rural populations, whose crops provide shrinking revenues, this phenomenon may reach a new magnitude.

Until a few years ago, in African countries in general, a secondary school student who became pregnant was automatically dismissed from school.[11] Yet her partner was not automatically punished; and if he happened to be a student, he had the opportunity normally to pursue his education. Although by and large pregnant students are no longer dismissed, the effects of pregnancy on students' academic careers are usually negative. The likelihood of repeated absence as a result of their condition contributes to lowering their academic performance. When the delivery occurs during the academic year, they take time off. Even in cases where a relative takes care of the baby, mothering makes it difficult to meet the requirements of full-time schoolwork, especially in a highly selective system. In some cases relatives take the baby with them in order to provide the student with the necessary time for her schooling activities. In addition to the physiological changes and difficulties that may accompany pregnancy, particularly for girls who do not have the resources to cover appropriate nutrition and health needs, the psychological and emotional strains constitute a hindrance to steady work and satisfactory performance in school. Usually, such students are considered the main persons, if not the sole ones, responsible for the pregnancy. Thus, they receive little understanding or sympathy from school, or from relatives, who tend to evaluate pregnancy in terms of the waste of resources already used for their education until the pregnancy.

Sex or population education has not been considered part of school responsibilities until recently. In fact, it has been introduced only in some elite schools. By and large, even when it is incorporated in the curriculum, it is not systematically discussed. Students rely on other sources—peers—for awareness. Even families in rural areas who still continue to practice certain initiation rites tend not to discuss sex issues openly, although they are sometimes discussed or taught during these ceremonies. The specific aspect of protection against pregnancy is usually addressed reluctantly. The main means for most of those adolescents to avoid pregnancy is abstinence. Furthermore, students do not always participate in those ceremonies, hence their special lack of awareness. Those who are aware of some modern methods (barrier methods and pills) may not have the means to acquire them. It must be stressed that although the responsibility for protection must be shared by both partners, as the negative impact of pregnancy is primarily on the female, her awareness and action are crucial in preventing pregnancy.

As all secondary schools are located in urban areas, students from rural areas are the ones who are the most likely to attend secondary school with little chance of parental supervision. And the risk of pregnancy is even greater for those students who do not have access to boarding facilities. Parents of higher socioeconomic status easily find solutions for their daughters in case of unwanted pregnancy.[12] On the whole, it is safe to assume that the lower the socio-economic status the higher the chances for a student to become pregnant, and the more negative the effects on the student and her academic future. Under these conditions, female students from socially disadvantaged origins face more obstacles in pursuing their education. As females are more likely to leave school (or be withdrawn from school) than males, especially in the lower grades, and if in addition to their low enrollment rates they are more likely to repeat their grades and/or to leave school in larger proportions, then the persistence of sex imbalance among socially disadvantaged groups is not likely to be eliminated soon. The statistics in the 1990s constitute an eloquent proof of these trends (UNESCO, 1991).

In the context of the ongoing economic constraints, boarding facilities are among the services targeted to be eliminated in the cost recovery strategies proposed by SAP (Structural Adjustment Program). Many African countries such as Togo have in fact complied with this policy of eliminating boarding facilities. A few countries like Côte d'Ivoire that have resisted may also comply. The proposal to eliminate these facilities indicates a lack of concern for the issues involved and the needs that they satisfy. As illustrated by Masemann (1974), the boarding school provides an environment for socialization parallel to the formal learning program based on the official curriculum. Allison has argued that boarding facilities have also been used as preventive means against female fertility; she states that "a well tried and tested formula, for example, has been the creation of separate schools or boarding facilities for male and female students" (Allison, 1985). Boarding schools are important for girls not only because they protect them from pregnancy but also because they provide a decent place to study after class, a place to sleep, time for homework, time to rest, and sufficient food—all elements that promote learning.

The real needs for boarding facilities follow social-class lines. As in some European traditions, African elite families learned to send their offspring to boarding schools for character building and other forms of socialization. From these Westernized African families, the necessary material and physical support, and probably some emotional support, are available in the towns/cities where the schools are. Their children do not need the boarding accommodations to concentrate on their work and perform well academically, and yet they use these facilities.

By contrast, the need for students of low socioeconomic status, especially those from villages with no adequate place to stay, to use the boarding facilities is motivated by economic constraints and distance of their homes and families. The fate of many students from rural origins who do not have access to boarding facilities is one of a precarious existence. The socioeconomic environment in which such students live is a reflection of general African conditions, characterized by a very small, rich, Westernized elite and middle class (bureaucrats and technocrats, the *fonctionnaires*) and a large proportion of rural and urban masses. But the constraints on female students in the urban context are even greater. Like those who live in the household they enter, the students must deal with the struggle of economic hardship, overcrowded rooms, and so on. They must struggle to take care of their homework while participating fully in the domestic work.

Although the urban population has increased rapidly, the Ivorian population is still predominantly rural. The majority of the rural dwellers are farmers, fishermen, traders, and the like.

Table 10.3
Distribution of Male Students by Size of Residence and Selectivity Indices of Students by Sex, 1963 and 1979

Size of Residence	Proportion of Ivorian Males		Sex Rates			
			Males		Females	
	1963	1979	1963	1979	1963	1979
Below 5,000 inhabitants	75.5	66.0	0.7	0.8	0.4	0.4
5,000 and above	24.5	34.0	1.6	1.2	2.8	2.0
Total	100.0	100.0				

Source: Assie, 1982, p. 210.

As is shown in Table 10.3, in 1963 as well as 1979 less than 35 percent of the students live in towns with more than 5,000 people. The selectivity indices (computed by dividing the proportion of students in a particular category by the proportion of the overall population in test category, with a coefficient of 1 indicating perfect representation) reveal that the rural residents are underrepresented among male as well as female students. The figures for urban dwellers show that they are overrepresented. In both samples, the inequality is greater among female students.

Table 10.4 shows the same pattern of unequal chances for access to the two types of academic secondary schools (*lycées* and CEG), with an overrepresentation of the urban population. The rural underrepresentation is more marked in the long stream (which includes two cycles of study) than in the short stream (only the first cycle).

Hyde points out that "area of residence is predictive of enrollment and attainment at all levels of education," as shown in a specific Ethiopian case, although "the impact of urban residence is misleading" (Hyde, 1991). She also argues that when the school, family, and other factors are controlled for, "the correlation between schooling attainment and size of the community vanishes, and in larger villages affects [only] primarily enrollment probabilities, while other factors explain level of education and time spent in school" (Hyde, 1991). However, in Côte d'Ivoire female students in CEG (with no boarding facilities) as well as in elite schools have fewer chances to pursue their education. Indeed, the social origins of nonelite *lycée* students and CEG students are similar. On the whole, students from poor social backgrounds and particularly those of rural origins who do not have their families and usual homes in the urban areas have to overcome higher obstacles to remain in school and to succeed academically.

Table 10.4
Selectivity Indices of Students by Size of Residence and Type of School, 1963 and 1979

Size of Residence	Long Stream		Short Stream	
	Long Academic* 1963	Lycee 1979	Short Academic* 1963	CEG 1979
Below 5,000 inhabitants	0.6	0.4	0.7	0.8
5,000 and above	1.7	2.0	1.6	1.4

Source: Assie, 1982, p. 211.

*Long academic and short academic are the names under which the long stream and short stream data were collected in 1963.

CONCLUSION

In most African countries, universal primary education has not been reached, despite commitments in the early years of independence, especially at the Addis Ababa Conference, and unprecedented expansion in the 1960s and 1970s. Regardless of the current African economic crisis, some states are still expressing their will to reach this target by 2000. However, secondary schools continue to be scarce in many countries as states are encouraged by structural adjustment programs to disengage themselves from the activities of building facilities as a result of privatization of the African economies. The argument of economy of scale is used to justify the policy of building secondary schools in urban communities in Africa, since they can serve the larger populations in the towns/cities and also several smaller communities around the urban centers. The location of secondary schools in urban areas has a profound ideological base, as the towns/cities symbolize and constitute the center of power of the ruling class. The economic crisis is hurting the educational institutions in the rural as well as urban centers. For instance, in Côte d'Ivoire, as in most African countries, there has been no new secondary school built by the state since the early 1980s. Yet, during this decade, students from the rural areas continued to enter secondary schools, and rural-urban migration may have been accelerated by the decline of the cocoa and coffee plantation economy.

The policy to centralize secondary schools in urban areas puts extra burdens on the students who have to leave their families and their rural communities to attend those schools. The urban settings have their own dynamics of socioeconomic constraints and social relations which make it difficult to provide an adequate learning environment to those students. Boarding facilities have been playing a key role in providing a truly needed living and study home for these rural students. In the current context of economic austerity, it is relatively easy to cut services of social groups which do not represent any major political threat. In other words, it is easier to eliminate a service for secondary school students than one for university students, the middle class, or the military officers. However, long-term socioeconomic impacts should be taken into consideration in these programs. In this particular case, it is important to analyze the impact of the absence of boarding schools on postprimary school attendance of youths of rural origin, particularly female students. The urban areas provide a unique opportunity for many rural students to see a wide variety of opportunities and diversified role models. However, for many the socioeconomic constraints do not enable them to fulfill their aspirations.

The situation of rural students in urban schools generally are worsening in Africa. In Côte d'Ivoire, for example, the boarding school system is threatened by the fiscal and monetary crisis of the state and society. To improve social conditions of females of rural origins in the urban secondary schools, there is a need for democratizing the distribution of the state and national resources and a need to introduce an adequate policy to help secondary schools by providing special assistance to those categories of students. The situation of the rural students in general, and particularly the females in the urban secondary schools, has to be addressed structurally and historically. The needs of these students must be understood as different from the unnecessary luxury and wastage that have characterized elite *lycées*. For further research, it would be advisable to follow a cohort of rural students to analyze the factors—some of which have been pointed out in this chapter—that enhance or hinder their chances for further education through and beyond urban secondary schools.

NOTES

1. This assured better surveillance and control over the movements of the masses. This is typical of periods when, due to the technological limitations regarding long-distance observation, it was necessary for the ruling class to live in higher places, often complemented by structures such as the donjon, which was practiced in medieval Europe.

2. This inequitable redistribution of lands and the whole repressive colonial situation, which took a particular tone in the settlers' colonies, led to the struggle for political independence, with its highest expression known as the "Mau Mau" movement. Within the rural and urban centers, the colonists occupied the highlands.

3. The *école primaire supérieure* had different tracks: In the beginning a *Cours Normal* offered a preparatory course for entrance to the federal *Ecole Normale de St. Louis,* Senegal, and the administrative and commercial track offered specialized divisions for future post office employees and telegraphists, accountants, typists, and also assistant doctors and assistant nurses. Vocational schools provided a two-year training for the *brevet d'ouvrier* or for manual work. A few pupils were selected for the higher-level vocational school, the *école professionelle centrale.*

4. The *Ecole Normale St. Louis* was created in 1907 and became William Ponty School after it was transferred to Goree Island in 1913. In 1916, the *Ecole de Médecine*

de Dakar was created. Many of the first "highly" educated Ivorians, like others in French colonies, attended federal schools—Ivorian president Felix Houphouet-Boigny, the only president since independence in 1960, graduated from the *Ecole de Médecine*—the majority having begun in the village schools and passed through all the stages of selection. The *Ecole des Pupilles Mécaniciens de la Marine* was also a federal school.

5. With the colonial law of native status created for the Africans, they were required, under the specific law of forced labor, to work without wages and under rough conditions in emerging urban centers.

6. This is where the first generation of Westernized elite live, while Cocody Les-Deux-Plateaux and Riviera III are preferred by younger professionals and high civil servants.

7. Bahamas, Burundi, Cambodia, Congo, Finland, India, Ireland, United Arab Republic, Senegal, Syria, and Thailand.

8. *Stranger* is used in the sense of either someone who is from outside of the community or a familiar person, including relatives, who no longer live or do not usually live in the community.

9. *Tuteur/tutrice* in this context is a new term created for the needs of the phenomenon of migration, particularly for the needs of students to have a surrogate parent.

10. Urban centers are in the process of a homogenization of diet habits. For example, rice is becoming the major staple even in countries where traditionally the majority of the population does not eat rice.

11. In the case of Zaire, the punishment of the boy depended whether the girl was under sixteen or not. If the girl was considered a minor, the boy was subjected to dismissal, imprisonment, or payment of a fine. But generally all this depended greatly on the social status of the parents of both the girl and the boy.

12. Such means include abortion, adoption, and transfer to a different school upon delivery.

REFERENCES

Allison, Caroline. (1985). "Health and Education for Development: African Women's Status and Prospects," in Tore Rose (ed.), *Crisis and Recovery in Sub-Saharan Africa* (Paris: OECD).

Assie, N'Dri. (1982). "Educational Selection and Social Inequality in Africa: The Case of the Ivory Coast," unpublished Ph.D thesis, University of Chicago, December.

Assie-Lumumba, N'Dri. (1983). "Equity and Public School Finance: Policy of Resource Allocation in the Ivory Coast," Institute for Higher Education Law Governance, University of Houston, *Monograph* 83–5.

———. (1985). "The Fallacy of Quota-Like Solutions to Unequal Educational Opportunity: The Case of Female Education in the Ivory Coast." Paper presented at the Twenty-ninth Annual Comparative and International Education Society Conference, Stanford, California, April.

———. (1987). "Females' Participation in Schooling and Their Educational Outcomes in Africa: The Case of Côte d'Ivoire." Paper presented at the Sixth World Congress of Comparative Education, Rio de Janeiro, Brazil, July.

————. (1992a). Beyond the Issue of Quantity: Gender Inequality in Educational Opportunity in Africa. *Africa Notes,* Institute for African Development, Cornell University, March.

————. (1992b). "Quality of Education for All in Africa: Legacies of Past Policies and New Prospects for the Female Population." Paper presented at the Thirty-sixth Annual Comparative and International Education Society Conference, Annapolis, Maryland, March.

Assie-Lumumba, N'Dri, and Tukumbi Lumumba-Kasongo. (1991). "The State, Economic Crisis, and Educational Reform in Côte d'Ivoire," in Mark B. Ginsburg (ed.), *Understanding Educational Reform in Global Context: Economy, Ideology and the State* (New York and London: Garland Publishing).

Assie, N'Dri, et al. (1978). *HARUBA: Modernisation de l'habitat rural en Côte d'Ivoire* (Québec: l'Editeur Officiel du Québec).

Bouche, Denise. (1975). *L'enseignement dans les territoires français de l'Afrique Occidentale de 1817 à 1920: Mission civilisatrice ou formation d'une èlite?* (Paris: Librairie Honoré Champion).

Hyde, Karin A. L. (1991). "Sub-Saharan Africa," in Elizabeth M. King and M. Anne Hill (eds.), *Women's Education in Developing Countries: Barriers, Benefits and Policy* (Washington, DC: World Bank).

Little, Kenneth. (1974). *Urbanization as a Social Process: An Essay on Movement and Change in Contemporary Africa* (London, UK: Routledge and Kegan Paul).

Lumumba-Kasongo, Tukumbi. (1990). "African Education Policies and Educational Development," in Mekki Mtewa (ed.), *Contemporary Issues in African Administration and Development* (New Delhi, India: Allied Publishers).

Masemann, Vandra. (1974). "The Hidden Curriculum of a West African Girls' Boarding School," *Canadian Journal of African Studies 6,* no. 3.

Pellow, Deborah. (1977). *Women in Accra: Options for Autonomy,* (Algonac, MI: Reference Publications).

UNESCO. (1970). Education et promotion de la femme. Paris: UNESCO.

UNESCO. (1991). Statistical Review prepared for the Sixth Conference of the Ministers of Education and Those Responsible for Economic Planning in African Member States, Dakar, July.

11

The Effects of War Trauma on Central American Immigrant Children

Magaly Lavadenz

The purpose of this chapter is to examine the effects that traumatic war zone experiences have on the school performance of Central American immigrant children (CAIC) in public schools. The objective is not only to document the differences in school performance, but also to determine what aspects of past traumatic war experiences continue to impact the daily lives of this population.

As a teacher, the author has personally witnessed the war zone trauma that children exhibit and the consequent difficulties in the schooling process. According to Kirst (1988), the school serves as the primary point of contact for resources for immigrant families. This project attempts to identify this one segment of the school population which historically has been underidentified and underserved. Along with the identification process, consideration for the types of experiences Central American immigrant children have in school and the extent to which their trauma interferes with or impacts their school experience will be pivotal to this investigation.

Data from both participant observation and interviews were analyzed to determine the extent to which both the actual traumatic experiences and their recollections impact classroom behavior, performance, and learning. The sample was selected from an elementary school population through a process of screening for country of origin (El Salvador) and the administration by a trained counselor of a Child Self-Report Scale, which yielded information on the possibility of the existence of Post Traumatic Stress Disorder (PTSD). Respondents whose scores indicated possible PTSD were selected for the three case studies.

The original research questions concerned the specific performance of CAIC in the area of language development: That is to say, the hypothesis was that traumatic war experiences would have the effect of delaying, interrupting, or creating an emotional barrier against both the oral language development and the literacy development of CAIC. However, as will be documented in a later section, CAIC did not exhibit significantly different delays in language development when compared to other Hispanic minorities in the same setting. What became evident through observation and particularly through the interview process was that CAIC experience significant episodes of memory interference in the form of daydreaming in the classroom. This results in breaks or gaps in attention span and concentration on direct instruction from the teacher and/or individual or group schoolwork.

The importance of conducting research in this area lies in the impact that the numbers of children from war-torn countries have on our educational system. Not only do they add to ever-increasing numbers of language minority students in this state (California) and nation, but they also differ significantly in the kinds of experiences they have endured prior to their arrival.

CENTRAL AMERICAN STUDENTS AND PERFORMANCE

It can be determined from recent psychological literature that war experiences, namely, being witness to murder, torture, or crime, victimization through sexual, physical, and emotional abuse, and forced immigration, alone or in combination can and do lead to traumatization in children (Terr, 1985). It is not necessary to have psychological expertise to realize that events such as those mentioned above can have detrimental effects on children. However, experts in the field who have investigated the psychological impact of war zone experiences generally conclude that many such children are suffering from Post Traumatic Stress Disorder (Lavadenz, 1991). Symptoms of this disorder include avoidance behaviors, loss of developmental skills (including language), difficulty concentrating, a restricted affect, and a foreshortened sense of the future (American Psychiatric Association, 1987). The preceding symptoms have been highlighted in this study and are particularly noticeable in the school setting.

To the author's knowledge, there is no school district which gathers information on children's mental health (including war zone experiences) as part of the intake process. Olsen and Chen (1988) charge that ''there is little or no support for students who are particularly traumatized and scarred due to war, political oppression or poverty'' (p. 74). At the point of entry into school, a vast number of Central American immigrant children continue to experience severe educational, social, and emotional adjustment problems.

Researchers who have studied Central American immigrants in public school settings have determined that many of them, particularly high school–aged students, have a greater tendency to succeed, in terms of both graduation rates and academic performance (Hamilton, 1990; Suarez-Orozco, 1989, 1990a). They have explored the apparent academic success of CAIC in comparison with other Hispanic minorities in the United States, such as Mexican-Americans and Puerto Ricans. The critical difference between CAIC and the other Hispanic minorities, according to Suarez-Orozco, is that many of the other Hispanic minorities have been incorporated into the United States against their will, either through the acquisition of territories in the Southwest or through Spanish colonization. He contends that CAIC have not yet experienced or internalized the effects of exposure to cultural and racial depreciation and discrimination to the extent that the other "caste-like" Hispanic minorities have (Suarez-Orozco, 1990b, p. 39). Therefore, CAIC in the Southwestern inner cities that served as the setting for that study exhibit characteristics similar to other first-generation immigrants. These characteristics include a dual frame of reference, in which immigrants compare their situation here in the United States with that of their homeland, which, due to circumstances, was generally worse; the belief that hard work will lead to increased benefits for themselves and their families; and the conviction that education is the primary vehicle for "getting ahead."

Suarez-Orozco utilizes anthropologist John Ogbu's cultural-ecological model (1987) as the framework with which to compare Hispanic subgroups. According to Ogbu, school success or failure cannot be studied separately from the wider sociohistorical and political context. Given this "emic" approach to the study of this immigrant group, Suarez-Orozco concludes that Central American immigrants have high levels of achievement motivation which enable them to overcome obstacles that other Hispanics are not able to overcome, and that increased rates of high school graduation are directly attributable to their achievement motivation.

Upon closer inspection, however, it becomes evident that success has been defined very narrowly (Trueba, 1983). Once the majority of Central American immigrant children have an arena in which to describe the unspeakable experiences they have endured, and once patterns of behavior within social settings are more closely scrutinized, obvious differences become apparent.

To an extent, Central American immigrant students initially perceive these barriers as obstacles to be overcome. However, upon a closer look at individual responses, factors such as working after school, the hurdles to be surmounted daily at school, and the separation from parents take their toll on these children. Many high school students were denied enrollment into higher-level math courses, not given credit for courses already taken, or otherwise ignored when requesting information for college entrance. Suarez-Orozco supports the need for looking at successful minorities, along with the need for normative patterns of behavior for cross-cultural comparisons. Nonetheless, the positive attributes ascribed to Central American immigrant students in regard to school achievement tends to gloss over the individual, as will be documented.

An additional point of interest discussed during an interview with Dr. Suarez-Orozco was his use and interpretation of the Thematic Apperception Test

(TAT). Critics have stated that this is a psychological measure which necessitates a trained psychologist to administer and interpret. Suarez-Orozco responded that De Vos, a psychological anthropologist at the University of California at Berkeley, assisted him in scoring and interpreting the test. He also stated that he utilized the test to obtain "surface content" through which cross-cultural comparisons could be drawn. He believes that the TAT is a "useful tool that allows kids to talk about things they normally would not talk about in a safer, less-threatening way" (Personal interview, April 1991). This was an interesting point. However, in conducting the interviews for this project I did not encounter any resistance to talking; on the contrary, I found that once students realized they had an interested audience, it was difficult for them to stop talking.

It is critical to point out here that the employment of any psychological tool outside the context for which it was intended limits its interpretive value and has implications for the validity and reliability of the results. The interpretations and generalizations made on the basis of the TAT reveal that CAIC are troubled by recollections of war experiences and have feelings of guilt over the family members left behind. These concerns were also revealed in the current study of elementary school children. Academically, both high school and elementary children do not experience severe lags or difficulties. The factors Suarez-Orozco attributes to motivation, namely, guilt and the dual frame of reference, do have an impact in the degree to which students perform academically; that is, there do appear to be differential patterns of achievement in comparison to other Hispanic groups. Notwithstanding this, upon closer examination of the actual experiences in the classroom, it becomes evident that CAIC are burdened with much more than striving to achieve. They have distinctively different patterns of behavior that became readily apparent through the observations and interviews. These patterns of behavior included daydreaming, which interrupts their train of thought and attention to the task at hand and which prevents full concentration on classroom activities.

RESEARCH QUESTIONS

The primary question for this investigation, as previously mentioned, is: How do traumatic war zone experiences affect school performance; more precisely, what specific classroom behaviors, such as daydreaming, attention, concentration, participation, and involvement, are exhibited by Central American immigrant children? The seemingly contradictory conclusion from a study of high school Central American immigrant children is that they are motivated to stay in school longer than their Mexican or Puerto Rican counterparts. Suarez-Orozco (1989) attributes this to the realization of the extent to which their parents sacrificed to bring them out of war-torn countries to the United States. While this study sheds a positive light as to length of and achievement during the public school experience, the author neglects to acknowledge the type and quality of either the internalization of the trauma or the school experience for those students. An example of this is the case of Oscar Cabrera, which appeared in the *Los Angeles Times* (Hamilton, July 1990). This is a student exemplified as an overcomer and survivor, having witnessed the murder of his father in El Salvador. After five years in the United States, Oscar received a full scholarship to the Webb School of California, "a prestigious, college-prep boarding school." In spite of his academic success, Oscar has no peer relations (very uncommon for a fifteen-year-old adolescent) and is plagued by recurrent nightmares wherein the execution of his father is replayed. He states that he often struggles with persistent thoughts and recollections of those traumatic events and consciously makes an effort not to think about them.

The point here is that although some Central American immigrant children differ in their school performance, the phantoms and shadows from their past greatly influence the quality of their school experience. The school experience may be deemed successful by some who view duration in school or graduation or even grade point average as measures of success. However, also necessary is a profound look into the quality of their emotional and social lives. A closer view of the informants in Suarez-Orozco's study (1989) reveals that while many high school students are superficially successful in school, the quality of their responses to the TAT portray themes similar to those revealed in the present study; that is, most Central American immigrant children are heavily burdened by the impact of their war zone experiences, to the extent that recollections of those experiences interrupt normal school functioning, especially in the area of staying on task, concentrating, and daydreaming.

METHODOLOGY

The exploration of the characteristics of the academic performance of war-traumatized children through analysis of school records, language, and literacy levels was the initial step taken in compiling a sample for this study. The determination of war trauma via the Child Self-Report Scale was the second step in the process. Respondents whose score indicated possible PTSD were selected for the case studies. All students were from El Salvador.

Participant observation and interview information constituted the third phase in determining the school experiences of Central American children in public schools. The case study methodology was selected primarily because the information could be elicited directly from the children in a setting within which they felt comfortable. In addition to the ability of this author to speak Spanish fluently, previous training in the field of counseling psychology proved to be beneficial in establishing a safe, nonjudgmental environment and for eliciting information from the children during the interviews. The case studies for this project were all at the elementary school where I was teaching. The school is a large, suburban k-6 elementary school within the Glendale Unified School District in Los Angeles County.

Phase One: Identification of Study Sample and Procedures

A search of school records for information regarding Spanish oral language levels and literacy levels revealed that many CAIC who had war zone experiences had very little differences in either oral language development or literacy development. The determination of oral language ability was established through measures of the Spanish LAS (Language Assessment Scales), while reading ability was assessed through placement and adequate performance in the Spanish basal reader.

Originally I believed, as mentioned at the beginning of the chapter, that during this first phase I would find that traumatic war experiences would negatively affect the language and literacy development of CAIC. Upon analysis of the data, however, this conclusion could not be drawn. Although some students were functioning at slightly below grade level in reading, this is not vastly different from the rest of the general school population. The same could be said for oral language (as determined by the Spanish LAS). In fact, while a few CAIC are limited in Spanish oral language and are two years below grade level in reading, many are fluent in their native language and functioning only slightly below grade level. This information led to a reexamination of what key features of school performance distinguish the school experience of traumatized CAIC. It was not until the case study interviews with the students and the teachers were conducted that the critical differences in performance became more apparent. These critical differences centered around specific patterns of attention (or lack thereof), daydreams, and a general difficulty in concentrating on schoolwork.

Phase Two: Child Self-Report Scale for PTSD

Upon identification of Central American immigrant children, those who were most limited in the LAS (score of 1 or 2), who were reading two or more years below grade level, or who were retained or placed or referred for special education were selected to complete a Child Self-Report Scale (Appendix A). In order to meet the criteria for Post Traumatic Stress Disorder (PTSD), children had to answer "yes" to three or more statements. Out of seventeen students who completed the scale, ten (or 58 percent) met the criteria for PTSD. The criteria for PTSD have been identified in both the *Diagnostic and Statistical Manual of Mental Disorders* (American Psychiatric Association, 1987) and Terr's (1985) research on traumatized children. The scales used were developed as part of this author's master's thesis. Of the ten children who met the criteria for PTSD, four were selected for the case studies in this project. In addition, classroom teachers were asked to complete a Teacher Observation Scale (Appendix B). This scale approximates the frequencies with which the teacher believes the student exhibits behaviors and drawings associated with PTSD. The behaviors are also consistent with the criteria in the *Diagnostic and Statistical Manual of Mental Disorders* and Terr's research.

Information was obtained from students, teachers, and parents. Interviews were conducted over a period of two weeks. Student interviews were conducted over two fifteen-minute sessions. The durations of interviews were determined according to the ages of the students, attention span being the primary concern with young children. Classroom observations were conducted during several forty-minute periods for each child. This time frame was selected in order to observe how the children reacted to shifts in the curriculum, such as changing from a teacher-directed lesson to independent practice. This type of information, in regard to reactions to change, proved useful in the analysis portion of the study.

Phase Three: Case Studies

Case Study 1: Enriqueta. Enriqueta is a six-year-old female student in the first grade at a large suburban elementary school in Glendale. She has been in the United States for two years. Enriqueta was selected for the case study because she scored 8 out of 10 on the Child Self-Report Scale for PTSD. The score indicates a very strong possibility of trauma, as evidenced by positive responses to items dealing with feelings that something bad happened, daydreams, inability to concentrate, and nightmares. She attended kindergarten at the same elementary school and her records indicate that she had a successful experience, both academically and socially. Enriqueta recently returned to El Salvador with her family for a vacation and to visit relatives that had remained. She was very willing to respond to questions and appeared comfortable and at ease. Enriqueta scored at the fluent level (4) on the Spanish LAS and is reading at the first preprimer level in Spanish.

Her most vivid recollection regarding her recent visit seems to center around her eleven-year-old cousin, who had been recruited for the war. She said she asked him, "Who let you do this?" and he answered that the soldiers were going to show him how to shoot a rifle and that he liked it. Enriqueta says that she thinks a lot about her cousin and hopes he can come soon. I asked her what her parents had told her about the war there and she said they had told her that you have to be careful of bullets because they fly in the air. When asked how she felt about that she said that "it was scary, especially one night when the bullets woke me up."

When I asked her about dreams, Enriqueta stated that she had dreamed that her cousin was stuck in a hole with water and they could not get him out. She also said that her family had tried to bring her cousin back with them, but they apparently could not get him through the border *(no la pudimos pasar)*. As it was, Enriqueta reported that they themselves had to use different names to get through. As is common with some Central American families, they return to visit family members that stayed behind. Enriqueta had originally immigrated at age three; many of her memories of that time were what is termed in the literature as "preverbal" (Terr, 1985). However, reexperiencing the war situation as well as the additional impact of reimmigrating had the effect of crystallizing previous traumatic events.

Enriqueta said that she tries not to think about war and bullets at school; however, sometimes she does anyway, especially about her cousin. Her teacher reports that she has made good academic progress throughout the school year in all subjects, but that she has to be reminded constantly to attend to her work. The teacher also reports that Enriqueta has many moments of "spacing out," but that she is very bright and usually completes her work correctly. During the classroom observations, much of what the teacher reported about Enriqueta's distractibility became evident. During the reading/language arts time block, in which students are to work independently on seat work until their small group is called for instruction, Enriqueta looked around several times, listened to what the small group was discussing, stared into space, and generally did not even begin working on her papers until after the teaching assistant had called her group to a round table and asked to see their work. The time elapsed was approximately twenty-five minutes. Eventually, Enriqueta completed her work correctly, but not until the teacher gave the ten-minute warning for recess. At this point, Enriqueta began work and completed two out of three work sheets. Enriqueta's teacher reports that she is able to complete her work only after constant reminders. Many of the responses for Enriqueta on the Teacher Observation Scale were in the "sometimes" and "always" categories, especially in classroom behaviors involving "staring," "confusion," and "seeming to be in another world."

Evidently, Enriqueta's classroom performance is negatively affected by aspects of PTSD. Although not seriously behind academically, she has extreme difficulty in staying on task without constant reinforcement by the teacher or teaching assistant. A brief conference with Enriqueta's mother indicated that since they returned from their vacation to El Salvador, Enriqueta wakes up more often at night and wants to sleep in the same bed as her parents. This is consistent with Enriqueta's report of dreaming of her eleven-year-old cousin. All the variables outlined in this case study—the sleep disorders, the lack of attention and concentration—demonstrate manifestations of PTSD. The ramifications of the general lack of knowledge of this phenomenon in the school setting will be addressed in "Conclusions and Implications," at the end of the chapter.

Case Study 2: Ricardo. Ricardo is a nine-year-old boy who has been in this country for two years. He speaks Spanish fluently and reads at the beginning of third grade level in Spanish, which is approximately 1½ years below grade level. Ricardo was able to verbalize and describe in greater detail the specific recollections about the war experiences he had witnessed. The memories which he said he thinks about the most are the lights in the hillsides, which were bombs exploding during combat between the army and the guerrillas. He said he was always very afraid because they could hit the village where they lived. Although he said no bombs actually fell in his village, he seemed to be bothered that soldiers were always coming through and telling everybody that "you'd better be careful." Ricardo did not go to school while he was in El Salvador because, he said, it was too dangerous. Sometimes his aunt would take him to the park, but would avoid going through "dangerous places" to get there.

Ricardo's nightmares and daydreams center around his fear that bad things will happen to his grandparents and aunts. I asked him what bad things he's afraid will occur, and he stated that the soldiers could take them away or a bomb could fall on them. He also has nightmares "that some people come into my house and want to kill me, and then, after my dreams, I can't go back to sleep." I asked him if soldiers had ever come to his house when he was in El Salvador. He said no, but that his aunts told him that the soldiers had come while he was not at home. Additional memories that he has about El Salvador mainly involve his sadness at being left behind by his mother for four years while she came to the United States to work and save enough money to send for him. He said he cried a lot, especially when his mother telephoned home. He reports that they do not talk much about the war at his house, and when he asks his mother a question, she doesn't like to talk about it "because it makes her worry more."

When questioned whether he thinks about the soldiers or the bad dreams while he is at school, Ricardo said that he thinks mainly about his grandmother, aunts, and cousins. He hopes that they can come soon so that he won't worry about them. Ricardo is aware of the times that he tends not to pay attention during school. He says that when he catches himself thinking about something other than what the teacher is saying or the work he is supposed to be doing, he tries to stop thinking about it and finish his work. He seems to have adopted some coping skills to deal with his tendencies to daydream in class. Ricardo's teacher reports that he is typically a very hard worker, but has difficulty staying on task. His performance is cyclical, some days being much better than others. Sometimes he just stares out into space. His drawings, as noted in the Teacher Observation Scale, are very immature for his age, appearing to be missing body parts and depicting war scenes.

Ricardo was observed several times in a variety of school contexts (recesses, language arts class, physical education). However, it was during an observation of a math lesson that the most obvious behaviors became apparent. The lesson was on place value. During the course of the lesson, he varied a great deal in the amount of attention paid to both the instructor and the task at hand. For example, at the beginning of the lesson, while the teacher was instructing and questioning the class as a whole, Ricardo initially followed along. After a few moments, while the teacher was still in front of the room, Ricardo began to look around, finally resting his observation on the butterfly mobiles hanging from the light fixtures. As soon as the teacher began moving around the room, however, Ricardo resumed paying attention to instruction. This type of fluctuation and variation of attention to the task at hand was common throughout the forty-minute observation. Other types of inattentive and distractive behaviors during this time included the following:

- Ricardo did not participate in oral recitation of place values. Instead, he looked around the room. He did occasionally glance at the blackboard while the teacher pointed to the numerals that were to be identified.
- Ricardo did not participate in volunteering answers during the brief (five-minute) session.
- Ricardo's posture during the course of the observation differed from that of the rest of the class: He leaned on his elbows and was hunched over his desk. His classmates were generally sitting up straight at their desks.
- During the course of the lesson, Ricardo was observed to be staring off at times, yet he usually turned his attention back to his work. This pattern of staring out the window and then returning to his work was repeated several times during the remainder of the observation period.

Because Ricardo was better able to verbalize his recollections and the impact he feels they have on his paying attention in class, a much clearer depiction of the linkage between war zone experiences and classroom performance can be established in his case. The extent to which he exhibited a higher level of cognitive awareness of his tendency to daydream frequently during class time, as compared with Enriqueta, can be primarily attributed to his age and development. Although this linkage was also observable in Enriqueta's case, Ricardo's was less because he was conscious of the disruptions these memories and concerns for family members had on his learning. These examples of awareness by CAIC of the total picture—worries about family members, mental lapses with glimpses of bombs falling, soldiers, and danger—are typical for these children, both at the elementary school level and at the high school level. The degree of awareness of the tendency to go off task, daydream and/or lose focus on instruction and learning varies from student to student; yet these behaviors appear readily noticeable to teachers and observers once they become knowledgeable about key factors affecting the classroom performance of CAIC.

Case Study 3: Paula. Paula is a twelve-year-old girl who has been in California for two years. She is a limited Spanish speaker (a score of 3 on the LAS) and reads $2^{1}/_{2}$ years below grade level. Paula was able to attend school in El Salvador. She has very vivid recollections of her experiences in her native land. She spoke very nonchalantly about seeing corpses along the road, especially of one man who she says was killed by blows from a machete. She was often told by her aunts to hide under the bed when the guerrillas would come through town trying to recruit adolescents. She said that her uncle was one of the "desaparecidos" (the disappeared). These "disappeared" are people, including men, women, and children, who for some reason or another are never seen or heard from again. A conference with Paula's aunt revealed that in actuality, Paula's uncle was killed by the guerrillas in front of his family, but that Paula was not told about it, merely that he had "disappeared."

In addition to these experiences, Paula reports that she was kidnapped by her grandmother's husband when he was drunk. She said that he used to like her and take her everywhere with him, but that he was always beating her grandmother up. She remembered that he took her over a bridge against her will. Although this episode was not directly connected with the war, this type of experience can also yield manifestations of PTSD (Arroyo, 1985) and, when added to the war trauma, can compound its effects.

Paula also remembered the bombs falling in her village and people running, screaming, and hiding. She said that her father speaks of returning to visit his sister, and she expressed fear at the thought, particularly in light of the fact that her father would take the whole family. She said she knows that if she goes she "won't make it back." She asks her father not to go, telling him that "todo esta muy feo" (things are very ugly). Paula says she worries about the possibility of her family's return to El Salvador when questioned as to what she thinks most about during the day.

Paula's classroom performance differs somewhat from those in the previous two case studies in that she is not doing as well academically. Despite the fact that she was able to attend school in El Salvador, Paula's teacher reports that she has severe lags in reading achievement (2½ years below grade level), not attributable to a learning disability, given that she was previously referred for evaluation for special education. Test results showed that she is of normal intelligence and ability. Paula's teacher reports that Paula rarely participates in class discussion or completes her work on time. The Teacher Observation Scale shows that Paula is usually withdrawn and that her drawings depict very dark settings.

During classroom observations, Paula was observed during the language arts time block. At the beginning of the lesson, the teacher gave directions and explanations for the independent seat work, much as had occurred in Enriqueta's classroom. At first glance, Paula appeared attentive to the teacher, but upon closer evaluation (which was possible because I changed seats to be more in proximity to Paula), it became obvious that Paula had a somewhat "glazed" look in her eyes. This glazed expression occurred approximately ten times during a thirty-minute period. Throughout the observation, Paula appeared to be very slow at getting around to actually doing her work. When the designated time was over, she had completed only half of her assignment. The teacher reports that this is the general trend for Paula.

It was not possible to ascertain via a postobservation interview whether the glazed expression could be imputed to the concerns for family and recollections of experiences. However, given that the criteria for possible PTSD was previously met through the Teacher and the Child Observation Scales, Paula's classroom behaviors (as well as those in the other case studies) consistently match those of others whose war experiences negatively affect classroom performance. In Paula's case, the efficiency with which she completed classroom tasks was significantly delayed due to daydreaming.

Discussion

In conjunction with the persistent and recurrent dreams and thought patterns, Central American immigrant children are struggling with the guilt and concern over those who are left behind. They and their families are happy to have gotten out; yet as evidenced by statements made by Enriqueta in regard to her eleven-year-old cousin, and by Ricardo about his grandmother, it is common for Central Americans not to forget or dismiss those who were not able to come. Often, as in Paula's case, family members in the United States express a desire to return to their motherland to visit with relatives. This concern is dominant for all children. Paula's fears about her father's return during war conditions are evident in her requests to him that he not do so. She fears for her own safety if the family were to return together. This fear of imminent return was portrayed in Paula's glassy-eyed expression during the classroom observation.

Parents of Central American students, although willing to talk to me, report that when their children question them, they usually pretend they don't hear, change the subject, or try to divert their child's attention. They feel that it is better not to talk about things that happened in the past and that since the children were young, they would probably forget about their war zone experiences. I found very little communication between families of Central Americans in our school. Even though they may have had children in the same classroom, they did not know each other, which created a sense of isolation. Parents reported that they don't have time to talk (because of work), yet underlying this lack of communication is their fear of the "death squads" which have been reported to have assassinated Salvadorans in the United States. It appears that the parents are also struggling with their own fears, nightmares, and other symptoms of PTSD.

In addition to the traumatization due to the actual war experiences, immigrant children from Central America have endured an additional trauma through the immigration process. Usually, immigration is accomplished illegally, through a "coyote," who is paid a fee. Even though a fee is paid, it is not a guarantee of passage through the border. Enriqueta demonstrated the tenuousness of the procedure and the regret that her cousin could not get through. The dynamics unleashed by war trauma are identified in Figure 11.1.

These cases are representative of the experiences of many Central American immigrants, children and adults alike (Arroyo, 1985; Suarez-Orozco, 1989). Older students who arrive with similar experiences are able to verbalize their experiences better, yet they exhibit similar types of problems, such as difficulty in concentrating and staying on task, daydreaming, and recurrent dreams. Simi-

Figure 11.1
Effects of War Trauma on Central American Immigrant Children

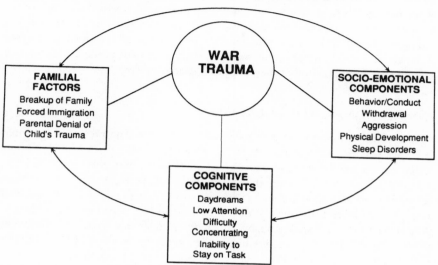

lar evidence is found in Suarez-Orozco's research (1989), in which high school students respond to cards in which particular scenes are depicted. Student responses are analyzed for themes in accord with the projective test (Thematic Apperception Test). Student responses were similar to responses from students interviewed for this project, yet the conclusions made by Suarez-Orozco were very different.

A comparison of the settings (urban versus inner-city) can be made in which students immigrating from war zones who come to live in inner cities exhibit different kinds of behaviors in schools (Arroyo, 1985). Instead of exhibiting difficulties in the areas of concentration and attention in the classroom, which are relatively unobtrusive and introspective, CAIC in inner-city areas where gang activity is very common tend to be aggressive, defiant, and more prone to acting out behaviors. These students tend to attract more attention from school staff because of their disruptive tendencies.

Juxtaposed to these aggressive students, who still receive little attention as to the underlying causes of their behaviors, are the majority of CAIC in our schools, who are classified by their teachers as more quiet and withdrawn. These types of students are often ignored by the teachers and other school staff. Most teachers, as evidenced by responses to interviews, are not even aware of the regional, ethnic, and cultural differences between Hispanic ethnic groups (for example, Mexican-American versus Guatemalan or Nicaraguan or Salvadoran), much less aware of the internal struggles of some of their students. Teachers have large class sizes (averaging between thirty and thirty-seven) and have little time for individual interaction with the more quiet students. Except for extreme cases, teachers usually classify Central American students as day-dreamers and "space cadets," sometimes punishing them for their lack of attention. Little do school personnel realize that their nightmares are extended to daytime, during which time traumatized children struggle with their straying thoughts and minds while simultaneously struggling with academic instruction and teacher perceptions that they are just "spacey or lazy."

CONCLUSIONS AND IMPLICATIONS

It is possible to surmise from the literature and the data presented here that the vast majority of Central American immigrant children in public schools today are not exhibiting severe academic problems, either in terms of oral language development or literacy development. As evidenced by their larger rates of graduation and other means of judging success, it can also be extrapolated from the literature and from the data presented in the case studies that Central American immigrant students have qualitatively different types of experiences in the schools. These qualitative differences occur on an internal level and are very much ignored by school personnel, who characterize these students as "hardworking space cadets." This was clear both at the elementary school level through teacher interviews, and in Suarez-Orozco's research at the high school level (1989), where themes and responses given by students demonstrated their internal struggles. Ernesto is an example from that study:

But then what happened to my cousins and my friends made me afraid. I said "Any time something will happen to me. El Salvador is a place where it is a sin to be young." Life became impossible; I could no longer live like that. . . . I would go to school and the students would be protesting about something, and the next day a few would be dead. . . . I was afraid I was going to be recruited into the army. There they teach you to be a criminal: they teach you to kill, kill, kill. They make you crazy. The death squads are sadists. They kill anyone. (Suarez-Orozco, 1989, pp. 61–62)

What is also readily apparent is that school officials are not attending to the struggles within.

Additional research is needed in the area of the impact of war experiences on children and the repercussions of struggling to adapt to the school environment on a daily basis. Specific actions on the part of those who come into immediate contact with Central American immigrant children, namely teachers, counselors, and researchers, are needed so as not to augment the struggles, but rather to understand their experiences and to find ways to ease their adjustment to a new setting. Some of these actions may be merely at the level of being aware of their experiences and withholding judgment as to their lack of attention. More direct actions involving searching for community resources as referrals for social and psychological services are also needed.

Other beneficiaries of the search for community resources will be the parents of these children, who very often have isolated themselves not only from each other, but also from their own children to an extent. They also have endured traumatic experiences and wish for their children to forget and go on with their lives in a new country, away from the war. The dreams that they have for their children revolve around getting an education and getting ahead. The problem remains that their children cannot forget.

While it is possible to generalize that the vast majority of Central American children who immigrated past the age of two will have experienced some degree of traumatization due to their war zone experiences, careful examination of each child remains critical. Children respond to stressors in a variety of ways; many develop coping skills, such as in the case of Ricardo, who consciously struggles with overcoming his tendencies to daydream and worry about his relatives. The teacher's role remains critical in the daily interactions with children like Ricardo. Labeling and negativity can augment daydreaming tendencies, while understanding, patience, and empathy will not only promote better teacher-student relationships, but will most likely assist Central American immigrant children in their adjustment to the academic environment, as well as in their adaptation to a new way of living in the United States.

The extent to which the vast majority of Central American immigrant students settle in larger urban areas, such as Los Angeles and San Diego counties (Suarez-Orozco, 1989), places an even greater burden on already overtaxed public school systems. Concerns for language minority students, including Central Americans, have risen in proportion to the increase in sheer numbers; however, many of these concerns have centered on academic performance and high school graduation rates. The degree to which CAIC have experienced greater academic success than their Mexican or Puerto Rican counterparts does not negate the fact that many CAIC are under emotional and psychological duress. This fact is also largely ignored by school officials. There remains a great need for continued research and intervention for this school population.

APPENDIX A: CHILD SELF-REPORT SCALE

		Circle One	
1.	I have been afraid to tell anyone about what happened to me.	Yes	No
2.	Something terrible happened to me but I don't know what it was.	Yes	No
3	I have bad headaches.	Yes	No
4.	I wake up a lot at night.	Yes	No
5.	I have a lot of bad dreams.	Yes	No
6.	Someone has done something bad to me.	Yes	No
7.	My teachers are always telling me to pay attention.	Yes	No
8.	I daydream a lot.	Yes	No
9.	I think I will be happy when I grow up.	Yes	No
10.	I know what I want to be when I grow up.	Yes	No

APPENDIX B: TEACHERS OBSERVATION SCALE FOR
CHILDREN WITH POST TRAUMATIC STRESS DISORDER

	Never	Sometimes	Always
Classroom Behaviors			
Stares	1	2	3
Gets confused often	1	2	3
Seems to be in another world	1	2	3
Does not want to be touched	1	2	3
Abilities to perform change	1	2	3
Behavior Observed on Playground with Peers			
Isolates and talks to self	1	2	3
Stares	1	2	3
Makes strange sounds	1	2	3
Terrified when other children are disciplined	1	2	3
Becomes aggressive suddenly	1	2	3
Withdraws suddenly	1	2	3
Afraid to go to certain places	1	2	3
Drawings			
Distinct separation of body parts	1	2	3
Picture with knives, blood, killings	1	2	3
Refuses to sign picture	1	2	3
Symbols Depicting Trauma			
Dark skies	1	2	3
Large mouths	1	2	3
Omissions	1	2	3
Males--vaginal shapes, looks trapped	1	2	3
Female--phallic objects	1	2	3

REFERENCES

American Psychiatric Association. (1987). *The Diagnostic and Statistical Manual of Mental Disorders*. Third edition, revised. Washington, DC.

Arroyo, William. (1985). Children Traumatized by Central American Warfare. In *Post Traumatic Stress Disorder in Children*. Ed. Spencer Eth and Robert Pynoos. Washington, DC: A.P.A. Press.

Hamilton, Denise. (12 July 1990). Oscar's Crash Course in Democracy. *Los Angeles Times*.

Kirst, Michael. (1988). *Policy Analysis for California Education (PACE): Condition of Children in California*. Berkeley, CA: Berkeley Press.

Lavadenz, Magaly. (1991). Post Traumatic Stress Disorder in Central American Immigrant Children. Unpublished master's thesis, California State University, Northridge, CA.

Ogbu, John U. (1987). Variability in Minority School Performance: A Problem in Search of an Explanation. *Anthropology and Education Quarterly* 18: 312–333. Berkeley, CA: Berkeley Press.

Olsen, Laurie, and Chen, Marcia. (1988). *Crossing the Schoolhouse Border: Immigrant Students and the California Public Schools.* San Francisco, CA: A California Tomorrow Research Report.

Suarez-Orozco, Marcelo. (1989). *Central American Refugees in U.S. High Schools.* Stanford, CA: Stanford University Press.

Suarez-Orozco, Marcelo. (1991). Personal interview, April.

Suarez-Orozco, Marcelo. (1990a). Speaking of the Unspeakable: Toward a Psychosocial Understanding of Responses to Terror. *Ethos 18:*353–383.

Suarez-Orozco, Marcelo. (1990b). Psychosocial Aspects of Achievement Motivation among Recent Hispanic Immigrants. In *What Do Anthropologists Say about Dropouts?* Ed. Henry Trueba, George Spindler, and Louise Spindler. Stanford, CA: Stanford University Press.

Terr, L. C. (1985). Children Traumatized in Small Groups. In *Post Traumatic Stress Disorder in Children.* Ed. Spencer Eth and Robert Pynoos. Washington, DC: A.P.A. Press.

Trueba, Henry. (1983). The Ethnography of Schooling. In *The Ethnography of Schooling.* Ed. Henry Trueba. Triffield: Nufferton.

12

Street Children and Their Education: A Challenge for Urban Educators

Adrian Blunt

This chapter discusses the education of street children, a rapidly growing, unique urban population that presents a major challenge for educators around the globe. The phenomenon of street children exposes the contradictions of urban life. Within sight of the economic and cultural riches of the city exists a social group whose everyday lives are a negation of the often-assumed benefits of urban life. As Stromquist writes in this volume, there is a need to take apart commonly held assumptions about urban life, especially in the educational context. The street children phenomenon raises disturbing questions about the wisdom of modernization and development models that favor urban development at the expense of rural development. This phenomenon also raises questions regarding national educational policies based on traditional forms of urban schooling. As this chapter will show, street children, and many children of the poor, are not served by urban public schools. The traditional model of city schools, with its middle-class curriculum, values, and social norms excludes, and is also rejected by, those who are "the poorest of the poor."

The street children phenomenon, although sensationalized by the popular media, has only recently emerged as the subject of systematic academic inquiry. The popular media have focused on the details of street childrens' lives to present graphic images of their poverty and exposure to violence, economic exploitation, and drug and substance abuse. Readers are left shocked and disturbed by reports, often supported by photographs, of child laborers, scavengers, teenage prostitutes, glue-sniffing preteens, and bodies of murdered children (see for example Dimenstein, 1991; Lee-Wright, 1990; Webber, 1991). These accounts have appealed to readers' emotions but have not contributed to a critical understanding of the underlying causes of street children as an urban phenomenon.

To move toward such an understanding, the literature on street children is examined in terms of structural factors which have shaped the conditions for the emergence of this population. A distinction is drawn between street children in the developing nations and those in developed nations in terms of how the literature ascribes underlying causes. I argue for a more dynamic and multifaceted understanding of the structural factors, economic, political, and social, which underlie the street children phenomenon in order to move away from "cultural" explanations. I also argue that educational programs for street children need to be critically examined to determine if they serve as instruments of social regulation and control, or are liberatory and emancipatory. Although structural forms are emphasized in the chapter I try to avoid viewing street children as victims of these urban structures. Educational programs which make "space" for resistance and liberatory possibilities need to be recognized. If "space" is taken in a productive sense (by this I mean space that both shapes identities and is in turn shaped by individuals acting in deliberate and conscious ways), then educators need to identify those processes and dynamics of successful street education projects that work to reshape the urban education interface in the most positive and beneficial ways for poor urban children. The chapter concludes with a discussion of issues for further analysis and research, and suggestions on how the work of street educators could be theorized.

WHO ARE THE STREET CHILDREN?

Childhood is a social institution constructed in different ways by cultures around the globe. In the West children are considered immature, dependent family members for considerably longer than in the developing nations. Compulsory school attendance in the West is generally required until age sixteen, after which adult roles such as full-time employment, driving, and marriage can be legally assumed. In many developing nations children are required to attend school only until age eleven or twelve and they are allowed, if not expected, to begin work or marry shortly afterward. In the West street children as young as eleven or twelve years old have been identified; however, the great majority are teenagers. Children as young as five years old live on the streets in the developing countries, and the majority range in age from ten to fifteen. Girls on the street are older than boys, as they frequently remain at home contributing domestic labor before being abandoned or running away.

It is not possible to provide accurate data on the numbers of street children globally, as there is no single objective definition used to report them. The most widely accepted definition has been proposed by the International Catholic Child Bureau and adopted by the United Nations Children's Fund (UNICEF):

"Street children are those for whom the street (in the widest sense of the word, including unoccupied buildings, wasteland etc.) more than their family has become their real home, a situation in which there is no protection, supervision, or direction from responsible adults" (Fyfe, 1985). From this definition two categories of street children have been created, "children-of-the-street" and "children-on-the-street." Children-of-the-street have no contact with their family members and live independently. Children-on-the-street maintain some contact with their family. They may work and sleep on the street and visit with family members at regular intervals, or they may make contact only at irregular intervals, such as when they are sick or in difficulty and need assistance. A third category, children-for-the-street, are all those who are at risk due to family breakdown leading to separation from their parents, or to family violence, or to extreme employment hardship, which may result in the decision to run away. While these *a priori* definitions are necessary to establish a consensus on the magnitude of the problem, it needs to be recognized that they tend to render invisible the actual cyclical and dynamic relationships that many street children are likely to have with their families.

Estimates of the numbers of children living in especially difficult circumstances have been developed by UNICEF (UNICEF, 1990). As many as 270 million, or 15 percent of the world's population of children, are estimated to be living under difficult circumstances: 100 million abused or neglected in their homes, or in state and community institutions; 100 million working in hazardous or exploitive conditions; 50 million living on the streets, and 20 million displaced by natural disasters and regional armed conflicts. From these estimates UNICEF reports that there are a minimum of 50 and possibly as many as 70 million children-of-the-street, an additional 100 million children-on-the-street, and a further 120 million children-for-the-street. Estimates vary between 15 and 30 percent as to the proportion of girls who are among the children-of-the-street and children-on-the-street populations. The great majority of street children, over 90 percent, are in the metropolitan areas of the least developed countries, including Rio de Janeiro, Mexico City, Nairobi, Calcutta, and Manila. Developed countries have far fewer street children than the least developed; however, numbers are increasing. Since 1972 the American Youth Work Center has published a directory of programs and agencies providing service for runaways, homeless youth, and families of missing children. The sixth edition (Hines, 1988) has 329 pages of resource information for the United States and Canada. It is estimated, for example, that there are over 200,000 children living on the streets of New York City. Similarly large populations are on the streets of European cities.

The street children phenomenon is ubiquitous, observing no political or national boundaries. Street children can be observed wherever the state's apparatus to control their presence is constrained by civil law or international moral persuasion. Shortly after the demise of the Communist Party in the former Soviet Union and the adoption of free market reform in the People's Republic of China, street children appeared in the downtown areas of Moscow and Beijing. Only on the well-controlled streets of states such as Cuba and Singapore are street children absent. However, while the phenomenon is global, the causes are reported to be different for the developed and least developed countries.

STRUCTURAL FACTORS INFLUENCING THE EMERGENCE OF STREET CHILDREN

In the least developed countries the descriptive literature attributes the occurrence of on-the-street children directly to family crisis and breakdown caused by extreme urban poverty. In the more analytical literature (see Agnelli, 1986; Boyden, 1991; Ennew and Milne, 1990; Espert and Myers, 1988; Felsman, 1989; Fyfe, 1985; Korten, 1990; Myers, 1991) this view is developed to recognize that the survival of the modern urban nuclear family has been placed at risk by several related factors including: (1) unprecedented global economic change causing national recessions, the imposition of international debt repayment programs, and the decline of social security programs; (2) continuing population increases and rural-urban migration; (3) declines in agricultural production and the failure to implement effective land reform; (4) natural disasters and climatic changes resulting in famine and the forced relocation of people; and (5) regional armed conflicts displacing populations and creating thousands of orphaned and abandoned children. Only the first three factors, which have an urban structural context, are considered in this chapter.

Economic Forces

For the urban poor in the least developed countries the extreme poverty and deprivation in their daily lives is seen to be a direct consequence of economic and social change far beyond their control or influence. Rural families who were encouraged to make the transition from subsistence to cash crop agriculture in the 1950s and 1960s were faced in the 1970s and 1980s with the collapse of international commodity prices and the continuance of national policies for low food prices to protect the urban populations earning subsistence wages. The commodification of food production pushed rural areas into economic stagnation, while cities appeared to promise employment, education, government assistance, and a more secure financial future. The global rural-urban migration accelerated in many of the least developed countries to become a migration out of control.

Since the 1950s, urban growth in Third World cities has occurred at such a rate that it has been equivalent to the construction of a new city of similar size to each old one, built on the outskirts or on top of the old cities, every ten to fifteen years (Hardoy and Satterthwaite, 1989). Cities have been unable to meet the demand for basic housing, education, and health services. The influx of "economic refugees" has overwhelmed the providers of services, and national governments have lacked the political will to act to halt the migration by implementing rural land and agrarian reforms. To compound the problem, the global economic recession has resulted in high unemployment and a halt to the development boom that encouraged urban growth in the first place.

Social Change in the City

In times of economic difficulty rural peasants relied for assistance on their extended family relationships, which existed within stable communities that valued cooperative effort. The cultural values of resource sharing, accepting responsibility to assist family members, and cooperative labor to achieve community objectives were reinforced in difficult times. However, the experience of urban poverty has proven to be unlike that of rural poverty. In the city close ties with extended family members in rural areas are rendered ineffective by distance and poor communications. Urban neighbors tend to be strangers and competitors for resources, so sharing becomes dysfunctional when not reciprocated. Crowding and a lack of sanitation, potable water, and quality housing bring disease. Sickness, unemployment, and hunger bring desperation, crime, violence, drug and alcohol abuse, and the exploitation of the weak and unprotected. In the urban slum, government assistance is negligible or nonexistent, and the organization of urban self-help and advocacy groups may be met with repressive acts from the state. In these circumstances the interests of the better-off focus upon their own protection, and the migrant family must rely entirely upon its own resources.

Over time densification and poverty provide the material conditions for extensive squatter barrios. The impossibility of owning land or a home for the rural migrants and the anemic conditions of the slums eventually operate to erode traditional patterns of social life. Many migrant families experience rapid, disorienting change from a rural culture, where children are likely to have been regarded as a blessing (certainly for males and often for females) and as security for parents in their later years, to an alienating urban slum existence where children may become a burden to threaten the immediate survival and future prosperity of parents.

Unemployment

Lack of employment forces some fathers to leave their families to seek jobs unencumbered by a spouse and children. Other families lose the financial support of male members owing to incarceration for petty crime, injury, illness, or death. Younger abandoned women with children, or with partners unable to support the family, have only four options: (1) to obtain paid employment with an income large enough to support the family, a highly unlikely prospect; (2) to replace the missing or nonproductive partner with one able and willing to maintain the family; (3) to find through illegal means, usually theft or prostitution, the income to support the family; and (4) to abandon the family. Initially, and with good intentions, parents might ask relatives or friends to care for their children until they are employed. Failure to find work may result in the temporary arrangements becoming a permanent responsibility for the foster parents. Alternatively, informal adoption, "bonding" to an employer, the sale of children, "shutting out" or even abandonment in a public place might be the parents' last desperate resort to reduce their family burden. Differently abled and impaired children are at high risk to abandonment if parents are unable to derive any benefit from the children's labor. Children who experience violence, abuse, or neglect in the home may run away. Older children who work and contribute to the family's income and who think they can have a better life away from their family sometimes decide to take their chances on the streets.

The literature ascribes the presence of street children in the developed countries, in contrast to the least developed countries, less directly to poverty in a material sense than to poverty in a values and moral sense. A large proportion of Western street children are from middle-class homes. Journalists and researchers, using a psychological perspective to frame their studies, have interviewed Western street children who report that they were estranged from their parents for several years before they left home. They claim that they left to escape not hunger and material deprivation, but emotional deprivation, parental alienation, and both psychological and physical violence. Their parents are reported not to love them. We are also told that frequently single parents struggling to cope on marginal incomes have been unable to provide the nurturing and loving care that their children may have needed. Many of those interviewed report having been "latchkey" children for years while their parent(s), from the children's perspective, placed greater emphasis on the material aspects of home life. Parents for their part report their children to be "out of control," disrespectful, uncaring, and ungrateful. While a significant proportion of children are on the streets as a consequence of family violence, including sexual abuse, the majority are reported to be there because they perceived their parents to be too controlling and essentially uncaring (see Janus et al., 1987; Webber, 1991; Lau, 1989). The impression emerges that this literature supports the popular perception that family values are in decline and the fault is largely parental. Unlike the literature about the developing countries, the literature on the street children in developed countries tends not to focus on the relationship between the occurrence of street children and the effects of structural adjustments in the economy and labor market. There is little analysis to counter the argument that individuals and families are to blame.

Street Children and Work

The urban poor frequently require welfare or social assistance. In the developed countries the state is able to provide this assistance in the form of money, goods, and services. Those of the least developed countries which are socialist states have adequate social welfare programs; however, in the developing nations with market economies social welfare programs are largely inadequate or nonexistent. In these countries a communal welfare system exists to support only those who are not estranged from their extended family or who live in communities which are organized, socially responsive, and have resources to share. Work in the absence of these conditions is the sole means of survival for the majority of Third World urban families. However, adult labor is frequently unable to meet the needs of the family, and child labor has become an essential component of the family economy.

Survival for the undereducated and unskilled urban family is achieved through long hours of physically demanding, poorly paid work. When both parents work children are frequently left to care for themselves, and girls at a very young age are left without supervision to care for infants. Low family incomes also mean compulsory schooling is an impediment to the family's attempts to gain financial security. In most of the least developed countries schools charge fees for tuition, textbooks, and supplies, and many require families to purchase school uniforms. However small the costs, for the poor these expenditures are a barrier to school attendance. In addition, children who attend school tend to contribute much less to family income. There is, therefore, an opportunity cost to the poor family who complies with compulsory education.

Street children need work to earn an income for themselves or their families. Most work made available to them is defined by the International Labor Organization (ILO) as exploitive, that is, threatening or limiting to physical, emotional, social, and mental growth and development (ILO, 1983). Around the world children work and are exploited in three economies: the formal, informal, and illegal. Millions of children work illegally in the formal economies of the developing nations where the conditions of work and the sites of production are regulated, but not inspected, by governments (Myers, 1991). Many of the garments we wear are produced in the sweatshops of the textile industry in Cairo, Manila, and Bangkok. Our homes are furnished with rugs woven in the back street factories of India and Pakistan. Automotive parts and accessories from the barrio industries of Mexico and Brazil are available in our suburban malls and discount shopping centers. Many of these goods are produced by children paid low wages for long hours of physically demanding, repetitive labor in dehumanizing and hazardous conditions. In the developed nations government enforcement of regulations prevents large-scale illegal unemployment.

More readily observable are the hundreds of thousands of children who work on the streets in the informal economy. In every major Third World city children sell flowers, newspapers, cigarettes, chewing gum, and candy in public places. At the busy traffic intersections the sellers are joined by windshield washers and in the car parks by "car watchers." At bus and railway stations and in public squares boys shine shoes. In the markets "carriers" move fruit, vegetables, and dry goods in homemade wooden carts. Lowest on the social ranking of street occupations in the informal sector are the foragers and garbage pickers. These child workers sort through neighborhood garbage containers and refuse sites in search of bottles, cans, metal, and any items that can be sold to scrap dealers.

Finally there is the illegal economy, where the most lucrative occupation is prostitution. Both female and male children are involved in the sale of sex to pedophiles in major cities around the world. The dollar value of the sex tourism trade has reached major proportions in cities such as Bangkok and Manila, where recruitment of children for prostitution is ignored by the state. Trafficking in drugs, petty theft, prostitution, pornography production, and violent crime are last resorts for children forced from the informal to the illegal economy in both the Third World and the West.

Although the participation of children in the illegal economy cannot be condoned, their participation in the informal economy appears to be necessary. Children are out of school largely because they must work; any education provisions for street children therefore must both recognize their rights to work and remove work as a barrier to participation.

NONGOVERNMENT STREET EDUCATION

Over the last two decades nongovernment organizations around the world have been working to provide basic education to street children. Initially projects were small, experimental, and ad hoc, managed by volunteers on "shoestring" budgets. Little if any research was conducted on the needs of the children, and the educators learned their pedagogy as they worked. Most church and community organizations began their work with projects which offered children shelter, food, clothing, and health services. Later crafts and basic literacy and numeracy classes were organized to establish street education. As the number of projects increased and developers began to network and organize their efforts, national and international organizations in the voluntary sector became involved. For a more detailed description of the origins and work of these international nongovernment organizations see Blunt (1993).

In particular, the United Nations Children's Fund (UNICEF) and the Catholic International Children's Bureau provided leadership to establish projects in Latin America and Africa. Through the advocacy of UNICEF, the United Nations declared 1981 to be the International Year of the Child (IYC) to focus global attention on the developmental needs of children. UNICEF in cooperation with the Brazilian National Child Welfare Committee (FUNABEM) established three projects for street children, which in 1984 had been expanded to over 200 communities. By 1987 projects in over 400 communities were providing assistance to over two million Brazilian street children.

In 1982, as a follow-up to its IYC activities, the International Catholic Child Bureau established the Inter NGO Program on Street Children and Youth, a global network of nine lay and religious NGOs (nongovernmental organizations). The program aimed to establish community-based demonstration projects for street children, disseminate information, and work cooperatively to raise public consciousness. Three years later over 240 projects had been started and governments, often reluctantly, began to recognize the work being done. Profiles of some Inter NGO projects were widely distributed, enabling a broad range of community-based models and strategies to be shared internationally (See Inter NGO, n.d.; Inter NGO, 1985; UNESCO, 1985). The momentum for international commitment was sustained by (1) UNICEF's Executive, which in 1984 commissioned a policy review paper on children in especially difficult circumstances, (2) the adoption by the United Nations General Assembly in 1989 of the Convention on the Rights of the Child (United Nations, 1989), and (3) the UN World Summit for Children, at which seventy-nine heads of state approved a ten-point Plan of Action (United Nations, 1990) to improve the lives of children in especially difficult circumstances.

As we have seen, street children are excluded from the public education system largely by the economic necessity to work. In addition, many poor families reject the public education system as irrelevant to their life priorities and as conflicting with the culture and values of their social class. But by not attending, street children end up not receiving the immediate benefits of formal education: literacy, numeracy, citizenship education, and the acquisition of their cultural heritage. They are also excluded from future access to adult and higher education opportunities provided by the state. The development of street education by nongovernment organizations has occurred because governments have failed to act. The NGOs have stated that their intentions are humanitarian and based on a view of social justice for the poor. However, little research is available to determine the degree to which street education is an alternative to public education processes, which achieve social reproduction and control. The extent to which street education is truly liberatory and emancipatory remains to be determined.

THREE MODELS OF STREET EDUCATION

Hundreds of community-based street education projects have been established, ranging in size from small volunteer efforts organized by two or three concerned members of a community group with minimal resources, to large NGO projects with budgets of hundreds of thousands of dollars and staff complements of over 100. Over 150 projects were surveyed by the writer during 1989 and 1990 to obtain information on their organizational structure, goals, and educational work. From an initial review of the materials collected, three projects were selected to highlight differences in the analysis of the problem, organization and goals of the project, and the relationship of the projects to the formal education system (Blunt, 1993).

The Philippines

The Joint Project in Street Children was established by a consortium of international and national NGOs and Philippine government departments in 1986 to provide services to 10,000 of the estimated 75,000 to 100,000 children in eight target cities (UNICEF, 1989; DSWD, 1988). The project was initiated by UNICEF Philippines, the Department of Social Welfare and Development (DSWD), the Council of Welfare Agencies Foundation of the Philippines, Inc. (CWAFPI, an association of NGOs involved in community development), and the National Economic Development Authority (NEDA). Three principles were stated to guide the project: (1) the context of existing basic urban social services would be recognized in planning, (2) project activity would build on existing government and NGO programs, and (3) the focus of project activity would be community-based. Phase two of the project began in 1988, adding a further eight cities and extending the target goal to reach 35,000 children-on-the-street and children-of-the-street.

Working committees in each target community surveyed the needs of the street children, identified resources, planned programs, and coordinated the activities of the groups and agencies involved. Two broad intervention strategies were implemented: center-based and community-based. The center-based projects involved institutions in providing food, shelter, clothing, medical care, and counseling. Community-based projects involved government agencies assisting community groups to organize parents to provide infant care, income generation projects, and alternative education programs. Street workers contacted children and established locations where children could meet and be free from harassment by the police and local businesses.

The street schools, which consisted of a large canvas awning and some wooden chairs and a table, were located in open spaces, often beside busy streets, adjacent to the barrios (Blunt, 1989). The curriculum focused on basic literacy and numeracy skills. Resource materials were made from newspapers, cartoon comic books, and consumer goods boxes. A few old school readers, some crayon slates, and chalk completed the inventory. Teaching focused on reading instructions, telling the time, and currency calculations. One parent was employed at each school to cook a simple nutritious daily meal from ingredients purchased by DSWD. Parents and older children were able to work, or to seek work, while the youngest family members were left in a safe environment. The teachers were mainly unemployed university students, or recent graduates, who may have had some teacher education training; their salaries were paid by the Department of Education, Culture and Sports (DECS). Social workers attached to the project worked with families to promote regular attendance at the street school and helped children to care for infants left in their care. When their economic circumstances improved, parents were encouraged to enroll their children in the local public school.

The Joint Project worked to stabilize the family and reduce the risk of child neglect, abandonment, and running away. By maintaining a link with the formal social support and education systems, the street schools constitute a strategy to prevent the further estrangement of the squatter families from society and the children from their parents.

Kenya

A second model of intervention is demonstrated in the work of the Undungu Society of Kenya (USK) (Gichuru, 1984 and 1987; Inter NGO, n.d.). The Society's origins date back to the mid-1970s when Father Arnold Grol, a Catholic priest working in the slums of Nairobi, organized services for "parking boys." From a small voluntary program relying on donations to feed and clothe boys, the project has grown to an internationally funded society with an annual budget exceeding $US 1 million. The Society first established a reception center to provide temporary shelter and meals and in 1975 purchased three houses as more permanent group homes for sixty boys. Social workers were employed to locate the boys' families, and between one quarter and one half of the boys would be reunited with their families after staying at the center for three months or less.

A basic education program was started for residents of the group homes, who were too poor to pay school fees from their earnings, too old to be placed in classes appropriate for their levels of education, and too independent to accept the rigid disciplinary and organizational structures of the public school. The boys were taught by volunteers for four hours each morning, and in the afternoons and evenings they worked on the street. Some used the services of the reception center and attended the basic education program while continuing to live on the street. By the late 1970s girls also began to appear as part of the street population and the Society extended its services to include them.

In 1982 the education project was operating in the four major Nairobi slum areas. The goals of the Undungu Basic Education Program (UBEP) were to enable the children to

develop social behaviours and grow towards the attainment of self sufficiency, . . . develop a constructive attitude towards life—hence develop good character and become responsible members of society . . . [to achieve] self employment or wage employment, [and] develop the spirit of self reliance and help the student to deal with the problems of life. (Gichuru, 1984, p. 6)

The curriculum provides a well-articulated alternative to the public elementary schools. Where the state schools require attendance for seven years between the ages of six and thirteen, UBEP requires ten- to fourteen-year-olds to attend for only four hours daily for three years. Relevance to the daily lives of the students is a major criterion in curriculum planning: technical subjects, basic literacy and numeracy, and social consciousness and community spirit are strongly supported. In contrast to the public schools, cooperation in learning rather than competition is a key organizing principle. Ten subjects are taught: Kiswahili, arts and crafts, mathematics, science, music, English, social studies, business education, physical education, and religious education. The two most important are science, which includes basic mechanics, small animal husbandry, health, and nutrition; and business education, which emphasizes small enterprise entrepreneurship. (For a personal description written by a former student, see Child Welfare Society of Kenya, 1990).

At first UBEP tuition was free; however, as the program expanded to meet the needs of the poor urban family, to reduce the risk that children working on the street would receive no formal education, fees were charged at a rate below that of public schools. The preferred teachers are those from low-income and social backgrounds similar to those of the students, as they are thought to be empathetically sensitive to the needs of the students. Teachers are encouraged to be tolerant of students' behaviors and weaknesses and to promote the strengthening of each child's self-concept. After three years students are expected to have achieved the equivalent of the formal education system Standard (Grade) 7.

As the project grew and funding from development agencies was secured, permanent UBEP school buildings were constructed by the students, teachers, parents, and community members. In 1979, under public pressure, representatives of the Kenya Institute of Education inspected the project, and in 1980 the UBEP certificate of graduation was granted official recognition as equivalent to the public school certificate of school completion. UBEP graduates are therefore able to enter government-sponsored technical training and adult education programs. Following this decision a vocational training facility constructed by the Society to offer courses including carpentry, auto mechanics, tailoring, leather work, and home economics was taken over by the government.

Today the Undungu Society has as its goal the strengthening of traditional values of Kenyan society and the family. By maintaining family and community values and social structures it reduces the causes of family breakdown. The Society provides a broad range of services to the community, organized on the broad principles of the Kenyan extended family. Programs for youth, women, and differently-abled persons are an integral part of the Society's work. "Elders" participate in decision-making roles on advisory committees, and the traditional relationships of seniors and youth in the tribal society are maintained. From its beginnings as a community nongovernment project responding to the survival needs of street children, the Society has been successful in securing the assistance of a reluctant government to establish a comprehensive preventive program and an alternative education system which receives state recognition.

Colombia

Bosconia–La Florida in Bogotá, Colombia, like the Undungu Society in the Kenyan case, was established by a Catholic priest, Father Javier de Nicola, who in 1967 established the first center for *gamines* (Agnelli, 1986; Dorfman, 1984; Shifter, 1985; Inter NGO, n.d.). A small project to assist homeless children has become a large alternative community with several levels of operation. First, through Operation Amistad (Operation Friendship) street workers contact *gamines* and encourage them to visit El Patio, a large courtyard where between 8:30 A.M. and 4:30 P.M. there are facilities for them to bathe, receive medical services, eat a free meal, and play games. Through regular contacts the street workers establish a relationship with the children built on assistance and trust. Those who are interested are offered the opportunity to enter one of two residential centers, Liberia and Camarin, where they can stay for up to thirty days. The goals of these centers are to help the residents determine whether they would benefit by entering the long-term program. The longer-term alternatives offered are to enter one of two residential centers, a vocational skills training center, Chibchala, or an elementary school program, Arcadia. Should the children wish to be admitted to this third level they must first return to the streets for three days; only if they return to "insist" on being accepted are they allowed to enter. A separate center has been established for female *gamines;* however, no information was available from the materials reviewed about the number of girls admitted.

The goal of the project's third level is to facilitate personal development and support the will to reject life on the street. At Arcadia boys up to the age of twelve learn basic literacy skills through a process in which they "learn to be, and to be useful, rather than to learn information" (Inter NGO, nd, p. 11). This center offers a radical alternative to the public school system: There are no formal classrooms, and small groups often learn in circles where the sidewalk and walls are convenient substitutes for blackboards. No marks or grades are given and the public school curriculum and instructional materials are not used, as they are judged to be inappropriate. Mathematics instruction is integrated into projects such as basic carpentry and purchasing food and materials required by the centers. Science and history are taught through comic strips developed by the teachers. Chibchala, the vocational center, is located in an industrial area of the city; its curriculum focuses on knowledge and skills required for work within a moral and political context. The boys learn to use tools to make products, including furniture required by the project centers. The centers have a zero-tolerance rule on drug and substance abuse. Sports, physical exercise, and a strong emphasis on music, art, and folk cultural activities are used to challenge the *gamines* to develop their artistic, cultural, and physical capabilities.

After three months at Arcadia and Chibchala the boys participate in a one-month leadership training course. Organized from groups of twenty-five, the course is physically and intellectually challenging. The boys live together in a building located away from the two centers. Together they study basic philosophy, history, community education, and theology. In addition to hard physical exercise they learn meditation techniques to help them discover their capacity for independent decision making and alternatives to drug use. Three options face the boys at the end of the course: to attend (1) La Industria, a project center which functions as a technical high school, (2) La Florida, a center with a strong academic focus, or (3) return to the community, their family, or the street. La Industria offers skills training in well-equipped vocational workshops where carpentry, construction, and mechanical repair are taught. The students can earn a diploma from the center.

Outside the La Florida complex of dormitories, workshops, and gardens in a barrio suburb of Bogotá the residents have erected the sign "República de Los Muchachos de La Florida." The center is governed by a "mayor" and five councilors elected by the five hundred residents to be responsible for all aspects of the center's operations, including the education program, and ensuring that the center is well managed and maintained. One resident is elected to serve as the public relations officer to provide information to visitors, community representatives, and the media. The residents police themselves, and the ultimate sanction for breaches of the community's code of behavior is expulsion. Under the direction of the elected representatives, a council of group leaders administers the center. The residents range in age from boys of fourteen to young men of twenty-three. As a group or clan they share their resources and work load, and they evaluate, promote, and demote each other through group processes. Often boys will choose to leave the center to try their chances on the street or return to their families. Illness, hunger, injury, or fear of violence or retribution for petty crimes committed result in some returning to seek readmittance.

Raising critical consciousness is an essential aspect of the program. La Florida's educators believe that a lack of critical consciousness among the poor about the causes of poverty and the possibilities for social change restricts the development of the poverty class. Cultural expression through music, art, literature, and the performing arts are also emphasized. Creativity and self-expression play a large role in building self-concept and a sense of group identity. Graduates of La Industria and La Florida enter the community to compete for scarce jobs against the credentialed graduates of the public schools. While La Florida builds character, independence, and a positive self-concept, frequently these characteristics are at variance with the traits preferred by employers—compliance, acceptance, and a repressed self-image. Over thirty "graduates" of the project have entered university, some doing so while continuing to live at La Florida. Others are employed with the project as street workers and educators.

While the Bosconia–La Florida Project works cooperatively with Colombian social service agencies, some of which contribute monthly per capita payments for the project's services, and receives grants from the State Lottery Foundation and the national telephone company, essentially the project remains independent from government. The project also receives grants from international NGOs and foundations to supplement livelihood projects which involve gardening, tree planting, and recycling waste materials.

Discussion

The three models reviewed are each based on a particular analysis of the nature of the problem and the community within which each project functions. In the Philippines a coalition of NGOs and government agencies collaborate to focus on the family at risk of breakdown and child abandonment. The street schools support the short-term survival needs of the barrio family by enabling parents and older children to seek work while providing a safe environment for the youngest family members. The primary goal of the school is to teach basic educational skills and to facilitate entry, or reentry, into the public school system when family circumstances improve.

The Kenyan model has its origins in the community work of the Catholic church, in which the initial focus was on the individual street child's survival needs. Today the Undungu Society is a broad-based community development organization working to return children to their families and prevent family breakdown. The Society's education program is an alternative to the public school and leads to a certificate accepted by the government as equivalent to a public school credential. While less well integrated with government agencies than in the Philippines, the Kenyan model delivers educational and social services which parallel those of government. The Colombian project also began as a church community effort to meet the survival needs of children-of-the-street. However, unlike the Philippine model it does not seek to integrate children into the public school system, nor, as in the Kenyan model, to offer an equivalent education with a government-recognized credential. Also unlike the Philippine and Kenyan models, which incorporate community and family norms and values, the Bosconia–La Florida project has developed alternative norms based upon a philosophy of personal empowerment and individual and collective responsibility to socialize the children into an alternative community. The children of Bosconia–La Florida are regarded as autonomous persons who have the opportunity to join a democratic, participatory community governed by fellow *gamines*.

There is little data available to confirm the numbers of street children served by the three projects or the proportion of the populations of street children in the communities who are reached. It appears likely that the Philippine project has reached its goal of providing services to approximately 35,000 children, yet the proportion of the population contacted is probably less than 5 percent. The Undungu Society provides accommodation for almost 300 children and services to at least five times that number. However, once again the population of children at risk who might benefit from the Society's services may be five or ten times larger. Similarly, over 800 children live at the project centers of Bosconia–La Florida, while at least twenty times that number remain on the streets of Bogotá. Even though hundreds of projects have been established, it is likely that less than 5 percent of children-of-the-street are participating in project activities on a regular basis. The need for additional projects remains urgent.

There are a wide variety of project sponsors delivering many different models of street education. The literature suggests that while models may not be replicated directly, the principles upon which "successful" models are based can be replicated. From the materials collected by the writer, and reports on the collective experience of street educators in Latin America (Childhope, 1987) and Africa (REDD BARNA, 1990), a number of principles of effective street education practice have been identified and can be highlighted here.

1. In practically every successful project the priority is the welfare and development of the children, not their reform.

2. Relationships between educators and children, regardless of age, are most productive when built on respect for the child's freedom of choice and independence.

3. The learned benefits of the street experience, including work skills and the abilities to endure hardship and conflict and to respond to life's challenges with ingenuity and adaptability, are important for building a working relationship and an educational program with each child.

4. The dignity of street children needs to be respected in the means by which services and information are provided.

5. The right to learn and earn needs to be respected. Employment is necessary and when it is not exploitive can be an important contributor to learning, socialization, self-esteem, and independence.

6. Basic services provided during initial contacts, including access to shelter, food, clothing, and medical and legal services, ought not to be made contingent upon promises that the child may be unable to keep.

7. Street education needs to be an alternative to public education, which largely reflects middle-class values, norms, and knowledge; perpetuates class, race, and gender biases; and results in class and cultural hegemony over the poor.

8. Street children have the right to know their legal human rights, and their educators have an obligation to teach them.

9. Informal, small group, and cooperative rather than competitive learning are the preferred instructional approaches.

10. Successful street schools provide opportunities for creativity, play, and the celebration of childhood.

11. The need to experience nurturing, sharing, and care-giving to others is important for all street children, as the role of their family in teaching values and family living skills has been nonexistent, distorted, or greatly diminished.

12. While zero tolerance of drug use and the exclusion of learners with severe behavioral problems may be necessary, successful projects have few barriers to participation.

Street children have been willing and successful learners where projects have incorporated these principles into their operations and have (1) used participatory approaches to develop curricula and resource materials which reflect the local community context; (2) aimed to develop basic educational knowledge and skills, including literacy, numeracy, communications, and livelihood skills; and (3) incorporated health education, play, and recreation as integral parts of the program. Many of the characteristics of successful street schools will sound familiar to progressive educators who would have little discomfort with the philosophy and principles of practice summarized above. However, little research has been conducted to advance our understanding of street education beyond descriptive and unsophisticated analysis such as that presented above. Little mention is made of how street educators make use of the urban environment to support learning. While the use of available materials for instructional purposes and a focus on the social and work context of the street are mentioned frequently, it is rare to read of street educators viewing the city as a rich laboratory for learning. Rather, the impression is left that the street school is a refuge from the city and that the public buildings and places which are often frequented by the uniformed public school students are avoided by the street children.

THE RESPONSE OF STATE EDUCATION SYSTEMS

Formal education systems in the least developed countries have largely ignored the problem of street children. For many years some governments denied that the numbers of street children were as high as advocacy groups claimed. However, studies conducted by international NGOs, and UNICEF's reports and situational analyses (Espert and Myers, 1988; UNICEF, 1990) in particular, have dispelled such denial. Still, most governments continue to be reluctant to allocate resources to street education. Their position appears to be that the state system of education is available to all children and that the refusal of parents to comply with requirements for compulsory attendance is the problem. Although there is a large body of evidence indicating that public school curricula are unsuited for poor urban children, that instructional practices are ineffective, that parents cannot afford the tuition fees and school uniforms, and that millions of children do not attend, school reform is not a priority for the majority of least developed nations. Consequently, leadership to provide street education remains with nonformal educators.

How are the refusals of governments to respond to the educational needs of street children to be understood? One possible set of explanations can be inferred by extending Carnoy and Samoff's functional analysis of the role of

education. Carnoy and Samoff (1990) studied the education systems and policies of states experiencing transition from colonial to socialist societies. They
concluded that these states held two competing views for national education
systems. One view is of a participatory, liberatory education which seeks to
increase access to education to socially transform society. The second view is
of an academic and technological education which seeks to develop human
resources and through skills acquisition to increase economic production. The
first view tends to give way over time to the second as short-term goals to
foster economic growth and increase GNP displace the longer-term goals of
building national identity and promoting equality in social relations. The reluctance of governments to address the educational needs of street children may
be evidence of a commitment to the instrumental use of education for economic
growth and the displacement of education as an instrument to foster social
equity.

The practical need of states to achieve economic growth during the global
recession and to implement the mandated economic policies of the World Bank
has required a commitment to increased funding for higher technological education and improvements in the quality of public education to facilitate skills
acquisition. Education has also had to compete for scarce state resources which
are targeted for investments likely to result in the highest economic returns.
The focus on modernization and economic growth has displaced other competing national priorities. The absence of millions of children from public schools
reduces state expenditures on education, and assists strategies to raise the quality of education, by removing from the system large numbers of learners who
by virtue of their social class and family background are those likely to require
the most assistance to achieve the intended school outcomes. The problem of
having a large number of illiterate adults is deferred for one or more genera-
tions, and the costs of future adult literacy campaigns are accepted, as they are
known to be less than the current costs of elementary education.

Further, as the state successfully promotes acceptance of the role of education as an instrument for economic growth, the system perpetuates an ideology
at the community level which also acts against funding for street education.
Competition in schools to achieve academic success and advance to higher
levels, where economic benefits from education become accessible, has become
widespread and has promoted individual competitiveness to the point where
community members who utilize the public school system recognize that the
fewer children who attend, the greater the opportunities are for the success of
their own children. That there has been no public outcry of concern or indigna-
tion that the state does not enforce attendance of the poor and working children
is evidence that community members recognize the advantage for their children
if the poorest children do not attend. Community groups have, however, frequently called for government action to remove street children from their neighborhoods and to prevent petty crime and property damage. Community interest

has all too frequently focused on the protection of property and neglected the developmental needs and human rights of street children. As with national goals, community goals have come to focus largely on economic interest and acceptance of competition as the strategy for achievement.

With a commitment to the use of education for economic growth have come standardization, centralization, and bureaucratization, and as Carnoy and Samoff (1990) have observed, inflexible structures reduce the capability of the state to experiment and innovate even if it wished to do so. It can be expected, therefore, that within rigid bureaucracies the additional problem of a scarcity of resources is likely to strengthen the resolve of administrators to fund only those programs which are identified as the highest national priorities. Further, as Fuller (1991) has pointed out, many states have worked to weaken and break down local institutions, depicting them as particularistic and traditional, while mass schooling has been presented as desirable to access the new social benefits of the nation. Universal public schooling has played a key role in the resocialization of families away from traditional local institutional loyalties. Consequently, in many countries the urban poor have few institutions to enable them to help themselves. The poor have become objects of the state's welfare agencies and their marginalization has increased. In these circumstances the reallocation of funds for projects which are outside the formal system and government control, and which are not even identified as a low national priority, is virtually impossible.

Third World governments use their education systems to build national consciousness and a commitment to development goals. Governments recognize that development is most successful when the population supports the systems for development implementation and the political parties managing the change. Education systems as instruments for national development have been used to signal intentions to move toward a modern society (Fuller, 1991). Consequently, it is argued here that to reject an education system is tantamount to rejection of a state's development program and vision of modernity. It is likely, therefore, that governments regard it as essential that they be successful in ensuring popular acceptance of the education system as an instrument of modernization and development. It is because the state is so committed to belief in the power of a centralized education system as an instrument of development that there is likely to be little support for an alternative community-controlled education system. To support an alternative education system is to support the opportunity for others to develop an alternative consciousness and identity, and to propose an alternative view of development. Most governments in the least developed countries fear counter-hegemonic movements. The stronger the belief by the governing party that education is an essential key to national development, the stronger will be the resistance of the government to providing support for alternative education systems and the greater the suspicion of those who do not support the formal public system. Where governments are forced by international and local advocacy to respond to the needs of street children and work in partnership with community agencies, it is likely that they will wish to co-opt and control the efforts of street educators.

BEYOND DESCRIPTION

The larger social context within which street education functions—the linkages to the economic, political, and cultural sectors of the society—merit detailed study if street education is to be supported and further enabled to become an extensive, alternative urban education system. Street schools ought not to continue to be studied in isolation from the larger social structures and patterns of unequal relations which exist in all those countries with large populations of street children.

Is street education another form of social regulation, or is it liberatory and emancipatory? Some projects are actively engaged in advocacy, promoting resistance, and developing curricula which teach human rights. Street schools, particularly the larger projects such as Bosconia–La Florida, are potential sites for the production and dissemination of alternative values, knowledge, and transformative educational practices which are oppositional to those of the public school system. It is because these projects are outside the control of agencies of the state that they are likely to be perceived as a potential threat. However, where a church or other establishment agency is involved, the state may be less concerned, as there would probably be a previously negotiated understanding in place, or a prior relationship, with regard to the agency's interest and role in supporting social justice and equity efforts. Also, only those projects which have community support could gain legitimacy to challenge the state education system, and many projects are located in relatively unsympathetic communities.

In Latin America, in particular, the response of many community residents, especially owners of small businesses, has been to regard the informal and illegal work activities, and frequently the mere presence of street children, as a threat to their well being and security. Off-duty policemen and members of the armed forces have served as vigilantes and death squad members who harass, torture, and brutally murder street children. Childhope (1990) describes how the names of 1,395 Brazilian street children who died from acts of organized violence at the hands of vigilantes and death squads were displayed during a conference on the plight of street children held in Brasilia. Very few of the murderers are brought to trial, even when staff members of organizations such as Covenant House are able to provide evidence for prosecution. (For details on the extent of violence against street children see Dimenstein, 1991; *Esperanza,* 1990; Serrill, 1990.) Wherever the state is able to grant economic opportunities and social status to a large proportion of public school graduates there is not likely to be a resurgence of popular support for community institutions to replace the state's role in education.

It is evident that in many countries the state does not regard the work of street educators benignly. While governments may have little interest in the economic role played by street schools, they are likely to have an enduring interest in their potential to offer a counter-hegemonic education. Where the state becomes involved in supporting street education, or at least allowing its expansion, it will be instructive to determine whether through co-optation, or a laissez-faire policy, a two-tier education system is reinforced or transformed. The postcolonial legacy of a bifurcated system, one for the elite and one for the middle class, may divide again into a tripartite system creating a lower, third level for the poor. Under such a system public schools might continue to emphasize economic and technological education to produce a hierarchically organized labor force, while the street schools might, for little cost, contribute a minimally educated labor force for occupations at the base of the hierarchy. The undeclared national goal of producing different classes of workers with different skills, values, and knowledge would be perpetuated by such an arrangement. In this scenario the fear of counter-hegemonic education is dissipated.

Street education projects have occurred in market economy states, often weak democracies, where the national education systems emphasize economic growth and individual competitiveness. The projects are community-based and organized through groups which act through loose coalitions to form a broad social movement. Street workers and educators are volunteers and low-wage, humanistic, socially aware, highly motivated, and idealistic young adults. Their focus is the individual learner and their goal is to facilitate the growth of a new person, socialized into the working-class community, and the achievement of social justice for all poor children. Does the street school have the potential to become a form of counter-hegemonic education to achieve social transformation for the poor—a goal congruent with that of the revolutionary and socialist education campaigns?

Among the most innovative projects, mainly in Latin America, are reflected some notions of postmodern education as described by Aronowitz and Giroux (1991), who write that from the dialectical relationship between knowledge and practice postmodern educators conclude that "the curriculum can best inspire learning only when school knowledge builds upon the tacit knowledge derived from the cultural resources that students already possess" (p. 15). This perception of curriculum is one of the essential features of street education. Further, the relations between teachers and learners, and the advocacy roles of the street workers, with their inclusionary practices and class consciousness, place them in opposition to the practices and beliefs of traditional educators. Just as the liberatory pedagogy of Freire evolved from the literacy campaigns of rural Brazil, it is possible that a liberatory postmodern education may evolve from the politicized, community-controlled street schools of Latin America. The further development of street schools under the control of popular democratic agencies, as opposed to traditional community agencies, may occur within a postmodern conceptualization of education and provide an opportunity for urban educators to contribute to the development of a postmodern educational theory:

> any viable educational theory has to begin with a language that links schooling to democratic public life, that defines teachers as engaged intellectuals and border crossers, and develops forms of pedagogy that incorporate difference, plurality, and the language of the everyday as central to the production and legitimation of learning. But this demands the reconstruction of a view of language and theory that establishes the groundwork for viewing schooling and education as a form of cultural politics, as a discourse that draws its meaning from the social, cultural, and economic context in which it operates. (Aronowitz and Giroux, 1991, p. 187)

The mission of street educators in the future may involve the development of such a theory of education.

CONCLUSION

How are street children to be understood as an urban phenomenon? The literature reflects two discourses. One is journalistic and targeted to mass audiences, performing advocacy and philanthropic functions to meet the immediate goals of establishing and supporting street projects. It is descriptive and atheoretical. The second is relatively sparse, research-focused, and analytical. It is aimed at promoting critical examination and understanding of the phenomenon and serves to influence longer-term goals of policy development and knowledge production. However, we still know very little about street education.

In this chapter we have seen how the literature ascribes causation of the street children phenomenon differently for developed and less developed countries. In the developed countries the literature focuses on the erosion of moral and spiritual values leading to family breakdown. However, in the least developed countries structural factors, including global economic restructuring, economic recession, commodification of food production, rural-urban migration, and unemployment are emphasized as contributory causes. In both situations there is strong support in the popular literature for the "culture of poverty" analysis, which emphasizes the individual's psychosocial context and the freedom of choice thesis. The poor, it is suggested, must accept some responsibility for their own predicament. Overall the literature reflects not only an inadequate theorization of the causes of urban poverty but the failure of governments to respond to the impact of poverty on children's lives.

What is missed by this type of dichotomous categorization is not only the similarities in forces at work in both the developed and developing countries but how the state intervenes in mediating their effects. For example, lack of employment as a cause of family breakdown is common to the experience of poor urban families globally. Youth unemployment in many areas of North

America and Europe is triple the rate of adult unemployment. The poverty of many Western street children, and their participation in the illegal economy, are attributable to their unemployment. The magnitude of the problem in the West is different simply because in liberal capitalist democracies the state accepts responsibility for the welfare of its citizens, including children, through social welfare programs. In the least developed socialist states there is political will to protect the poorest citizens from the worst offences of poverty, but governments lack the economic resources for effective social welfare systems. In other less developed nations with free market economies neither the political will nor state welfare services are present to protect the poor family from failing economies and the negative effects of poverty.

We can conclude that as an urban phenomenon, street children will continue to pose a problem for urban educators. The existence of street children needs to be seen in a broad context of processes of urbanization within a shifting global economy. Educational responses to the phenomena need to be critically examined. In considering some nonformal educational responses, visited through secondary sources, I have identified some principles of effective practice. But these voluntary efforts by NGOs represent a minuscule response to the enormous numbers of children-of-the-street and children at risk. Formal education systems in both the developed and developing countries have largely ignored the educational needs of street children. Ironically, perhaps, I argue that the principles underlying many innovative street education projects exemplify characteristics of a "liberatory post-modern education" suggested by Aronowitz and Giroux (1991).

Urban educators need to turn their attention to street children not only because of the magnitude of the need, but also because of the opportunities for innovation in street education and the possibility for the transformative model of education which could emerge.

REFERENCES

Agnelli, Susan. (1986) *Street Children: A Growing Urban Tragedy*. Independent Commission on International Humanitarian Issues. London: George Weidenfeld and Nicolson.

Aronowitz, Stanley, and Giroux, Henry. (1991) *Postmodern Education: Politics, Culture, and Social Criticism*. Minneapolis: University of Minnesota Press.

Barker, Gary. (1990) Undungu Society Tops Informal Sector to Assist Nairobi's Street Children, *Esperanza 2*, Childhope, USA.

Blunt, Adrian. (1989) Street Schools: On the Road to Universal Urban Elementary Education, *International Education 19*, 1: pp. 5–11.

Blunt, Adrian. (1993) Street Children. In Vincent D'Oyley and Adrian Blunt (eds.), *Development and Innovation in Third World Education*. Vancouver: Pacific Educational Press.

Boyden, Jo, with Holden, Pat. (1991) *Children of the Cities*. Atlantic Highlands, New Jersey: Zed Books.

Carnoy, Martin, and Samoff, Joel. (1990) *Education and Social Transition in the Third World*. Princeton, NJ: Princeton University Press.

Child Welfare Society of Kenya, Nairobi. (1990) Life on the Street. A Personal Account, *Sasa*, October/December.

Childhope. (1987) *Educating Children in the Street and in the Community*. Regional workshop report, Guatemala, June 1987, mimeo.

Childhope. (1990) *Annual Report 1989–1990*. Childhope, The International Movement on Behalf of Street Children.

Dimenstein, Gilberto. (1991) *Brazil: War on Children*. London, UK: Latin American Bureau.

Dorfman, Ariel. (1984) Bread and Burnt Rice: Culture and Economic Survival in Latin America, *Grassroots Development 8*, no. 2.

DSWD. (1988) The Situation of Street Children in Ten Cities. Manila: Department of Social Welfare and Development (DSWD), National Council of Social Development Foundation of the Philippines, Inc., and UNICEF, mimeo.

Ennew, Judith, and Milne, Brian. (1990) *The Next Generation: Lives of Third World Children*. Philadelphia, PA: New World Publishers.

Esperanza. (1990) Guatemalan Street Children Face Death Squads: Amnesty International Releases Report on Extra-judicial Executions, *Esperanza 2*, October, Childhope USA.

Espert, Francisco, and Myers, William. (1988) *Situational Analysis: Latin American and the Caribbean Regional Programme*. Children in Especially Difficult Circumstances Outreach Series No. 1. Bogotá: UNICEF.

Felsman, J. Kirk. (1989) Risk and Resiliency in Childhood: The Lives of Street Children. In Timothy Dugan and Robert Coles (eds.), *The Child in Our Times: Studies in the Development of Resiliency*. New York: Burres/Mozel.

Fuller, Bruce. (1991) *Growing Up Modern: The Western State Builds Third-World Schools*. London, UK: Routledge.

Fyfe, Alec. (1985) *All Work and No Play: Child Labour Today* Trades Union Congress in collaboration with the UK Committee for UNICEF.

Gichuru, F. X. (1984) *Undungu Basic Education Programme: An Innovative Approach to Educating "Parking Boys" of Nairobi*. Univet for Cooperation with UNICEF and WPF, UPEL 9. Paris: UNESCO.

Gichuru, F. X. (1987) Basic Education for Street Children in Nairobi, *Prospects 27*, 1: pp. 139–143.

Hardoy, Jorge, and Satterthwaite, David. (1989) *Squatter Children: Life in the Urban Third World*. London, UK: Earthscan Publications.

Hines, Virginia. (ed.) (1988) *The North American Directory of Programs for Runaways, Homeless Youth, and Missing Children*. Washington, DC: American Youth Work Center.

Inter NGO. (nd) *Programme on Street Children and Street Youth. Project Profiles Series No. 1*. Geneva: Inter NGO Secretariat.

Inter NGO. (1985) *Programme on Street Children and Street Youth. Project Profiles Series No. 2*. Geneva: Inter NGO Secretariat.

International Labor Organization (ILO). (1983) *Child Labor*. Report of the Director-General to the International Labour Conference, 69th Session. Geneva: International Labor Organization.

Janus, Mark-David, McCormack, Arlene, Burgess, Anne, and Hartman, Carol. (1987) *Adolescent Runaways: Causes and Consequences*. Lexington, MA: Lexington Books.

Korten, David. (1990) Symptoms versus Causes: Observations and Recommendations on UNICEF's Urban Child Programme, *Environment and Urbanization 2*, 2: pp. 46–57.

Lau, Evelyn. (1989) *Runaway: Diary of a Street Kid*. Toronto: Harper and Collins.

Lee-Wright, Peter. (1990) *Child Slaves*. London, UK: Earthscan Publications.

Myers, William (ed.) (1991) *Protecting Working Children*. London, UK: Zed Books.

REDD BARNA. (1990) *Summing Up of Our Experiences in Work with Street Children*. Harare: REDD BARNA Regional Office.

Serrill, Michael. (1990) Slaughter in the Streets, *Time International*, September 24.

Shifter, Michael. (1985) Majito and Carlos Alberta: The Gamin Legacy, *Grassroots Development 9:* pp. 42–47.

UNESCO. (1985) *Courier 38*, no. 6.

UNICEF. (1989) Meeting the Needs of Street Children: The Philippine Experience. Joint DSWD-NCSD-UNICEF Project. Manila: UNICEF, mimeo.

UNICEF. (1990) *Children and Development in the 1990's, A UNICEF Sourcebook*. New York: UNICEF.

United Nations. (1989) *United Nations Convention on the Rights of the Child*. New York: United Nations.

Webber, Marlene. (1991) *Street Kids: The Tragedy of Canada's Runaways*. Toronto: University of Toronto Press.

Index

About the Editor and Contributors

NELLY P. STROMQUIST is Professor of International Development Education at the University of Southern California in Los Angeles. She has taught at Stanford University and worked for the International Development Research Center (IDRC, Canada). A specialist in gender and education, research methodologies, and evaluation, her most recent publications are *Women and Education in Latin America: Knowledge, Power, and Change;* and *Daring to Be Different: The Choice of Nonconventional Fields of Study by International Women Students.*

N'DRI ASSIE-LUMUMBA is an Assistant Professor at Cornell University, where she was first a Fulbright Senior Research Fellow and a Ford Foundation/ Africana Center Fellow. Prior to Cornell, she taught and did research in several institutions, including Abidjan University, CIRSSED (Togo), the University of Houston, Vassar College, Bard College, the Ministry of Education of Mali, and the UNESCO-International Institute for Educational Planning. Her teaching and research interests include access to schooling, women and gender issues in development, history and social change in Africa, and the African diaspora.

ADRIAN BLUNT is Associate Professor in the College of Education at the University of Saskatchewan, where he teaches courses in adult, continuing, and postsecondary education. Currently, he serves as coeditor of the *Canadian*

Journal for the Study of Adult Education. His research interests focus on marginalized learners in literacy, community development, and adult education programs.

ROGER BOSHIER is Professor of Adult Education at the University of British Columbia. He is interested in the theoretical foundations of adult, lifelong, and comparative education, particularly in Asia and the Pacific, educational campaigns (such as those on AIDS and boating safety), motivational orientations, adult learning, and the training of adult educators.

GERALD GRACE began the first graduate program in Urban Education in the United Kingdom in 1976. His books include *Teachers, Ideology and Control: A Study in Urban Education* and *Education and the City: Theory, History and Contemporary Practice.* He taught at King's College, University of London, the Cambridge University (where he was a Fellow of Wolfson College), and Victoria University in Wellington, New Zealand. He is currently the head of the University of Durham School of Education, United Kingdom.

DEIRDRE M. KELLY is Assistant Professor in the Department of Social and Educational Studies at the University of British Columbia. Her interests include gender and schooling, alternative education, and adolescent subcultures. She is currently doing an ethnographic study of two programs for teenage mothers, one in a rural setting and the other in an urban setting. She recently authored *Last Chance High: How Girls and Boys Drop In and Out of Alternative Schools.*

MAGALY LAVADENZ was born in Cuba and is currently a doctoral candidate at the University of Southern California in Los Angeles and a Visiting Assistant Professor at Loyola Marymount University in Los Angeles. She received her M.A. degree in educational psychology, guidance, and counseling from California State University at Northridge in 1991. Her experiences with Central American immigrant students began while she was teaching bilingual first-graders.

W. O. LEE is a lecturer in the Department of Education at the University of Hong Kong. His teaching and research interests cover comparative education, educational philosophy, and values education. He is the author of *Social Change and Educational Problems in Japan, Singapore, and Hong Kong* and articles and book chapters on education in China, Hong Kong, and Japan. He is at present conducting a project comparing school education in Guangzhou and Hong Kong.

LI ZIBIAO is Director of Guangzhou Educational Science Institute and has extensive teaching and administrative experience in schools in Guangzhou. He is the coeditor of *Studies of the Development of Secondary Education in Guangzhou* (in Chinese) and the author of articles for such Chinese journals as *Educational Research* and *Guangdong Social Science*. He is at present co-editing a book on school education in Guangzhou and Hong Kong with W. O. Lee.

ROSLYN MICKELSON, a former high school teacher, is Associate Professor of Sociology and Adjunct Associate of Women's Studies at the University of North Carolina at Charlotte. Her research deals with the effects of race, class, and gender on educational processes and outcomes. With Carol Ray and Stephen Smith, she is examining business-led school reforms and their implications for educational equity.

MALONGO R. S. MLOZI is a lecturer with the Department of Agricultural Education and Extension, Sokoine University of Agriculture, Morogoro, Tanzania. He is currently pursuing a doctoral program at the University of British Columbia.

NELLY MOULIN is Professor of Research Methodology in the Graduate School of Education, State University of Rio de Janeiro. She serves as coordinator of the Board of Evaluation Consultants for the Study of Official Educational System Evaluation, carried out by the Rio de Janeiro State Department of Education.

ISABEL PEREIRA is a high school teacher of science and biology in the public schools of Rio de Janeiro State. Her primary research interest is in the area of organized social movements and the movement of high school students and the struggle for public schooling.

CAROL RAY taught at the University of North Carolina at Charlotte and at Loyola University of Chicago. She now works as Assistant Professor of Sociology at San Jose State University. Her publications concern business leaders' ideologies, perceptions, and attempts to control managers, workers, and "pre-workers," that is, high school students.

STEPHEN SMITH is Assistant Professor of political science at Winthrop College in South Carolina, where he teaches the politics of education, public policy, and urban politics. He has investigated the effects of governmental violence on political participation in the United States.

R. MURRAY THOMAS is Emeritus Professor of Educational Psychology at the University of California, Santa Barbara, where he served as head of the International Education Program over the 1961–91 period. Books he has edited recently include: *Oriental Theories of Human Development* (1988), *The Ency-*

clopedia of Human Development and Education (1990), *International Comparative Education* (1990), *Education's Role in Learning Difficulties* (1989), *Counseling and Life Span Development* (1990), and *Comparing Theories of Child Development* (third edition, 1992). He is the author of *What Wrongdoers Deserve* (Greenwood, 1993).